Insights into Language Education Policies

FOREIGN LANGUAGE TEACHING IN EUROPE

Edited by
Manuel Jiménez Raya, Terry Lamb and Flávia Vieira

VOL. 18

Zu Qualitätssicherung und Peer Review der vorliegenden Publikation

Die Qualität der in dieser Reihe erscheinenden Arbeiten wird vor der Publikation durch Herausgeber der Reihe im Blind-Verfahren geprüft. Dabei ist der Autor der Arbeit den Gutachtern während der Prüfung namentlich nicht bekannt.

Notes on the quality assurance and peer review of this publication

Prior to publication, the quality of the work published in this series is blind reviewed by editors of the series. The referees are not aware of the author's name when performing their review.

PETER LANG

Manuel Jiménez Raya
Terry Lamb
Borja Manzano Vázquez
(eds.)

Insights into Language Education Policies

PETER LANG

Bibliographic Information published by the Deutsche Nationalbibliothek
The Deutsche Nationalbibliothek lists this publication in the Deutsche Nationalbibliografie; detailed bibliographic data is available in the internet at http://dnb.d-nb.de.

Library of Congress Cataloging-in-Publication Data
A CIP catalog record for this book has been applied for at the Library of Congress.

Printed by CPI books GmbH, Leck

ISSN 1437-3157
ISBN 978-3-631-71606-9 (Print)
E-ISBN 978-3-631-81014-9 (E-PDF)
E-ISBN 978-3-631-81015-6 (EPUB)
E-ISBN 978-3-631-81016-3 (MOBI)
DOI 10.3726/b16861

Peter Lang Edition is an Imprint of Peter Lang GmbH.

Peter Lang – Frankfurt am Main · Bern · Bruxelles · New York · Oxford · Warszawa · Wien

This publication has been peer reviewed.

www.peterlang.com

Contents

List of contributors

Bertha Du-Babcock
City University of Hong Kong, China

Kristine M. Harrison
University of Wisconsin-Whitewater and Deep Institute, USA

Manuel Jiménez Raya
University of Granada, Spain

Terry Lamb
University of Westminster, UK

Borja Manzano Vázquez
University of Granada, Spain

Maria Alfredo Moreira
University of Minho, Portugal

María Luisa Pérez Cañado
University of Jaén, Spain

François Victor Tochon
University of Wisconsin-Madison, USA

José Manuel Vez Jeremías
University of Santiago de Compostela, Spain

Flávia Vieira
University of Minho, Portugal

Manuel Jiménez Raya, Terry Lamb, and Borja Manzano Vázquez

Perspectives on language education policy

"To learn a language is to have one more window from which to look at the world"

Chinese proverb

Abstract: The increasing globalisation our world is experiencing has increased the number of intercultural contact situations, underlining the need for individuals to develop the capacity to use several languages appropriately and effectively. Plurilingualism has become a major asset in our present-day society. Our world is also characterised by the linguistic diversity present in many countries due to the coexistence of different local and migration languages. The problem, however, is that many of these languages tend to remain as minority languages, spoken by a small part of the community and neglected in schools and local administrations. The present chapter underlines the key role that education and, consequently, language education policies can play in encouraging language learning as well as contributing to preserving, revitalising and recognising local and migration languages. It concludes by providing an overview of the main contents addressed in each of the chapters included in the present book.

Keywords: Language education policy, language education, plurilingualism, minority languages

One of the main characteristics of the 21st century is the increasing globalisation which currently our world is experiencing, leading countries to become more and more connected and people to engage more frequently in intercultural contact situations. This phenomenon underlines the pressing need for every citizen to acquire competence in using different languages. Plurilingualism has thus become an important attribute to be developed by learners and a fundamental component to be incorporated into educational policies. The importance attached to plurilingualism can be observed, for example, in the various documents issued by the European Union (European Commission, 1995, 2004, 2005, 2008) to encourage (foreign) language learning in education.

Another important characteristic of our contemporary world is the co-existence of different languages in one geographical area. Many countries encompass a great diversity of cultures, customs and languages. One example is Spain, where Spanish co-exists in some regions of the country with other local languages such as Basque, Catalan, and Galician. This diversity is nowadays being enhanced by migration. The world is witnessing one of the largest migratory flows in history. More and more people are leaving their countries (some escaping from war, hunger, or poverty) in order to settle in another country where they can have better living and working conditions. The problem is that many of these local and migration languages tend to remain as minority languages, being spoken by a small part of the community and neglected in schools and local administrations. In this sense, education can play a key role in addressing this situation as well as encouraging social cohesion. Apart from incorporating foreign languages into the curriculum, one of the greatest challenges schools and, consequently, language education policies face is to cater for this linguistic diversity, that is, to encourage the learning of local languages as well as recognising and building on the languages that learners of a migrant background bring to the classroom.

The main purpose of the present book is to provide the reader with critical insights into language education policies in different countries around the world: the United States, China, Portugal and Spain. The different chapters included in this book analyse what is done (or not) in these settings to promote (foreign) language learning from different perspectives (for example, the preservation of indigenous languages at schools, the promotion of CLIL [Content and Language Integrated Learning] instruction in education, or the situation of migration and minority languages in curriculum policies), underlining their merits and flaws as well as suggesting future avenues and courses of action to be adopted in order to enhance plurilingual education in these contexts. We therefore believe that, although modest in its scope, this book will be of particular interest to policymakers, academic researchers and teaching professionals concerned with language education.

Overview of the book

In the first chapter of the present book Flávia Vieira and Maria Alfredo Moreira analyse language curriculum policies in primary and secondary education in Portugal in order to discuss their potential (or lack of it) for enhancing plurilingual education, focusing on the teaching of foreign languages as curriculum subjects as well as migration and minority languages. The chapter begins by examining the main foundations and implications of the European idea(l) of plurilingualism. Next, it describes the changes effected by recent language policies in Portugal that promote the development of a multilingual curriculum which is dominated by English and in which concepts such as intercultural competence and plurilingualism are excluded. Finally, the chapter concludes by analysing the current situation of migration and minority languages in Portuguese academic settings and underlines the pressing need for adopting a plurilingual approach so as to cater for the educational inclusion of these languages.

The next three chapters of the book analyse the language education policies of three different Spanish contexts. The chapter by María Luisa Pérez Cañado provides a detailed rendering of the plurilingual education model developed in Andalusia, officially a monolingual community in the south of Spain. It answers a series of wh-questions which aim to canvass the past, present and future of the two main plans enacting this model: the Andalusian Plan for the Promotion of Plurilingualism (APPP) and the *Plan Estratégico de Desarrollo de las Lenguas en Andalucía* (PEDLA). The chapter begins by expounding on *why* the APPP and the PEDLA have been developed. It then describes *how* they are being implemented in practice, mapping how their overarching guidelines are reflected in on-the-ground practice. The chapter analyses the outcomes of the APPP and the PEDLA, focusing on *who* has done stocktaking on the way in which these plans are working and *what* results have been yielded by the research conducted thus far. It concludes by exploring *where* those outcomes lead, identifying the main challenges to be addressed and setting an agenda for the future.

José Manuel Vez Jeremías examines the language policies developed in a Spanish bilingual community: Galicia. The chapter begins by analysing the Galician linguistic landscape in which Galician, once a linguistic variety of low prestige, has gained more social status through different political measures. These measures, however, have not prevented the drastic decline of L1 Galician speakers among adolescents. To reduce this language deficit, the Galician Government has enacted various educational measures, which are reviewed in the chapter. These measures have aimed to promote the learning of Galician through its incorporation into the school curriculum, both as a subject and as a language of instruction. In recent years, however, Galicia has experienced a shift towards a trilingual model in education (based on teaching a third of the school subjects in Galician, Spanish and English respectively). While supporters of this model regard it as a promising tool for increasing learners' foreign language skills, detractors argue that its development is a potential threat to the revitalisation of the regional language.

The chapter by Borja Manzano Vázquez is also framed in a Spanish bilingual community, in this particular case, the Basque Autonomous Community. On the one hand, the chapter describes the different language policies and initiatives implemented to promote language education in the Basque school system. In this sense, it examines the development of bilingual education (Basque-Spanish) in the community and discusses how CLIL (Content and Language Integrated Learning) has been implemented in Basque schools. On the other hand, the chapter explores the findings of the main studies conducted in the Basque Autonomous Community on the impact of CLIL on learners' language learning. In doing so, it identifies potential flaws and shortcomings in these studies to be addressed in future research. To conclude, the chapter suggests different courses of action which can be adopted in the future so as to enhance multilingual education and the implementation of CLIL in this region.

Next, the focus shifts to language policy in the United States. Using the Hesitation Waltz as a metaphor, François Victor Tochon describes the back and forth movements that characterise language education policies in the United States. These policies have shifted, in varying degrees in the different states, from tolerance to repression, from restriction to expediency, and from absence of support to promotion or indeed the reverse. The chapter thus begins by discussing two examples of the current situation of the United States regarding language education policies targeted at the Native American population and the Ebonics controversy, illustrated with the case of the Oakland California School Board. Next, it focuses on analysing modern language education policies after 9/11, the progressive opening to measures helping Hispanic heritage learners, the detrimental effect of the No Child Left Behind Act on foreign language education, and the 'Hesitation Waltz' experienced in higher education. The chapter concludes by expounding on the influence of dialectical and cultural substrates on language education policies.

The chapter by Kristine M. Harrison analyses the effects of the monolingual, English-only policy of the United States on Native Americans and immigrants. It indicates that for Native Americans this language education policy has entailed forced education in boarding schools and language shift to English, whereas for immigrants it has resulted in first language attrition. This monolingual approach has been reinforced by the English as a Lingua Franca movement, which has contributed to the spread of English globally. To revitalise native languages in the United States, a Native American movement emerged, which led to the passing of the Native American Languages Act. The chapter describes the main implications of this Act for native languages and the difficulties it has encountered. It concludes by presenting the MEMES (Making Empathetic Multilingual Environments in School) project, an ambitious initiative aimed at creating a network where teachers and policy-makers can interact and share resources which contribute to fostering multilingual education.

In Chapter 7, Bertha Du-Babcock discusses the current language policy in Hong Kong and its relationship with, and effect on, language use. The author first expounds different background factors relating to the Hong Kong language environment and summarises, from a critical perspective, available information on various assessments measuring the language use and ability of Hong Kong residents to communicate in Cantonese, English, and Mandarin. Next, she outlines governmental, educational and business language policy in Hong Kong, putting special emphasis on business and commerce. Using the language-based communication zones model, the author analyses different communication situations which develop in the business sector and show how varying language competence levels are required to communicate successfully in these situations. Finally, the chapter concludes by tying together Hong Kong language policy and its relationship with present and future language use in the area.

References

European Commission. (1995). *White paper on education and training. Teaching and learning: Towards the learning society*. Brussels: European Commission.

European Commission. (2004). *Promoting language learning and linguistic diversity: An action plan 2004-2006*. Brussels: European Commission.

European Commission. (2005). *A new framework strategy for multilingualism*. Brussels: Commission of the European Communities.

European Commission. (2008). *Multilingualism: An asset for Europe and a shared commitment*. Brussels: European Commission.

Flávia Vieira and Maria Alfredo Moreira

From European to national policies in language education: Plurilingualism and the case of Portugal[1]

> *There can be no question that the freedom of choice of language is a fundamental cultural right. Furthermore, in multilingual settings, it seems just as urgent that people can participate in public communication without being subject to dominant language use. Therefore the right to use one's own language and communicative competence (of various degrees) in other language(s) must be seen as complementary elements for democratic citizenship. (Breidbach, 2003: 21)*

Abstract: This chapter examines the different language policies enacted in primary and secondary education in Portugal with the aim of analyzing their potential or lack of it for improving plurilingual education in the country. In this sense, it will particularly focus on the teaching of foreign languages as curriculum subjects and migration and minority languages. On the one hand, the chapter describes the impact of recent language policies which place emphasis on the teaching of English but neglect concepts such as intercultural competence and plurilingualism. On the other hand, it analyses the current situation of migration and minority languages in the Portuguese school system. In doing so, the chapter seeks to raise issues that are locally relevant but may also resonate elsewhere.

Keywords: plurilingualism, foreign language education, minority languages, migration languages

1 Introduction

Plurilingualism has been a major concern in European language policies that challenge language hegemonies and advocate the promotion of linguistic diversity, democratic citizenship and social cohesion, with significant implications for language pedagogy and teacher education.

---

1 Paper produced in the Research Centre on Education, projects UID/CED/1661/2013 and UID/CED/1661/2016, Institute of Education, University of Minho, through national funds of FCT/MCTES-PT.

Several types of arguments to support linguistic diversity have been advanced (e.g. Skutnabb-Kangas, 2002), but utilitarian concerns prevail at an administrational and economic level, where the use of English and a few other bridge-languages is favoured. That is also the case with scientific activities like access to knowledge, participation in conferences, publication, research networks, funding programmes, etc. As regards language pedagogy and teacher education, we are still very far from having plurilingual curricula that promote linguistic diversity, intercultural competence and the development of hybrid linguistic repertoires. Moreover, migration and minority languages are often excluded from academic settings.

Nevertheless, European recommendations have been very influential upon research. In the case of Portugal, plurilingualism has been an important focus of language education research for more than a decade and research reviews indicate that many researchers defend a 'plurilingualism didactics' so as to give prominence to cross-curricular educational and social values and competences, thus seeking to challenge and transform dominant school practices (Alarcão et al., 2004; Alarcão & Araújo e Sá, 2010).

According to a review study covering the period from 2006 to 2011 (Vieira, Moreira, & Peralta, 2014), research findings suggest that teacher and learner images of languages and cultures are often instrumental, ethnocentric, monolithic and stereotyped, which reinforces hegemonic understandings of the value of languages and a limited view of their social, cultural, political and identity role; however, the findings from intervention studies carried out in teacher education and pedagogical settings show that plurilingual approaches can help reconstruct teacher and learner identity and promote openness to diversity, metalinguistic awareness, plurilingual and intercultural competence, and language-friendly school environments. As regards the specific case of Portuguese as a non-native language (PNNL), which covers the teaching and learning of Portuguese to speakers of other languages, findings indicate that there needs to be a more comprehensive view on the sociolinguistic situation of non-native learners in Portugal, as well as greater investment in policies, resources and teacher education programmes; experiments show that PNNL learning (and bilingualism in general) is a desired and valuable experience that can be put at the service of inclusive democratic citizenship and globalisation.

The studies indicate a huge distance between policies and practices, and two major constraints are pointed out: the established school cultures, where a fragmented, monolingual approach to language education prevails, and the lack of appropriate teacher education. However, national policies are also part of the problem and will be the main focus of the present paper. We start with a brief presentation of the European idea(l) of plurilingualism and then analyse language curriculum policies in primary and secondary education in Portugal so as to discuss their (lack of) potential for enhancing plurilingual education. We will refer to (1) foreign languages as curriculum subjects and (2) migration and minority languages, seeking to raise issues that are locally relevant but may also resonate elsewhere.

2 The European idea(l) of plurilingualism in language education

The idea(l) of plurilingualism in language education became popular nearly two decades ago when the Council of Europe (CoE) published the *Common European Framework of Reference for Languages* – CEF (CoE, 2001). However, CoE policies for plurilingualism can be traced back to the *Convention for the Protection of Human Rights* (CoE, 1950), where commitment to political democracy and the need for a common understanding and observance of universal human rights is assumed, and also to the *European Cultural Convention* (CoE, 1954), whose purpose was to enhance Europe's common cultural heritage, the appreciation of cultural diversity, and the study of European languages and cultures. Over the decades that followed, the CoE and the European Commission have developed language policies intended to promote plurilingualism in connection with linguistic diversity, mutual understanding, democratic citizenship, and social cohesion[2].

Although the terms 'multilingualism' and 'plurilingualism' are often used as synonyms, the former refers mainly to the knowledge of different languages or to the existence of different languages in the same society, and "it may be attained by simply diversifying the languages on offer in a particular school or educational system, or by encouraging pupils to learn more than one foreign language, or reducing the dominant position of English in international communication" (CoE, 2001: 4). As for plurilingualism, it entails much more than that:

- an awareness of why and how one learns the languages one has chosen
- an awareness of and the ability to use transferable skills in language learning

2 European policies regarding cultural diversity, democratic citizenship and social cohesion are not limited to language education. For example, in 2016, the CoE published a document that proposes a cross-disciplinary conceptual model of the competences to be developed by learners so as to foster participation in culturally diverse democratic societies, aimed at supporting educational decisions "for the preparation of learners for life as competent democratic citizens" (CoE, 2016: 9).

- a respect for the plurilingualism of others and the value of languages and varieties irrespective of their perceived status in society
- a respect for the cultures embodied in languages and the cultural identities of others
- an ability to perceive and mediate the relationships which exist among languages and cultures
- a global integrated approach to language education in the curriculum[3]

As Lenz and Berthele (2010: 17) put it, "Plurilingual and intercultural education is basically concerned with all language and (inter-)cultural learning but is particularly interested in plural, transversal and integrative approaches to language and culture." The authors note, however, that although knowing various languages may expand intercultural experience, this experience is not necessarily linked to the knowledge of languages and can also be enhanced by the use of a *lingua franca* (p. 6).

Plurilingual education requires the development of intercultural competence, whose components are presented by Byram, Gribkova, and Starkey (2002: 11–13) as follows:

- *Attitudes (savoir être)*: curiosity and openness, readiness to suspend disbelief about other cultures and belief about one's own.
- *Knowledge (savoir)*: of social groups and their products and practices in one's own and in one's interlocutor's country, and of the general processes of societal and individual interaction.
- *Skills of interpreting and relating (savoir comprendre)*: ability to interpret a document or event from another culture, to explain it and relate it to documents from one's own.
- *Skills of discovery and interaction (savoir apprendre/faire)*: ability to acquire new knowledge of a culture and cultural practices and the ability to operate knowledge, attitudes and skills under the constraints of real-time communication and interaction.
- *Critical cultural awareness/political education (savoir s'engager)*: an ability to evaluate critically and on the basis of explicit criteria perspectives, practices and products in one's own and other cultures and countries.

A plurilingual approach calls into question the way language curricula are usually organised and put into practice (see Beacco et al., 2010). A central issue regarding its feasibility is: How can the specific content and aims of plurilingual

3 http://www.coe.int/t/dg4/linguistic/Division_EN.asp.

and intercultural education be identified and integrated within the curriculum, while also respecting the specific content and aims of teaching individual languages? (ibid.). In response to this question, a major challenge is to expand language teachers' co-operation, with implications for how different languages are planned and taught across the curriculum. This includes foreign and classical languages, language(s) of schooling, regional languages, minority and migration languages, which can be taught "as subjects" or as "languages in other subjects" (p. 40).

Lenz and Berthele (2010: 5–8) discuss the implications of a plurilingual approach for assessment and propose a long list of components of plurilingual and intercultural education that might be worth assessing, organised into five groups: a) the overarching goals of plurilingual and intercultural education; b) competences that help learners to participate successfully in social life; c) competences and attitudes that help learners to develop as critical intercultural individuals and citizens; d) competences that help learners to take responsibility and develop as language users and learners; and e) competences that help learners to acquire new knowledge in their studies in plurilingual settings. The assessment of intercultural competence should have pedagogical purposes and its results should be used formatively, supporting the improvement of teaching and learning practices (p. 26).

A plurilingual approach further implies substantial changes in pre-service and in-service teacher education so as to develop new types of expertise including a plurilingual repertoire, knowledge about how bilingual/plurilingual individuals function, and how teaching can be planned and carried out so as to promote plurilingual and intercultural competence (see Beacco et al., 2010; Kelly et al., 2004; Willems, 2002). Moreover, a school-based approach would entail the preparation of all teachers, and not just language teachers, as well as a whole-school commitment to plurilingualism as a political project (Pereira, 2014).

Broadly speaking, plurilingualism can be associated with four key competences for lifelong learning defined by the European Commission (2007): communication in the mother tongue; communication in foreign languages; social and civic competences; and cultural awareness and expression[4]. Most European countries have implemented either national strategies or large-scale initiatives to promote the first three competences (European Commission/EACEA/Eurydice, 2012)[5],

4 The other four key competences are: mathematical competence and basic competences in science and technology; digital competence; learning to learn; and sense of initiative and entrepreneurship.

5 The Eurydice report does not include data on cultural awareness and expression.

but that does not mean that plurilingualism has been implemented as a new paradigm in language education. Western education and curriculum planning have always emphasised homogeneity rather than diversity, and national curricula have always tried to reinforce national cultures so as to produce subjects with a national identity (Macedo, Dendrinos, & Gounari, 2006: 55). As regards foreign language education, policies have been largely determined by hegemonic interests and we need to ask whose language is important enough to be integrated in the curriculum and why, and what counts as legitimate language knowledge, thus rejecting a vision of language education as an ideologically neutral task (p. 57).

Plurilingualism can also be related to the promotion of inclusive education, an ambitious goal that requires, among many other things, a special attention to linguistic and cultural diversity:

> An inclusive curriculum takes gender, cultural identity and language background into consideration. […] Multilingual approaches in education, in which language is recognized as an integral part of a student's cultural identity, can act as a source of inclusion. (UNESCO, 2009: 18)

As regards less-favoured groups (e.g. migrants, people with a communicative handicap, elderly people, people affected by relations between major and minority languages, and poor or illiterate people), the Civil Society Platform on Multilingualism (2011: 10) points out that "the learning of languages will not be a goal in itself, but will be an instrument within a more far-reaching objective: social empowerment of these groups, assuring competences which allow full participation and integration in society". However, shortcomings are observed as regards the fulfilment of this objective in Europe and several recommendations are made, including the teaching of "intercultural competencies as an integral part of language learning in preschools and schools to create an inclusive society, to combat xenophobia and discrimination" (p. 13).

The driving force for promoting plurilingualism is not exclusively linked to linguistic, cultural and social concerns. It is also strongly tied to innovation, economic growth and sustainability as envisaged by the EU. The priority of the EU 2020 strategy is to surpass the current economic crisis through "smart growth" (developing an economy based on knowledge and innovation), "sustainable growth" (promoting a more resource efficient, greener and more competitive economy), and "inclusive growth" (fostering a high-employment economy delivering social and territorial cohesion) (European Commission, 2010: 3). Education is one of its main targets so as to reduce the distance between the world of education/training and the world of employment, and the promotion of multilingualism is one of the European Commission's policies to make the European Union more competitive in the knowledge society[6]. Nevertheless, economic interests (among others) also rest on, and promote, the status of English as a global language, which poses dilemmas as regards plurilingualism and democratic citizenship. Therefore,

> [...] language education policies for plurilingualism should include considerations about the role of English against the backdrop of Europe as a polity in which citizenship means both a multitude of (linguistic) identities and the capacity to enter public discourse on various levels of the communicative sphere. (Breidbach, 2003: 18)

Overall, the idea(l) of plurilingualism is extremely complex. It draws on various rationales and has quite radical political and educational implications, and perhaps this is the main reason why it has been so difficult to put into practice. On the other hand, because European policies have been developed with the support of research experts, they present a theoretical density that may appeal to other researchers, but not necessarily to practitioners. Moreover, they are not mandatory and the way they are integrated into national curricula is always a matter of national sovereignty. Furthermore, they tend to be oversimplified and reduced to a set of rhetorical devices with little or no impact. Therefore, we should ask: what is their *real* impact?

The following section seeks to explore answers to this question in the case of Portugal, with a primary focus on language curriculum policies.

3 The case of Portugal: Languages across the curriculum

3.1 Foreign languages as curriculum subjects[7]

Current European policies recommend the inclusion of three European languages in the school curriculum – the native language and two foreign languages (FLs).[8] This has long been implemented in the Portuguese schooling

6 The five targets set by the EU 2020 strategy are R&D investments, education, energy/climate change, employment rate, and reducing poverty. For an overview of EU policy initiatives and outcomes regarding the framework *Education and Training 2010* see http://ec.europa.eu/education/policies/2010/doc/compendium05_en.pdf.

7 Portuguese as the language of schooling will be discussed in the following section in relation to policies regarding migration and minority languages.

8 This target was set by the European Commission in 1995 in the White Paper on Education and Training (Comissão Europeia, 1995).

system[9]. English and French were first introduced in secondary education in 1836, together with German as an optional subject. From 1905 to 1973, French was compulsory as FL1. Since 1973, English could also be chosen as FL1 and the importance of French and German declined progressively as English became a global, hegemonic language. Spanish was introduced more recently, in the 1990s[10]. In 1995 English was already the most taught FL in Portuguese schools. From 2006 onwards primary schools were obliged to offer English as an extra-curricular subject that was optional for students, and in 2015–16 English was integrated into the primary curriculum and became mandatory in grades 3 and 4 (2 hours a week), remaining optional in grades 1 and 2. More recently, the Portuguese Ministry of Education, with the support of the Government of the Republic of China, has been implementing pilot projects for Mandarin as an optional fourth foreign language. In 2015 the curricular guidelines for Mandarin as a third foreign language in Humanities courses in upper secondary education were published, to become effective from 2015–16 onwards.

At present, all students learn at least two FLs in basic compulsory education (grades 1–9, ISCED[11] 1 and 2). They learn English as an optional subject in the first two years of primary education and as a mandatory FL1 in grades 3 to 9. Students learn a second FL in grades 7 to 9, where they can choose one of the other three FLs depending on the school offer. In upper secondary education (grades 10–12, ISCED 3) they may continue learning the FL1/FL2 or initiate a third FL, depending on the vocational learning paths they choose.

Table 1 below presents the percentage of students who were learning FLs in 2014 (European Commission/EACEA/Eurydice, 2017: 169–170):

The first issue to consider here is the dominance of English over other FLs, and this is common to nearly all European countries, where English is by far the

---

9 Also in higher education, where the range of FLs taught in different graduate and post-graduate degrees is much wider (e.g. in the areas of Humanities, Political Sciences, Engineering, Economics, Music, etc.).

10 Given its similarity with Portuguese, Spanish was never introduced before in the formal curriculum. Actually, in the Middle Ages Portuguese and Castilian were considered as varieties of the same language and there was a lot of bilingual literary production. However, after the Portuguese revolution that put an end to the Iberian Union under the rule of the Hispanic monarchy (1580–1640) the Spanish language was marginalized and French has been more valued since then (Pinto, 2010).

11 International Standard Classification of Education (ISCED). ISCED 1 corresponds to what is known in most countries as Primary Education, ISCED 2, to lower secondary education, and ISCED 3 to upper secondary education (see http://uis.unesco.org/en/topic/international-standard-classification-education-isced).

Table 1: FL learning in Portuguese schools (2014 data)

	ISCED 1 Primary education	**ISCED 2 Lower secondary education**	**ISCED 3 Upper secondary education**
English	35.9*	95.4	72.4
French	0.3	64.7	6.7
Spanish	—	20.8	7.1
German	—	0.8	1.5

* English is not mandatory in the first two years at this level although it is sometimes offered by primary schools

most taught FL at all educational levels and a mandatory foreign language for more than 90 % of students, at least in one of the three levels of school education (97.3 % in lower secondary education; 79.4 % in primary education, and 85.2 % in upper secondary education). English is followed by French, while Spanish and German come in third place (European Commission/EACEA/Eurydice, 2017). The fact that English was elected as the only FL to be introduced at primary schools follows the general pattern in Europe: "the early learning of languages has benefited English almost exclusively" (Truchot, 2002: 8). Breidbach (2003: 22) argues that "sustainable cultural and political inclusion, which can lead to opportunities of participation in multilingual Europe, requires a holistic language education policy inclusive of English *and* linguistic diversity." What is envisaged is then "an open-ended cultural affiliation" that is not based on a single language and "develops an openness to languages – an awareness of the diversity of European plurilingual repertoires and a shared but plural manifestation of identity/ies" (Beacco 2005: 21). This leads us to a second issue: how is FL education carried out?

As regards FL education at the primary level, it was primarily conceived as an opportunity to sensitize children to language and cultural diversity and no specific language was indicated when a national curriculum was designed in 2001. Even though English was later elected, the specific guidelines for teaching it still recommend a language-awareness, cross-curricular approach (Bento et al., 2005). According to a study by Edelenbos, Johnstone, and Kubanek (2006), there is no consensus regarding approaches to early language learning across Europe and four models are in place:

> i) roughly one hour per week for teaching a particular language, mainly based on given course-book and other material; ii) as for i) but with a more flexible syllabus based to

> some extent on relating the modern language to other aspects of the curriculum, e.g. science and geography, but still within limited time provision; iii) a language awareness model, not dealing with one additional language alone but instead giving access to a number of languages and cultures, in order to develop underlying qualities such as meta-linguistic awareness and intercultural sensitivity; iv) provision of increased time and intensity in the form of bilingual or partial immersion education. (Edelenbos, Johnstone, & Kubanek, 2006: 11)

The authors recommend a combination of models ii) and iii) as the most feasible and appropriate approach, which is in tune with our policies. The problem is that initial teacher education programmes for teaching English to young learners were only created in 2015, after English became compulsory and a new recruitment group for primary English teachers was established. Until then, English has been mostly taught as an isolated subject by English teachers hired at a local level, who worked in different schools and had no job stability. With the new initial teacher education programmes, practices are expected to distance themselves from model i), which appears to be in place in most situations as teachers tend to follow textbooks and conform to traditional assessment practices (Leslie, Moreira, & Mourão, 2018).

FL syllabi for all school education levels draw on a communicative paradigm, including the development of sociocultural and intercultural competence, with a focus on communication as a social interaction phenomenon and a means for enhancing respect for others, co-operation, and citizenship. However, in Portugal as elsewhere, languages are taught in isolation by different teachers with separate educational backgrounds, with different resources and assessment systems, which hampers the development of language teacher co-operation as envisaged by Beacco et al. (2010), even though language departments in schools integrate teachers of different languages.

A major problem school education faces in our country, with implications for language education, is that curriculum policies have been pervaded by a conservative, performative, outcomes-based ideology that tends to undervalue the moral and political dimensions of teaching. In late 2011, the national curriculum for compulsory education, which subscribed to progressive educational values like democratic citizenship, autonomy, meaningful learning, formative assessment and cooperative learning (Ministério da Educação, 2001), was withdrawn, the term "competence" was rejected, and "content" is now defined in terms of subject-specific knowledge and ability. Standards regarding what teachers must teach and assess (essential content) have been defined for all school subjects – *Metas Curriculares* (Curriculum Goals) – specifying the objectives and performance descriptors for each level. Old syllabi are still in operation in this transition phase, but they must be articulated with the new Curriculum Goals.

In order to illustrate the implications of these changes, we looked at the Curriculum Goals for English in lower secondary education (grades 5–9), published in May 2013 (Cravo, Bravo, & Duarte, 2013). They consist of lists of contents (objectives and performance descriptors) organised according to levels based on the CEF and divided into seven areas: Listening, Reading, Spoken Interaction, Spoken Production, Writing, Intercultural Domain, and Lexis and Grammar. The Intercultural Domain is presented as follows:

> **Intercultural Domain** – This domain presents the thematic areas to be explored. The specific nature of the subject, especially in the 8th and 9th grades, does not imply the teaching of isolated, mandatory thematic contents, but rather the exploration of areas of learner interest that can enhance him/her as a human being. In an increasingly diversified and complex world where English is the global language, the contents aim to raise youngsters' awareness of their own identity and the identity of others through descriptions and comparisons of social and cultural settings. (Cravo, Bravo, & Duarte, 2013: 5)[12]

This statement is quite abstract and also illustrative of the refusal to assume the political dimension of interculturality, namely as regards its relation to democratic citizenship. The fact that no reference is made to intercultural competence is striking (the word *competence* is now forbidden), and English is described as *the* global language in a diversified and complex world – why then consider language diversity and plurilingualism? Needless to say, the terms *plurilingual* or *pluriligualism* are absent from this document.

The way the Intercultural Domain is conceived becomes clearer when we look at how it is translated into lists of performative contents. The focus is on declarative knowledge about the target culture and on understanding cultural differences, but no reference is made to intercultural skills and know-how defined in the CEF as regards cultural sensitivity, mediation and the ability to overcome stereotyped relationships (CoE, 2001: 104–105). As Lenz and Berthele (2010: 27) point out, "defining the contents of a cultural-knowledge syllabus is not a straightforward task, and there is an inherent risk of codifying stereotypes whose real-world basis is in the process of decomposition." For these reasons, it would be important to embrace a broad notion of culture as social knowledge that integrates *knowing that*, *knowing of* and *knowing how* (Riley, 1989, quoted in Willems, 1996, 2002). The current guidelines include the first and second types

12 This and other quotations from Portuguese sources were translated into English.

of knowledge in a rather limited way and there appears to be a lack of focus on values, theories or convictions underlying world visions, as well as on strategic abilities that facilitate intercultural encounters and a critical analysis of one's own culture in relation to those of others. As regards the components of intercultural competence proposed by Byram, Gribkova, and Starkey (2002), the skills of interpreting and relating (*savoir comprendre*), the skills of discovery and interaction (*savoir apprendre/ faire*), and critical cultural awareness/ political education (*savoir s'engager*) are largely absent.

Although the authors of the new Curriculum Goals claim to have based their work on European language policies, namely the CEF, the only visible influence is in the definition of language descriptors and proficiency levels, which is in tune with a performative, outcomes-oriented rationale. The CEF is referred to as a descriptive document that allows teachers to choose the approaches that they find more appropriate in their context, which is true, but no reference is made to those approaches or to the way language education practices might enhance the construction of democratic citizenship. Actually, no pedagogical recommendations are made. There is no reference to language assessment principles either, but the recent increase of external assessments and the outcomes-oriented ideology permeating curriculum reform may induce a return to test-based assessment and undermine previous orientations that emphasised formative assessment (including self-assessment) and the use of instruments that cover both language and language learning competences. High-stakes tests are becoming a "*de facto* language policy" (Suárez-Orozco & Suárez-Orozco, 2009: 67), as they tend to shape curriculum and daily instruction more than ever. This may clearly reduce the possibility of assessing plurilingual and intercultural competence since that would require an exploratory approach to assessment with a focus on its formative purposes (Lenz & Berthele, 2010).

Overall, we have a multilingual curriculum that is dominated by English and has been developed in a rather 'monolingual' way. Recent reforms seem to reinforce rather than transform the current situation. We now turn to migration and minority languages and how Portuguese as a non-native language (PNNL) is dealt with.

3.2 Migration and minority languages

Portugal is still perceived, by nationals and foreigners alike, as essentially a monolingual country, a perception that draws on a direct equation between language and nation, according to which "monolingualism [is seen] as natural, normal and desirable" (cf. Ellis, Gogolin, & Clyne, 2010: 440). This view does not account for linguistic diversity and tends to "exclude the large groups of immigrants, the new minorities who contribute to enormous changes in 'the linguistic public spheres' of our societies" (Gogolin, 2002a: 7).

Actually, Portugal is anything but monolingual and a plurilingual approach is needed so as to cater for the educational inclusion of migration and minority languages.

Portuguese is the official national language, the legitimate language with the highest symbolic power and status, even though there is a recognition of Mirandese[13] as an official language with the status of a regional minority language, and of Portuguese Sign Language (PSL) as the L1 for deaf people. In the case of Mirandese, in 1999 the community's linguistic right to use it in official documents and schooling was recognised, which allows Mirandese children to choose it as an optional subject in the curriculum. Regarding PSL, deaf children have a right to effective bilingual education in specific reference schools[14].

Besides these national minority languages, we can also identify ancient and newly immigrated languages. However, they hold the status of *illegitimate* languages as their speakers' linguistic rights, namely the right to develop literacy in their L1, are not acknowledged. Only in 2001 was it officially recognised that students who do not have Portuguese as their native language should be offered specific classes of PNNL.

In 2004, the Eurydice report on integrating immigrant children in schools in Europe pointed out the training of teachers to work with immigrants as a priority of in-service training (European Commission, 2004). In 2007, a Resolution by the Council of Ministers stated the need for teachers to develop intercultural competences, and in 2011 the Framework for the Teaching of Portuguese as a Foreign Language abroad (Grosso et al., 2011) was established by the Ministry of Education, mainly to support the bilateral agreements on mother tongue tuition for Portuguese-speaking children in several host countries. Teacher education institutions have been offering a variety of courses on different aspects of PNNL

13 A regional language spoken in the Northeast in the region of Miranda do Douro, recognized in the Law n. 7/99, January 29. Nobody has accurate figures for the number of speakers. In 1995, the numbers were estimated in less than 30,000 speakers of Mirandese (Nelde, Strubell, & Williams, 1996); currently, the numbers are estimated to be smaller (between 6,000 and 10,000).

14 The Law Nr.3/2008, January 7, gives parents the right to choose bilingual education for their children. PSL is recognized as mother tongue for deaf students and Portuguese as L2. In 2011 a national syllabus for PL2 for deaf people was published by the Ministry of Education (Baptista et al., 2011).

and intercultural competences, mostly at the postgraduate level, but training in this area is almost non-existent in initial teacher education.

Overall, there are four types of measures to help integrate minority language students in Portuguese schools[15] (Duarte, Moreira, & Flores, 2013):

1) Measures to compensate for the students' language needs. Intensive teaching of PNNL is the most favoured one as they are exposed directly to the target language and receive intensive tuition, individually or in small groups (special linguistic support) during normal school hours.
2) Measures aimed at addressing the students' learning needs in certain areas of the curriculum. The content and teaching methods of the mainstream curriculum may be modified, curriculum support is organised, and assessment procedures may be adjusted.
3) Inclusion-oriented projects in the areas of literacy and cultural diversity, or in other related areas defined by the school. At the pre-school level, as well as in compulsory education, these projects entail adjusting teaching and learning processes to the different needs of each student and each school context.
4) Mediation and tutoring carried out by specially trained sociocultural mediators who establish links between home, the school and the community. Their role consists of promoting the integration of immigrants and ethnic minorities in order to strengthen intercultural dialogue and social cohesion[16].

Despite these measures, the Council of Europe's Commission against Racism and Intolerance still places gypsies and immigrants as the most vulnerable groups in Portugal (ECRI, 2002). We will now look more closely at each of these groups.

3.2.1 Roma

The Roma community (usually referred to, by themselves, as gypsies) is estimated between 40,000 and 50,000 individuals and constitutes the largest ethnolinguistic minority group in Portugal (Casa-Nova, 2008). A study by the Ministry of Education reported on the school year 1987/88 stated that there were 4,082 gipsy students in compulsory education, corresponding to 30 % of the school age population in this group (Leite, 2002). Ten years later, the estimates were 5,896 individuals, but not all completed their studies (Casa-Nova, 2008). NGO sources in Portugal have reported that by 2007 there were fewer than 10 Roma students in higher education (Council of Europe, Commissioner for Human Rights, 2012: 120), while in 2018 the estimates are for 29 individuals only (Pereira,

---

15 Decree-Law 219/97; Decree-Law 74/2004; Decree-Law 319/ 91; Decree-Law 6/2001.

16 Sociocultural mediators can fulfil their duties in a variety of public or private bodies beyond schools, like health or social security institutions.

2018). More recently, another study by the Ministry of Education (DGEEC, 2017) involved 69.6 % of the schools and school clusters in the public sector and revealed that there were only 12,963 gypsy students enrolled in all school levels, a number that can be regarded as clearly below the expected enrolments for Roma children under 18.

Compared with Portuguese native students, Roma students present the highest levels of academic underachievement, grade repetition, and school drop-out in compulsory education (Casa-Nova, 2005), displaying an alienation from school that shares the features already evidenced in many other countries (Casa-Nova, 2008; Leite, 2002). A study by the Ministry of Education (DGEEC, 2017) revealed that 48.1 % are retained and that 28.4 % are retained in the same school year more than once. This is mainly due to the segregation they are subjected to. When they are included within mainstream schools, they are often regarded as lazy, as the school routines and cultures from the majority are regarded as 'foreign' in their social environment (Casa-Nova, 2008; see also Leite, 2002)

Even though Portuguese public authorities report that Roma attendance rates have risen since sociocultural mediators were introduced (Council of Europe Commissioner for Human Rights, 2012: 119), the status of mediators is not clearly defined and they do not get the necessary financial support to carry out their job. Their role is often misunderstood by school administrators and local authorities, who perceive them as additional teachers who should take care of Roma pupils instead of mediating between the families, the dominant population, the school and the authorities (cf. Silva et al., 2010).

The absence of 'real' and effective schooling for these students, along with their low literacy skills in their L1, leads to a lack of social and discursive competences that works against the intended intercultural dialogue and inter-ethnic social skills (Casa-Nova, 2005). The recently approved National Strategy for the Integration of Roma Communities recognises that society at large has been unable (or unwilling) to provide for their effective inclusion and access to material and symbolic services and goods. Several reasons are indicated: "social exclusion, discrimination, difficulty in mobilization, resistance to schooling, loss of economic resources, traditional labour activities in decline, high rates of detention and obedience to strong internal rules" (Council of Ministers' Resolution 25/2013, April 17)[17]. In spite of covering various areas of inclusion (like education,

17 In 1996 a working group for the Equality and Integration of Roma Communities was created (Leite, 2002). In 1996 the High Commissioner for Immigration and Ethnic Minorities was established by a Decree-Law. It became, in 2007, the High Commissioner for Immigration and Intercultural Dialogue and, in 2014, the current

health, employment, justice, etc.), the Strategy still fails to ensure the respect for this community's linguistic rights. The section on education addresses several measures like improving access to school, literacy rates and social and technological competences, as well as reducing school drop-out and increasing the participation of families, but it does not mention any measures that would ensure cognitive justice and linguistic rights. The approach is integrative, not inclusive, transformative, plurilingual and intercultural.

3.2.2 Immigrated languages

The first wave of immigrants took place in the mid-1970s and was formed by Portuguese nationals from Portuguese ex-colonies in Africa, where Portuguese was the official language. Therefore, the African students' lack of academic success was explained mainly in socio-economic and cultural terms (Casa-Nova, 2005), not in linguistic terms. Only after 2001, when massive waves of immigrants from Eastern countries had started to arrive in Portugal, did the issue of language gain public visibility and political attention. Only then was there a recognition that coming from an official Portuguese-speaking country did not necessarily mean that children would have Portuguese as their first language or that it was used in the family. In addition, the quality of the schools these children attend is often below national standards, and their families have a low income and live in poor neighbourhoods (cf. Klugman, 2009).

The submersion (sink-or-swim) monolingual model is the norm in schools. Upon their arrival, immigrant students are placed in school according to their age and the level of instruction in their country of origin, together with native students, learning the same national curriculum in Portuguese. They should attend PNNL classes if the results of a diagnostic test on their competence in Portuguese places them at a beginning or intermediate level (A1, A2 or B1). Since 2011, the teaching of PNNL for beginning and intermediate students is done in replacement of the regular Portuguese lessons, with about 45 minutes per week allotted to the teaching of Portuguese as the vehicular language for the remaining subjects. However, these classes only function if there is a minimum

High Commissioner for Migrations. Only recently did the European Union approve a set of recommendations for the full inclusion of Roma and Travellers in Europe (December 2013), following a 2011 recommendation for the development of National Strategies that would fight exclusion and discrimination. Portugal only developed its national strategy in April 2013.

of 10 students in the same level. Otherwise, the school has to provide alternative support activities for learning PNNL.

In a study that reports on the school year 2012/13 (Madeira et al., 2013), there were a total of 9,240 PNNL students (1.8 % of the total students in the inquired schools) from 95 different nationalities and speaking 76 different first languages, the majority being Cape-Verdian (15.8 %), Portuguese (10.6 %), Romanian (9.4 %), Ukrainian (9.2 %) and Guinean (8.9 %) (Madeira et al., 2013); 24 % of these students (from A1 to B1 proficiency levels in Portuguese) attended regular classes and did not get any additional support for PNNL or any instruction in their first language.

As pointed out by Vieira, Moreira, and Peralta (2014), PNNL is an emerging research field of inquiry in our country. Therefore, not much is known about the school population, non-formal schooling contexts, teachers' qualifications, learner needs and successful practices that may be disseminated and expanded, with a backwash effect on teacher education. Research signals a growing awareness of the sociolinguistic landscape and underlines the need for more educational innovation at the policy and practical levels, namely as regards teacher education.

Education in a language other than Portuguese is mostly offered for the socially privileged in a few private schools where instruction is provided in English, French or German as a form of CLIL (Content and Language Integrated Learning)[18]. These schools follow *regular bilingual models* (cf. Caels & Mendes, 2008) and reinforce the power of a few European languages by accepting their official status as curricular languages (cf. Gogolin, 2002a). There has also been a residual offer of *two-way bilingual* (dual language) programmes, carried out partly in the language of instruction and partly in the native language of minority language pupils. These programmes are supported by the Ministry of Education and other official organisations, and by private institutions (Calouste Gulbenkian Foundation), under the responsibility of the Institute of Computational Linguistics of the University of Lisbon. Two programmes in preschool and in primary education were conducted: *Nursery Policy and Practice within a Bilingual Context* (1998–2000) and *Bilingual Class* (2008–12). These were part of research projects on bilingual education using Portuguese and Cape

18 CLIL started with a few elite private schools and with pilot projects undertaken in a few schools with the collaboration of the British Council, but it has been gradually expanding to primary and secondary public schools (see, for example, http://www.tvi24.iol.pt/videos/sociedade/ha-uma-escola-secundaria-com-aulas-bilingues-em-varias-disciplinas/5824cf760cf29175b3ab3822).

Verdean Creole in the Lisbon area (Pereira, 2014; Pereira, Martins, & Antunes, 2013) and are the only examples of additive bilingualism in Portugal we know of, since the minority native language that children speak is not in danger of being replaced by the language(s) of instruction.

Because there is no established bilingual provision in the public system, incorporating linguistic diversity is generally perceived as a 'problem' to schools. The situation mirrors what Gogolin (2002b: 127) observes: "the fundamental myth of uniformity of language and culture among a people also permeates the structures, forms and contents of European school systems." Even though there have been political efforts in line with European recommendations to support linguistic and cultural diversity as regards minority and immigrated languages, as well as the cross-disciplinary development of education for citizenship in schools, a monolingual/ monocultural framework prevails, according to which the students' languages are *not* school languages. Actually, FLs as curriculum subjects enjoy a much higher status than the languages spoken by non-native students.

4 Final remarks

The idea(l) of plurilingualism seems to indicate conditions for building "a vibrant and open society without discrimination, benefiting us all, marked by the inclusion of all residents in full respect of their human rights" (CoE, 2008: 3), even if this kind of society can only be anticipated at present. The *White Paper on Intercultural Dialogue* (ibid.) sets some preconditions for intercultural dialogue to thrive, which are not yet in place:

> the democratic governance of cultural diversity should be adapted in many aspects; democratic citizenship and participation should be strengthened; intercultural competences should be taught and learned; spaces for intercultural dialogue should be created and widened; and intercultural dialogue should be taken to the international level.

These goals appear to be both desirable and unfeasible. We may think they are too idealistic, and perhaps they are, but the bottom line is: *what kind of society do we envisage and stand for?*

We agree with Pereira (2014) when she argues that each school can create conditions for sustainable language education that promotes plurilingualism (not just language teaching). To that end, as Gogolin (2002b: 128) argues, we need to build "a linguistic self-conception different from today's: not a 'monolingual', 'monocultural' but a 'multilingual habitus'", which means "not only to observe and recognise that a cultural and linguistic multiple public sphere exists already, but also to accept its potential and legitimacy." We further need to address the low impact of European discourses on curriculum policies and practices, as well as the disempowering effect of neoliberal rationales, and find strategies to keep on struggling for a more humanistic education.

References

Alarcão, I., Andrade, A. I., Moreira, A., Sá, C. M., Pereira, L. A., Canha, M. B., ... Pinto, S. (2004). Percursos de consolidação da Didáctica das Línguas em Portugal. *Investigação em Educação, 3*, 237–302.

Alarcão, I., & Araújo e Sá, M. H. (2010). *Era uma vez… a didáctica de línguas em Portugal: Enredos, actores e cenários de construção do conhecimento.* Cadernos do LALE, Série Reflexões 3. Aveiro: University of Aveiro.

Baptista, J. A., Santiago, A., Almeida, D., Antunes, P., & Gaspar, R. (2011). *Programa de Português L2 para alunos surdos: Ensinos básico e secundário.* Lisboa: Ministério da Educação, Direção Geral de Inovação e Desenvolvimento Curricular.

Beacco, J-C. (2005). *Languages and language repertoires: Plurilingualism as a way of life in Europe.* Strasbourg: Council of Europe. Retrieved April 15, 2014 from http://www.coe.int/t/dg4/linguistic/Liste_EN.asp#TopOfPage.

Beacco, J-C., Byram, M., Cavalli, M., Coste, D., Cuenat, M. E., Goullier, F., & Panthier, J. (2010). *Guide for the development and implementation of plurilingual and intercultural education.* Strasbourg: Council of Europe. Retrieved April 15, 2014 from www.coe.int/lang.

Bento, C., Coelho, R., Joseph, N., & Mourão, S. J. (2005). *Programa de Generalização do Ensino de Inglês no 1º Ciclo do Ensino Básico.* Lisboa: Ministério da Educação.

Breidbach, S. (2003). *Plurilingualism, democratic citizenship in Europe and the role of English.* Strasbourg: Council of Europe. Retrieved April 17, 2014 from www.coe.int/lang.

Byram, M., Gribkova, B., & Starkey, H. (2002). *Developing the intercultural dimension in language teaching: A practical introduction for teachers.* Strasbourg: Council of Europe. Retrieved April 17, 2014 from http://www.coe.int/t/dg4/linguistic/source/guide_dimintercult_en.pdf.

Caels, F., & Mendes, M. (2008). Diversidade linguística na escola: Uma problemática global. In M. H. M. Mateus, D. Pereira & G. Fischer (Eds.), *Diversidade linguística na escola portuguesa.* Lisboa: Fundação Calouste Gulbenkian. Retrieved April 25, 2014 from http://www.iltec.pt/divling/_pdfs/cd1_diversidade_linguistica.pdf.

Casa-Nova, M. J. (2005). (I) Migrantes, diversidades e desigualdades no sistema educativo português: Balanço e perspectivas. *Ensaio: Avaliação e Políticas Públicas em Educação, 13*(47), 181–216.

Casa-Nova, M. J. (2008). Tempos e lugares dos ciganos na educação escolar pública. In M. J. Casa-Nova & P. Palmeira (Eds.), *Minorias* (pp. 7–55). Lisboa: Ministério do Trabalho e da Solidariedade Social e PETI. Retrieved March 29, 2014 from http://repositorium.sdum.uminho.pt/bitstream/1822/8657/1/M%20J%20CN-10anos_PETI-Livro8%20MJCN%2002.pdf.

Civil Society Platform on Multilingualism. (2011). *Policy recommendations for the promotion of multilingualism in the European Union*. Brussels: Executive Summary.

Comissão Europeia. (1995). *Livro branco sobre a educação e a formação. Ensinar e aprender. Rumo à sociedade cognitiva*. Bruxelas: Comissão Europeia. Retrieved March 20, 2014 from https://infoeuropa.eurocid.pt/registo/000037230.

Council of Europe. (1950). *Convention for the protection of human rights and fundamental freedoms*. Retrieved March 20, 2014 from http://human-rights-convention.org/the-texts/the-convention-in-1950/.

Council of Europe. (1954). *European cultural convention*. European Treaty Series – No. 18. Retrieved March 20, 2014 from http://conventions.coe.int/Treaty/Commun/QueVoulezVous.asp?CL=ENG&NT=018.

Council of Europe. (2001). *Common European framework of reference for languages: Learning, teaching, assessment*. Cambridge: Cambridge University Press.

Council of Europe. (2008). *White paper on intercultural dialogue. Living together as equals in dignity*. Council of Europe: Strasbourg. Retrieved March 20, 2014 from www.coe.int/t/dg4/intercultural/publication_whitepaper_id_en.asp.

Council of Europe. (2016). *Competences for democratic culture – Living together as equals in culturally diverse democratic societies*. Strasbourg: Council of Europe.

Council of Europe, Commissioner for Human Rights. (2012). *Human rights of Roma and travellers in Europe*. Report drafted by Claude Cahn & Gwendolyn Albert. Strasbourg: Council of Europe Publishing. Retrieved March 20, 2014 from http://www.gitanos.org/upload/43/39/RightsOfRoma_Consejo_de_Europa.pdf.

Cravo, A., Bravo, C., & Duarte, E. (2013). *Metas curriculares de Inglês – Ensino Básico: 2º e 3º ciclos*. Lisboa: Ministério da Educação e Ciência.

DGEEC (Direção Geral de Estatísticas de Educação e Ciência). (2017). *Perfil escolar da comunidade cigana. 2016/17*. Retrieved May 5, 2018 from http://www.dgeec.mec.pt/np4/906.html.

Duarte, J., Moreira, M. A., & Flores, C. (2013). Bilinguismo e educação: Um novo currículo para a formação de professores. In R. Bizarro, M. A. Moreira & C. Flores (Eds.), *Português língua não materna: Investigação e ensino* (pp. 111–128). Lisboa: LIDEL.

ECRI, European Commission against Racism and Intolerance (Comissão Europeia contra o Racismo e a Intolerância). (2002). Segundo relatório sobre Portugal. Strasbourg: Council of Europe. Retrieved March 21, 2014 from http://www.gddc.pt/direitos-humanos/portugal-dh/relatorios-ce/CBCRelatorioPortugal_2002.pdf.

Edelenbos, P., Johnstone, R., & Kubanek, A. (2006). *The main pedagogical principles underlying the teaching of languages to very young learners. Languages for the children of Europe. Published Research, Good Practice & Main Principles*. Final Report of the EAC 89/04, Lot 1 study. European Commission. Retrieved March 23, 2014 from http://www.poliglotti4.eu/php/language-research/index.php?doc_id=1212&lg=en.

Ellis, E., Gogolin, I., & Clyne, M. (2010). The Janus face of monolingualism: A comparison of German and Australian language education policies. *Current Issues in Language Planning, 11*(4), 439–460.

European Commission. (2007). *Key competences for lifelong learning. European reference framework*. Luxembourg: Office for Official Publications of the European Communities.

European Commission. (2010). *Europe 2020. A strategy for smart, sustainable and inclusive growth*. Brussels: Communication from the European Commission.

European Commission/EACEA/Eurydice. (2004). *Integrating immigrants' children into school in Europe*. Brussels: European Commission.

European Commission/EACEA/Eurydice. (2012). *Developing key competences at school in Europe: Challenges and opportunities for policy*. Eurydice Report. Luxembourg: Publications Office of the European Union. Retrieved March 20, 2014 from http://eacea.ec.europa.eu/education/eurydice.

European Commission/EACEA/Eurydice. (2017). *Key data on teaching languages at school in Europe. 2017 Edition*. Eurydice Report. Luxembourg: Publications Office of the European Union. Retrieved May 5, 2018 from https://publications.europa.eu/en/publication-detail/-/publication/73ac5ebd-473e-11e7-aea8-01aa75ed71a1/language-en/format-PDF.

Gogolin, I. (2002a). *Linguistic diversity and new minorities in Europe. Guide for the development of language education policies in Europe: From linguistic diversity to plurilingual education. Reference study*. Strasbourg: Council of Europe. Retrieved April 16, 2014 from http://www.coe.int/t/dg4/linguistic/Source/GogolinEN.pdf.

Gogolin, I. (2002b). Linguistic and cultural diversity in Europe: A challenge for educational research and practice. *European Educational Research Journal, 1*(1), 123–138.

Grosso, M. J., Soares, A., Sousa, F., & Pascoal, J. (2011). *QuaREPE. Quadro de referência para o ensino do português no estrangeiro. Documento orientador (vol. 1). Tarefas, actividades, exercícios e recursos para a avaliação (vol. 2)*. Lisboa: Ministério da Educação, Direção Geral de Inovação e Desenvolvimento Curricular.

Kelly, M., Grenfell, M., Allan, R., Kriza, C., & McEvoy, W. (2004). *European profile for language teacher education – A frame of reference*. A report to the European Commission Directorate General for Education and Culture. Retrieved from http://www.scuole.vda.it/english/images/library/teacherprofile.pdf.

Klugman, J. (2009). *Human Development Report 2009 – Overcoming barriers: Human mobility and development*. Hampshire & New York: Palgrave Macmillan & United Nations Development Programme. Retrieved April 20, 2014 from http://hdr.undp.org/en/media/HDR_2009_EN_Complete.pdf.

Leite, C. M. F. (2002). *O currículo e o multiculturalismo no sistema educativo português*. Lisboa: Fundação Calouste Gulbenkian & Fundação para a Ciência e a Tecnologia.

Lenz, P., & Berthele, R. (2010). *Assessment in plurilingual and intercultural education*. Strasbourg: Council of Europe. Retrieved April 17, 2014 from www.coe.int/lang.

Leslie, C., Moreira, M. A., & Mourão, S. (2018). School cluster assessment criteria and implications for primary English education in Portugal. Lecture in the Young learners & very young learners APPI Conference, Porto, 26th January.

Macedo, D., Dendrinos, B., & Gounari, P. (2006). *A hegemonia da língua inglesa*. Mangualde: Pedago.

Madeira, A., Teixeira, J., Botelho, F., Costa, J., Deus, S., Fiéis, A., ... Pessoa, I. (2013). *Avaliação de impacto e medidas prospetivas para a oferta do Português Língua Não Materna (PLNM) no Sistema Educativo Português*. Lisboa: ME/DGIDC.

Ministério da Educação. (2001). *Currículo nacional do ensino básico. Competências essenciais*. Lisboa: Ministério da Educação.

Nelde, P., Strubell, M., & Williams, G. (1996). *Euromosaic – The production and reproduction of the minority language groups in the European Union.* Luxembourg: Office for Official Publications of the European Communities.

Pereira, A. C. (2018). Em 19 anos duplicou o número de ciganos na escola obrigatória [Newspaper article]. *Público*, April 9. Retrieved May 3, 2018 from https://www.publico.pt/2018/04/09/sociedade/noticia/quase-duplicou-o-numero-de-alunos-ciganos-na-escola-obrigatoria-1808751.

Pereira, D. (2014). Para uma cultura linguística de escola. In M. A. Moreira & K. Zeichner (Eds.), *Diversidade linguística e justiça social na formação de professores* (pp. 77–97). Mangualde: Pedago.

Pereira, D., Martins, P., & Antunes, V. (2013). Educação bilingue e aprendizagem do português em contexto multilingue. In R. Bizarro, M. A. Moreira, & C. Flores (Eds.), *Português língua não materna: Investigação e ensino* (pp. 129–143). Lisboa: LIDEL.

Pinto, P. F. (2010). *O essencial sobre política de língua.* Lisboa: Imprensa Nacional-Casa da Moeda.

Silva, A. M. C., Caetano, A. P., Freire, I., Moreira, M. A., Freire, T., & Ferreira, A. S. (2010). Novos actores no trabalho em educação: Os mediadores socioeducativos. *Revista Portuguesa de Educação, 23*(2), 119–152.

Skutnabb-Kangas, T. (2002). *Why should linguistic diversity be maintained and supported in Europe? Some arguments.* Strasbourg: Council of Europe. Retrieved April 15, 2014 from www.coe.int/lang.

Suárez-Orozco, M. M., & Suárez-Orozco, C. (2009). Globalization, immigration, and schooling. In J. Banks (Ed.), *The Routledge international companion to multicultural education.* New York: Routledge.

Truchot, C. (2002). *Key aspects of the use of English in Europe.* Strasbourg: Council of Europe. Retrieved April 15, 2014 from www.coe.int/lang.

UNESCO. (2009). *Policy guidelines on inclusion in education.* Retrieved April 20, 2014 from http://www.inclusive-education-in-action.org/iea/index.php?menuid=47.

Vieira, F., Moreira, M. A., & Peralta, H. (2014). Research in foreign language education in Portugal (2006-2011): Inquiring into its transformative potential. *Language Teaching, 47*(2), 191–227.

Willems, G. (1996). Culture in language learning and teaching: Requirements for the creation of a context of negotiation. In G. Willems (Ed.), *Issues in cross-cultural communication – the European dimension in language teaching.* Nijmegen: Hogeschool Gelderland Press.

Willems, G. (2002). *Language teacher education policy promoting linguistic diversity and intercultural communication.* Strasbourg: Council of Europe. Retrieved April 15, 2014 from www.coe.int/lang.

María Luisa Pérez Cañado

The what's, why's, who's, and how's of Andalusian plurilingual education

Abstract: The present chapter aims to provide a detailed rendering of the plurilingual education model developed in the autonomous community of Andalusia (Spain) since 2005. To this end, it raises and answers different wh-questions which attempt to canvass the past, present and future of the two main plans enacting this model: the Andalusian Plan for the Promotion of Plurilingualism (APPP) and the *Plan Estratégico de Desarrollo de las Lenguas en Andalucía* (PEDLA). The chapter begins by explaining *why* the APPP and the PEDLA have been developed. Next, it describes *how* both plans are being practically implemented. Then, the chapter analyses the main outcomes of the APPP and the PEDLA, expounding on *who* has assessed the way in which these plans are working and *what* results have been yielded by the research conducted so far. It concludes by discussing *where* these outcomes lead us, identifying the main challenges to be addressed and setting an agenda for the future.

Keywords: Plurilingual education, CLIL, implementation, research

1 Introduction

It is an uncontested fact that we are currently confronted with a "language challenge" (Tudor, 2013: 22) in our increasingly multilingual and multicultural society. Language education is in turmoil (Lorenzo, 2010) and we are living what Mehisto (2008) terms a period of disjuncture, characterized by the tension between the previous order and a new approach which changes the *status quo*. The need for what Aronin and Hufeisen (2009: 105) denominate "a new linguistic dispensation" arises, where *polylanguaging*, *translanguaging*, or *plurilingualism* surface as key concepts. This necessity for novel language education policies which respond to the changing landscape acquires a particularly sharp relief in an autonomous community such as Andalusia, in the south of Spain, characterized by a deep-seated monolingual tradition, lack of extramural exposure to languages other than the mother tongue, and deficient levels of foreign language (FL) mastery. The shift from a monoglot to a polyglot mentality in this region has implied "fairly major upheavals for education" (Lorenzo, 2010: 4) in the last decade, and has been channeled via the Andalusian Plan for the Promotion of Plurilingualism (henceforth, APPP) and the *Plan Estratégico de Desarrollo de las*

Lenguas en Andalucía[1] (henceforth, PEDLA), two milestone documents which have provided a solid top-down push to plurilingual education in the autonomous community.

The present chapter will strive to paint a comprehensive picture of the plurilingual education model, which has been operative in the autonomous community of Andalusia since 2005, when the APPP was officially approved. In doing so, it will raise and attempt to answer a series of *wh-* questions which will allow us to canvass the past, present, and future of the Plans which have been set in motion to promote plurilingualism in a region with a firmly entrenched monolingual model. The chapter will begin by expounding on *why* the APPP and the PEDLA have burgeoned, tracing their origins from 1998 to 2004 and showcasing how they conform to the *zeitgeist* of broader European policies and regulations. It will then describe *how* they are being practically implemented by charting how their overarching guidelines trickle down to on-the-ground practice. The way in which they are working will subsequently be analyzed by focusing on *who* has done stocktaking on the way in which the APPP and the PEDLA are playing out and by reporting on *what* results have been yielded by the research carried out in our context. The chapter will conclude by exploring *where* these outcomes lead us by identifying the chief challenges to conquer and by mapping out an agenda for the future. This overview of plurilingual education in Andalusia will offer insights into the strengths and weaknesses of the APPP and the PEDLA and will explore the threats and opportunities they face in order to contribute to the successful implementation of these ambitious language policies.

2 *Why* have the APPP and the PEDLA burgeoned? Origins and backdrop

As Macaro et al. (2018: 64) have recently underlined, the growth of bilingual programs "appears to be top-down policy driven, rather than bottom-up and promoted by enthusiastic key stakeholders (teachers and students)". This is exactly what has occurred in Andalusia. The APPP and the PEDLA have provided the strong institutional support required for bilingual education to be firmly put into place in a community with a deep-seated monolingual tradition. These two foundational documents can be framed within the broader backdrop of a series of pivotal European documents which have shaped the continent's linguistic landscape for the past two decades: the 1995 EC White Paper on Education and

1 Strategic Plan for the Development of Languages in Andalusia.

Training (European Commission, 1995), which established the mother tongue + 2 initiative; the Council of Europe's encouragement of plurilingualism; the ECML's (European Centre for Modern Languages) support for the implementation of innovative language teaching reforms across member states; the Lisbon Summit's (2000) emphasis on the need to improve the quality and efficiency of education systems; and the worrying outcomes of successive Eurobarometers in terms of Spaniards' language competence[2].

In line with the above-mentioned activities, four clear-cut phases can be discerned in the implementation of bi- and plurilingual education in Andalusia. The first one corresponds to the experimental bilingual sections which were initially established from 1998 to 2004 in 26 Andalusian schools with three FLs: English, French, and German. In 2005, this initiative became a full-fledged plan with the official approval of the APPP, which brought about an exponential increase in the number of bilingual schools from 140 in 2005–2006 to 519 in 2008–2009. From 2009 onwards, the onus was on the implementation of the Bilingual Schools Program, which has continued to establish Content and Language Integrated Learning (CLIL)[3] across the autonomous community, reaching 1,260 bilingual schools in 2016. Finally, the PEDLA (2016–2020) has further sharpened and refined the previous stages, with over 1,400 bilingual schools now being operative in Andalusia and with a target number of 1,500 being set for 2020. Andalusia now has more bilingual schools than any other monolingual community in Spain and has earned the European Language Label Award in 2006 for its contribution to multilingualism.

Both the APPP and the PEDLA have entailed a substantial reconfiguration of Andalusian schools (Lorenzo, 2019), which has impinged on methodology, curricular organization, types of groupings and teaching modalities, teacher profiles, and evaluation and assessment. The overarching goals of these documents are two-fold: to improve mother tongue language skills while concomitantly

---

2 Indeed, according to the latest Eurobarometer (European Commission, 2012), Spain is on "the bottom rung of the foreign-language knowledge ladder" (Lasagabaster & Sierra, 2009: 7), with 54 % of its citizens admitting to being monolingual and only 18 % being capable of holding a conversation in two other languages.

3 CLIL is defined as "a dual-focused educational approach in which an additional language is used for the learning and teaching of both content and language" (Marsh & Langé, 2000: 2). The emphasis on both teaching and content points to the very hallmark of CLIL: it involves a "two for one" approach (Lyster, 2007: 2), where subject matter teaching is used at least some of the time as a means of increased meaningful exposure to the target language.

harnessing plurilingual and pluricultural competence amongst the Andalusian population.

The APPP (Junta de Andalucía, 2005) is based on 13 objectives, 61 actions, and five pillars or subprograms. They involve increasing the number of bilingual schools in the community (the *Bilingual Schools Program*); reconfiguring Official Language Schools to provide enhanced language teacher education (the *Official Language Schools Program*); expanding teacher training initiatives through the sharing of good practices and the provision of study licenses and exchanges (the *Teachers and Plurilingualism Program*); increasing extramural exposure to English (the *Plurilingualism and Society Program*); and setting in place measures to cater for the more vulnerable and underserved student population (the *Plurilingualism and Cross-culturalism Program*).

In turn, the PEDLA (Junta de Andalucía, 2017) updates and realigns the APPP with the most pressing concerns of the current Andalusian linguistic scenario. It has four broad goals and hinges on six lines of action. The latter entail a continuous commitment to up-skill Andalusian students' FL level (according to Lorenzo [2019], 69.2 % of bilingual schools students in this autonomous community now have a B1/B2 level at the end of Compulsory Secondary Education (CSE), as opposed to non-bilingual schools students, who only attain an A1/A2 on average). The PEDLA also pushes for increased teacher education (which now centers on methodological issues in addition to linguistic ones), continues to favor increased extramural exposure to the FL and attention to diversity, and steps up research into the effects of bilingual education and their evaluation. This goal will be fueled by bringing back study licenses and creating educational innovation projects through which universities and schools carrying out grassroots practice can collaborate.

3 *How* are the APPP and the PEDLA being practically implemented? From regulations to on-the-ground practice

How do these overarching guidelines laid out in the APPP and PEDLA documents filter down to on-the-ground practice? The implementation of these actions has been channeled via a set of regional Orders and Instructions. The *Order of July 24th, 2006* (Junta de Andalucía, 2006a) sets forth the basic organizational principles, which guide all curricular aspects of the *Bilingual Schools Program*. It establishes that bilingual schools are those infant, primary, secondary, and vocational training schools which teach from 30 % to 50 % of the curriculum (this was raised to a minimum of 50 % by the *Order of June 28th, 2011* [Junta de Andalucía, 2011]) of two to four content subjects through CLIL in the first

FL. Bilingual branches or sections can co-exist with regular, mainstream groups who only receive input in the target language in FL classes. The CLIL stream must receive daily exposure to the first FL in both primary and secondary education. CLIL teaching takes place 1 to 2 hours per week, alongside FL instruction (3–4 hours a week), L1 classes (3–5 hours per week), and L3 classes from the second cycle of primary education (2–3 hours a week), with a view to developing plurilingual intercultural competence (Jáimez Muñoz, 2007). Depending on the available teachers' profile, each school is able to determine the subjects taught through the first FL, although at least one must belong to the area of natural and social sciences. The most common ones being implemented via CLIL include science, art, and physical education at primary level, and social and natural sciences, mathematics, physical education, and technology in secondary education.

In order to become a bilingual school, a project needs to be drafted and presented in a consultancy phase[4], which, if granted, gives way to a so-called 'year zero', where preparation for CLIL teaching takes place. A bilingual section coordinator is appointed and participating teachers engage in intensive linguistic and pedagogical training through courses provided by the Official Language Schools, Teacher Training Centers, and conferences or conventions. An integrated curriculum of language and content is elaborated, specific materials are designed, and the European Language Portfolio (ELP) is incorporated for use in the following year, when CLIL teaching is launched.

Four types of teaching figures come to the fore within bilingual sections: bilingual project coordinators, language teachers, nonlinguistic area teachers, and teaching assistants (TAs). It is essential that they all work in a collaborative manner. As established by the *Order of July 24th, 2006* (Junta de Andalucía, 2006a), coordinators receive teaching reductions in order to fulfill the following functions:

- Oversee the adequate implementation of the new curricular model;
- Coordinate meetings to elaborate the integrated language curriculum;
- Coordinate teaching activities;
- Establish a timetable for TAs;
- Communicate with other bilingual centers and the provincial coordinators;
- Coordinate all initiatives within the overarching APPP.

4 As of 2010, schools are no longer allowed to apply for bilingual sections; the latter are directly granted by the *Junta de Andalucía* in accordance to its priorities.

Language teachers, in turn, must prioritize communicative teaching, work cooperatively with other language colleagues, and participate in the development of the integrated language curriculum, following the recommendations of the CEFR and using the ELP. Nonlinguistic area teachers also have a two-hour reduction in hours, and primarily need to contribute to the elaboration and adaptation of the integrated language curriculum and to design appropriate CLIL materials. Important innovations have been introduced by the *Instrucciones de 31 de agosto de 2010* (Junta de Andalucía, 2010) regarding the requirements which nonlinguistic area teachers must meet in order to be considered eligible for public bilingual sections. They must now be permanent teachers with at least a B2 level in the target language (the PEDLA foregrounds that it will be pushed up to a C1 in the near future), provisional teachers who obtain a bilingual teaching post through a regulated selection process, or permanent teachers who have successfully completed official recognition courses at B1 level and who make a formal commitment to acquire a B2 level. When none of the above are available, FL specialist teachers will be appointed to teach subject content. This new requirement for a higher English level, coupled with the also recently established imperative to teach the majority of the subject in English, resorting to the mother tongue only when strictly necessary, is going to require substantial changes in the implementation of the APPP at all levels, quite possibly yielding different outcomes from the ones obtained in studies hereto conducted (Hughes, 2010).

TAs have their own regulations (*Order of June 20th, 2006* [Junta de Andalucía, 2006b]; *Order of September 14th, 2007* [Junta de Andalucía, 2007a]; *Instrucciones de 17 de julio de 2009* [Junta de Andalucía, 2009a]). For 12 hours a week, they complement and support CLIL teachers, fostering oral conversation practice, providing correct pronunciation and grammatical models, collaborating in materials design, and constituting a gateway into their home country's culture. They can also be assigned further functions or tasks by the regional authorities, but must always be accompanied in class by the teacher whose activity they are supporting and can never substitute for him/her. In infant education, one TA is assigned per school; at primary level, one TA is designated to schools with one to five bilingual units and two to those with six or more; and in secondary education, one TA is allotted to centers with one to three bilingual units and two to those with four or more. Official Language Schools also receive one TA if they have up to 24 English groups and two if they have 25 or more. In 2009–2010, for example, 1,044 TAs worked in Andalusia, 75 financed by the Ministry of Education and 969 provided by the *Junta de Andalucía*. As of 2009, ERASMUS students and final year students in Philology and Teacher Training degrees at Andalusian universities can also be appointed as TAs.

These diverse types of teachers need to adapt to a learner-centered, communicative methodology, underpinned by constructivist theories of learning. Task-based teaching, reflection on the mother tongue, and the connection between languages should all be emphasized (*Order of July 24th, 2006* [Junta de Andalucía, 2006a]). Materials should also reflect these principles, presenting didactic innovation, reflecting CEFR principles, and catering for diversity (*Order of March 7th, 2008* [Junta de Andalucía, 2008a]). Specific awards have been granted to those originally designed materials which most embrace these principles. Evaluation procedures should also be in line with this communicative approach: they need to incorporate CEFR and ELP recommendations, prioritize content knowledge over linguistic expression, and assess both communicative competencies and compensatory communication strategies (*Order of July 24th, 2006* [Junta de Andalucía, 2006a]). These curricular guidelines are not static, but adjusted and fine-tuned through yearly 'instructions' (e.g. *Instrucciones de 21 de septiembre de 2007* [Junta de Andalucía, 2007b], *Instrucciones 31 de julio de 2008* [Junta de Andalucía, 2008b], *Instrucciones de 24 de julio de 2009* [Junta de Andalucía, 2009b], *Instrucciones de 31 de agosto de 2010* [Junta de Andalucía, 2010], *Instrucciones de 19 de junio de 2013* [Junta de Andalucía, 2013]).

4 *Who* has done the stocktaking? Key figures and types of publications

The flurry of interest and sweeping changes generated by the APPP and the PEDLA have spawned a remarkably broad array of publications on CLIL in the Andalusian community. They can be classified into five broad categories: *practitioner accounts*, *quantitative research*, *qualitative investigations*, *studies with a mixed research design*, and *critical evaluations* to the research conducted.

Within the initial category of *practitioner accounts*, a notable number of publications are primarily theoretical descriptions of CLIL in Andalusia. Roldán Tapia (2005), Madrid Fernández (2006), Jáimez Muñoz (2007), Luque Agulló (2009), or Pérez Torres (2009a) all attempt to characterize the CLIL model being applied through the APPP, framing it within the broader bilingual education picture. Another set of authors expound on the traits of different models or methodologies which can be used within successful CLIL: Ávila López (2009) centers on cooperative learning and the role of affective factors as a CLIL touchstone; Salaberri Ramiro (2009) and Morilla García and Gallagher (2009) focus on Multiple Intelligence Theory; and Gerdes (2009a, 2009b) fleshes out the origins, theoretical underpinnings, and steps of the SIOP (Sheltered Instruction Observation Protocol) model. Méndez García (2009), in turn, offers some theoretical recommendations for the inclusion of intercultural education in the CLIL classroom, while Pavón Vázquez (2009) develops a framework for the introduction of CLIL in tertiary education that spans all curricular levels.

This theoretical discussion of Andalusian CLIL is offset by the description of practical experiences, which can also be located in the specialist literature. Alameda Hernández (2002), for instance, signposts relevant practice in implementing science through CLIL at primary level. López Cabrera (2009), in turn, describes how the integrated curriculum has been approached at a high school in Baza, outlining its step-by-step implementation and providing samples of the materials generated for its implementation.

The organizational aspects of setting up bilingual sections have also attracted considerable attention in our autonomous community, perhaps because, as Ruiz Gómez and Nieto García (2009) emphasize, "[…] en la actualidad continuamos conviviendo con múltiples dificultades organizativas de diversa índole en la implantación y desarrollo de nuestras secciones bilingües, diferencias que aún no han sido resueltas de forma satisfactoria […]"[5]. Precisely with a view to circumventing these potential hurdles, García Jiménez and Cobo López (2009), Ruiz Gómez and Nieto García (2009), or Román Fernández and Moreno Álvarez (2010) lay out problems, formulate questions for debate, and provide suggestions to overcome potential difficulties, which, in their prior experience, have been encountered in the organization and implementation of CLIL programs.

Given the many lacunae associated with materials design reported in the specialist research literature (e.g. lack of availability, poor quality, or insufficient guidelines for materials adaptation or design), it is not surprising that it has become a major area of interest in Andalusian publications. Actual instances of originally designed or adapted materials are presented: Espinosa Zafra (2009) offers examples of materials designed for the integrated curriculum in primary education (class vocabulary and rules, songs and poems, class labels, or posters), and García Jiménez (2009) and Tomlinson and Masuhara (2009) do the same for the subject of science and the content area of football, respectively, to entice learners into English. Entire units of work or excerpts from them are offered by Benítez Castro and Adán Nieto (2007) (for 1st grade CSE science), Luque Agulló (2009) (for 3rd grade CSE biology), and Clegg (2007) (for 3rd grade primary education science). Finally, specific types of originally designed materials

---

5 "[…] currently we continue to face multiple organizational difficulties concerning the implementation and the development of our bilingual sections in schools. No sastificatory solution has been found for these differences/These differences remain unresolved."

are also presented, such as a bilingual dictionary on mathematics (Casares Fernández, 2009) or others based on the ELP (Hornillo Estrella, 2009; Medrano Dorantes, 2009; Rocha Martín, 2009a, 2009b).

With regard to the latter type of materials, ICT merits special attention, as it has occupied many pages in Andalusian publications. Pérez Torres (2009b) provides a general overview of available multimedia software, webpages, reference materials, treasure hunts, webquests, authentic materials, and Web 2.0 tools (wikis, blogs, chats, e-mail, international portals, or e-Twinning) for CLIL instruction, expounding on their many assets. Del Moral Villalta (2009a) narrows the scope down to the advantages of Web 2.0 and focuses on wikis, blogs, RSS, podcasts, Googledocs, and spreadsheets. In another article, she focuses specifically on wikis (Del Moral Villalta, 2009b) and their definition, traits, use, and effectiveness in the CLIL classroom. Malagón Gallego, Dunmall Connor, and Moral Martos (2009), in turn, concentrate on e-Twinning, highlighting its innovative character and intercultural benefits, and providing a step-by-step account of how to introduce it in the CLIL class. Finally, García Jiménez (2009) describes the utility, features, and merits of Open Office.

The new roles which stakeholders must be ready to take on are not disregarded in the official literature and constitute a further field of interest in Andalusia. Julián de Vega (2007) centers on bilingual program coordinators, not only identifying their main tasks, which she considers are multiplied in the grassroots implementation of the APPP, but also highlighting those abilities which they must harness in order to be effective, and which include leadership, technical, methodological, and social competencies. Ortega Cebreros (2009) shifts her attention to the TA within the APPP, charting the traits, social characteristics, and pedagogical potential (s)he must garner. The author concludes that they particularly assist learners in the development of their oral competence and allow attention to diversity based on empathy with the student body.

Despite this clear predominance of practitioner accounts in the Andalusian bibliography on CLIL, there have also been *quantitative studies* conducted into its functioning in our immediate context. Here, the work of the research groups led by Francisco Lorenzo in Pablo de Olavide University and by Daniel Madrid at the University of Granada deserves to be foregrounded. The investigation, which has undoubtedly had the greatest dissemination and impact in our region, is that conducted by Lorenzo et al. in the academic year 2006–2007 (Casal & Moore, 2008; Lorenzo, Casal & Moore, 2009; Lorenzo et al., 2009). These authors, commissioned by the *Consejería de Educación* of the *Junta de Andalucía*, administered skills-based language tests to 1,768 students participating in English, French, and German bilingual sections in 61 randomly selected schools across the whole of Andalusia. The French and German language cohort had received CLIL education since primary level, as it was part of the pilot program for bilingual sections implemented prior to the APPP, whereas the English language sections had only been running for a year and a half when the study was conducted. It is an instance of cross-sectional research, as it applied these tests to 4th-grade primary students and 2nd-grade CSE students. This quantitative data was complemented by questionnaires administered to teachers, students, and parents, and with SWOT analysis interviews with coordinators.

Many of the limitations of this investigation were addressed by a study coordinated by Madrid (Madrid & Hughes, 2011). Conducted by 6 researchers and 10 collaborators, this three-year investigation provided valuable information on the effects of CLIL programs in primary and secondary education on the L1, L2, and subject matter knowledge. It also probed their repercussions on cultural competence and attitudes towards the target language and culture. The data collection phase took place in 2007–2008 and worked with a random and non-probabilistic sample of 314 students, 146 in 6th grade of primary education and 168 in 4th grade of CSE. It compared CLIL and non-CLIL strands in bilingual public schools with a private school where 50 % of instruction takes place in the L2 and with a semi-private monolingual school, all of them in the city of Granada. English and Spanish language and subject matter tests (natural and social sciences at primary level and social sciences in secondary education) were carefully designed and piloted, and subsequently applied. In the case of the English test, the four skills were sampled.

The most recent large-scale quantitative investigation has been conducted at the University of Jaén and led by Pérez Cañado (Madrid Fernández & Barrios Espinosa, 2018; Pavón Vázquez, 2018; Pérez Cañado, 2018a, 2018b; Rascón Moreno & Bretones Callejas, 2018). It has explored the effects of CLIL programs within the English bilingual sections of three of the monolingual communities in Spain which have the least experience of bilingual education (Andalusia, Extremadura, and the Canary Islands). To this end, it has studied the effects of CLIL on English language competence, Spanish language competence, and content knowledge of those subjects taught through the FL of primary (6th grade) and secondary (4th grade of CSE) education students. The study has involved 20 researchers from all Andalusian universities, the University of Extremadura and the University of Las Palmas de Gran Canaria. It has worked with a total of 53 public, charter, and private schools in the twelve provinces of these three autonomous communities and with a sample of 2,245 students, 333 teachers, and 595 parents. It addresses the limitations of previous investigations through the size of its sample (the largest in studies hitherto conducted), through guaranteeing the homogeneity of bilingual and non-bilingual schools students, through the intervening variables it has factored in, through its longitudinal focus, and through its timing, as it has measured the impact of CLIL after 10 years of implementation.

These investigations have been complemented *qualitatively* through needs and SWOT analyses and case studies. Rubio Mostacero (2009) carried out needs analysis interviews with 20 teachers in 4 secondary schools in the province of Jaén in June 2005, with a view to designing a training course for nonlinguistic area teachers on the basis of her outcomes. She initially drafted a course model based on her prior experience and subsequently revised it in two successive phases: after conducting the needs analysis and after subjecting it to the critical scrutiny of the interviewees and the local teacher-training center. In turn, Cabezas Cabello (2010) interviewed over 100 teachers and 30 coordinators in 30 primary and secondary schools implementing English, French, and German bilingual sections in the APPP in all eight Andalusian provinces. His aim was to carry out a SWOT analysis of APPP implementation and to contrast top-down and bottom-up approaches to the Plan. Finally, Tobin and Abello-Contesse (2013) worked exclusively with TAs participating in English bilingual sections in public schools of Andalusia to determine how they were used and to investigate the cultural component of their job. Longitudinal case studies were carried out with seven informants, using guided, semi-structured interviews which were repeated three times over an eight-month teaching period.

Research-wise, a final set of investigations (Pérez Cañado, 2016a, 2016b; Lancaster, 2016) can be classified as following a *mixed research design*, since they are instances of survey research, which Brown (2001) characterizes as mid-way between qualitative and statistical research. Both have designed, validated, and administered original questionnaires to geographically comprehensive samples (574 respondents in Pérez Cañado and 745 informants in Lancaster), using multiple triangulation (data, investigator, and location), factoring in intervening variables for each of the cohorts involved, and carrying out both within- and across-cohort comparisons. Pérez Cañado (2016a, 2016b) conducted a needs analysis of language teacher training for bilingual education across the whole of Europe in order to identify the current proficiency level and training needs which pre- and in-service teachers, teacher trainers, and bilingual coordinators had on five main fronts: linguistic and intercultural competence, theoretical underpinnings of CLIL, methodological aspects, materials and resources, and ongoing professional development. In turn, Lancaster (2016) focused on stakeholder perspectives of CLIL development in the monolingual province of Jaén and polled teacher and student perceptions of the way CLIL schemes are playing out vis-à-vis teacher and student competence, methodology, materials, resources and ICT, evaluation, mobility, improvement and motivation towards English, and coordination and organization. Finally, Pérez Cañado (2018c) administered three sets of questionnaires and conducted semi-structured interviews with 2,633 teachers, students and parents in Andalusia, as well as other monolingual communities in Spain, in order to carry out an in-depth analysis of where we stand in the process of implementing CLIL methodology, materials and evaluation.

The final series of publications worthy of mention is also very recent and comprises *critical evaluations* of the studies carried out on CLIL in the Andalusian context. They have been primarily led by Bruton (Bruton, 2011; Bruton, 2012; Bruton, 2013; García López & Bruton, 2013), Pérez Cañado (2011, 2012), and more recently, Cenoz, Genesee, and Gorter (2013).

5 *What* have the results been? Research outcomes

What are the overarching conclusions to be drawn from the research outcomes on CLIL programs within the APPP and the PEDLA? To begin with, as *assets* or *strengths*, the quantitative studies (Lorenzo et al., 2009; Madrid & Hughes, 2011; Pérez Cañado, 2018a, 2018b) conducted reveal an unequivocal support for a CLIL route over traditional language-driven instruction. Indeed, CLIL groups invariably outstrip their non-CLIL counterparts on FL competence; content knowledge taught through the FL is not watered down, as CLIL students also perform satisfactorily in the subject matter taught in the L2, assimilating this knowledge at the same high level as the monolingual control groups; and the development of the native language is not at all curtailed, even when the amount of L2 exposure is increased to 50 %. Furthermore, cognitive, cultural, social, affective, and intellectual benefits for students participating in bilingual programs have been documented (Cabezas Cabello, 2010), together with increased motivation towards FL learning (Lancaster, 2016). Methodologically, student-centered pedagogies are being incorporated to a greater extent, especially task-based, project-oriented and cooperative learning options (Pérez Cañado, 2018c). Materials are considered to be more authentic, communicative, interesting, and innovative, and they are incorporating ICT to a much greater extent, which is furthermore more readily available. Coordination and collaboration among teachers is equally being stepped up, especially in the elaboration, adaptation, and implementation of the integrated language curriculum. Opportunities to travel and to experience multicultural contact have also increased for both students and teachers, and encouragement to participate in exchanges, visits, or projects abroad is documented. Finally, teacher training has also been enhanced: there is greater attendance at teacher training courses on CLIL, completion of linguistic upgrade courses in

Official Language Schools, and participation in linguistic study abroad programs. The overall picture, which transpires from the studies conducted in Andalusia, is that CLIL programs within the APPP have been enthusiastically embraced by participating stakeholders and have garnered acceptance and prestige in the community. Indeed, research outcomes evince a tangible commitment and preparedness to invest time and resources in the CLIL enterprise, with traditional monolingual education being increasingly equated with second-rate education, "drip-feed education" (Vez, 2009: 8) or a slow track to language learning (cf. Cabezas Cabello, 2010; Lancaster, 2016; Pérez Cañado, 2016a, 2016b).

There are, however, many *weaknesses* or *challenges*, which still need to be addressed (cf. Cabezas Cabello, 2010; Pérez Cañado, 2016a, 2016b, 2018c; Lancaster, 2016; Rubio Mostacero, 2009; Tobin & Abello-Contesse, 2013). There are conspicuous weaknesses in terms of the linguistic and intercultural competence of teachers: pronunciation in the FL needs to be improved, both BICS (Basic Interpersonal Communication Skills) and CALP (Cognitive Academic Language Proficiency) (Cummins, 1999) need to be worked on, and a focus on form needs to run through CLIL programs. Furthermore, the vast majority of bilingual teachers are still not familiar with the theoretical underpinnings of CLIL, evincing an almost complete lack of knowledge vis-à-vis the precursors of CLIL: its origins, driving forces and models; its features, assets, and pitfalls; the theory of language and learning underlying it; or the effects and functioning of CLIL in evidence-based research. Further guidelines also need to be provided with regard to materials and resources for the design and adaptation of materials, the elaboration of the integrated curriculum, the implementation of collaborative teaching, and the use of Web 2.0 tools. Methodologically, considerable strides still need to be taken in order to incorporate student-centeredness fully, ensure homogeneity in the development of CLIL programs, cater for diversity, and prepare TAs to work with students and teachers. Ongoing professional development is another major area for future work, as attendance at university conferences and Masters on CLIL needs to be fostered, together with the award of study leaves for further studies or research, and participation in exchange and mobility programs and methodological upgrade courses. Finally, a series of false myths or misconstrued perceptions (cf. Pérez Cañado, forthcoming for a full account) need to be debunked for progress to be made on the CLIL front, including the erroneously held beliefs that content and L1 learning lag behind in CLIL programs (a theory which research has shot down), that language teachers now take a back seat (their role is more heightened than ever in preparing students to cope successfully with the grammar and lexicon covered in the content classes), or that subject-matter lessons should merely summarize contents in the FL. This led to what Lasagabaster & Sierra (2010) termed the 'Valencian fiasco'.

Together with these pitfalls, certain flaws detected in the existing research also need to be addressed. Indeed, although the studies thus far conducted are invaluable endeavors commendable for contributing to pushing the field forward, they present potentially serious *methodological problems*, which could skew the results obtained. Bruton (2011, 2012, 2013), García López and Bruton (2013), Pérez Cañado (2011, 2012), or Cenoz, Genesee, and Gorter (2013) have all pinpointed the chief criticisms which can be leveled at these studies and which require action in order for "CLIL to evolve […] in a pedagogically coherent fashion and for research to play a critical role in its evolution" (p. 5). These attested shortcomings can be classified into three main categories:

In terms of *variables*:

- One of the most worrying problems presented by prior studies is that none of them have guaranteed the homogeneity of the experimental and control groups involved. Given the well-documented level of self-selection in CLIL groups, this could invalidate the results obtained thus far. Hence, the treatment and comparison groups need to be matched in future studies for verbal intelligence, motivation, level of English, or socio-economic background, among other variables.
- Intervening or moderator variables have not been factored in or controlled for in prior investigations and, consequently, need to be taken into account.
- The L1 and content knowledge of the subjects taught through CLIL have not been considered as dependent variables and should thus become a prime area of attention.

Vis-à-vis the *research design*:

- Some of the prior investigations have not employed pre- and post-tests or control and experimental groups, thereby not truly carrying out a comparison of CLIL and non-CLIL strands.
- None of them have been longitudinal, as they have all been cross-sectional endeavors without delayed post-testing phases.
- They have not combined both quantitative and qualitative research methods.
- Within the qualitative part of the study, multiple triangulation has very rarely been employed.

Finally, concerning *statistical methodology*:

- Some of the studies in question have made sweeping statements without statistical confirmation. For example, they have based their conclusions regarding the effects of CLIL on the L1 or subject content acquisition on

teacher's appreciations, and not on an empirical analysis with different types of variables (dependent – independent – moderator).
- They have furthermore not employed ANOVA and the t-test, together with multivariate procedures (factor analysis and discriminant analysis) and thus have been unable to identify the causes of the linguistic gains, merely assuming they were due to CLIL.

Furthermore, largely discrepant findings have been yielded by top-down and bottom-up investigations: while the former have sung the praises of CLIL (e.g. Lorenzo et al., 2009), the latter (e.g. Cabezas Cabello, 2010) have been a reality check. Thus, a balance needs to be orchestrated between both views and further research, which overcomes the aforementioned limitations, needs to be conducted[6]. Indeed, the single most widely consensual affirmation in the specialized literature is that solid empirical research is still sparse and that, consequently, the field is very much open to scrutiny. In García López and Bruton's (2013: 269) words, "[...] there is still much research to be undertaken to offer a representative picture of the benefits and drawbacks of the implementation of CLIL classes in public schools in Andalusia".

6 *Where* do these outcomes lead us? The agenda for the future

On the basis of progress so far, there are four chief lines of action, which the Andalusian regional government has set for the PEDLA by 2020. The remit is to have the program continue to *grow* by increasing the number of bilingual schools and expanding bilingual streams in vocational training and Baccalaureate. A second objective is to *upgrade* participating teachers' linguistic proficiency, by requiring they meet a C1 rather than the present B2 level, as well as participating schools' offer of languages, by moving from bilingual to plurilingual schools, where an L3 is also taught through CLIL. Another chief goal is to *homogenize* CLIL models across schools; the fact that CLIL is being applied in variegated ways across Andalusia may cause the concept to be internally ambiguous, not clearly defined, and difficult to pin down, as Cenoz, Genesee, and Gorter (2013) have argued. Finally, there is a willingness to *learn* from the research conducted

6 Two governmentally-financed research projects have just been set in motion precisely with the aim of carrying out a large-scale, longitudinal study into the effects of CLIL in monolingual regions (including Andalusia) and which supersede all the aforementioned shortcomings (cf. *Proyecto FFI2012-32221 del Ministerio de Economía y Competitividad* and *Proyecto de Excelencia P12-HUM-2348 de la Junta de Andalucía*).

hitherto, by taking into account its outcomes in shaping future decisions and continuing to do stocktaking of the way the APPP is playing out.

How to go about attaining these lofty goals? We propose going about it by fostering what we have termed '*the six –tions*'. A necessary starting point is to promote *reflection*. In order to build a solid template for the future, it is incumbent upon stakeholders and gatekeepers to be up-to-date with the way the APPP is developing, as well as to carry out self-assessment of teaching practices from a critical perspective.

The best way to continue moving the CLIL agenda forward is to engage in *investigation* as a device that drives the aforementioned reflection. Both top-down and bottom-up stocktaking should be encouraged and teachers should increasingly take responsibility for classroom-based enquiry in order to truly have ownership of CLIL pedagogies.

The outcomes of such research should then be shared by fostering *communication*. Forums for debate should be articulated (e.g. the latest *Jornadas Regionales de Plurilingüismo*, which took place in Seville in September 2013), online platforms should foster the dissemination of good practices (e.g. *LinguaRed*[7] or *Vandelvira*[8]), and both horizontal and vertical coordination should be promoted.

This communication will undoubtedly increase the amount of *information* reaching key players in CLIL programs. It behooves all participants to stay abreast of the way they are working by being aware of the conferences, courses, book series, and specific journals which relay their results.

This ties in directly with *education*, the key to any future vision for bilingual education. This is, in our view, where CLIL will stand or fall in terms of sustainability. Teacher training needs to be escalated via linguistic and methodological upgrade courses, specialized conferences, study periods abroad, job shadowing programs, or specific CLIL Masters, such as the one currently being coordinated by the University of Jaén.

And, finally, ensuring participant *motivation* is equally pivotal. Providing incentives, course release, and stability for teachers, and guaranteeing support from gatekeepers are essential for the successful implementation of the APPP. In this sense, we fully concur with Fernández and Halbach (2011: 262) in that, more than on any other aspect, the success of CLIL schemes "ultimately relies on teachers' commitment and motivation", which, consequently, need to be sustained.

---

7 *LinguaRed: Red Profesional de Formación para el Profesorado de Centros Bilingües* (http://ulises.cepgranada.org/moodle/course/view.php?id=937#section-3).

8 Vandelvira: Plataforma Provincial de Plurilingüismo (http://www.cepjaen.es/vandelvira/).

7 Conclusion

The present chapter has provided a detailed rendering of the language policies, which have been put in place in Andalusia, a monolingual community striving to become more plurilingual. Two ambitious and forward-thinking Plans (the APPP and the PEDLA) have been heralded as a "welcome innovation" and "a major step forward" (Tobin & Abello-Contesse, 2013: 224) in attaining the balanced bilingualism pursued by the Andalusian educational authorities in response to European mandates. Five *wh-* questions have been addressed in order to chart the theoretical and methodological foundations that underlie the Plans. Their recent history has been explored by presenting their origins as a proactive response to reinforce Andalusia's levels of multilingualism. Their present has been examined by describing how they are being practically implemented, who has taken stock of the way they are playing out, and what the research outcomes reveal vis-à-vis their achievements. Finally, the future agenda of the Plans has also been set out by unraveling the chief lines of action envisaged for 2020 and by suggesting measures to successfully step up to them. As with any innovative initiative, "hard work must be done to make certain that the goals are achieved" (Tobin & Abello-Contesse, 2013: 225). This hard work needs to be compounded with ongoing stocktaking, stalwart research, solid training, and unfailing motivation, and it may indeed pay off, particularly considering that the APPP and the PEDLA - and CLIL within them - may well prove to be the lynchpin to tackle the current FL deficit in our region.

References

Alameda Hernández, A. (2002). Content-based language teaching: Some practical issues. *GRETA. Revista para Profesores de Inglés, 10*(2), 37–40.

Aronin, L., & Hufeisen, B. (2009). Methods of research in multilingualism studies: Reaching a comprehensive perspective. In L. Aronin & B. Hufeisen (Eds.), *The exploration of multilingualism. Development of research on L3, multilingualism and multiple language acquisition* (pp. 103–120). Amsterdam: John Benjamins.

Ávila López, J. (2009). Factores afectivos: La piedra de toque del AICLE. In V. Pavón Vázquez & J. Ávila López (Eds.), *Aplicaciones didácticas para la enseñanza integrada de lengua y contenidos* (pp. 91–112). Córdoba: Junta de Andalucía, Universidad de Córdoba, CETA.

Benítez Castro, M. A., & Adán Nieto, M. (2007). Teaching science in CLIL: A sample lesson plan for the non-linguistic areas. *GRETA. Revista para Profesores de Inglés, 15*(1&2), 47–59.

Brown, J. D. (2001). *Using surveys in language programs*. Cambridge: Cambridge University Press.

Bruton, A. (2011). Are the differences between CLIL and non-CLIL groups in Andalusia due to CLIL? A reply to Lorenzo, Casal and Moore (2010). *Applied Linguistics*, *32*(2), 236–241.

Bruton, A. (2012). Is CLIL so beneficial, or just selective? Re-evaluating some of the Research. *System*, *39*(4), 523–532.

Bruton, A. (2013). CLIL: Some of the reasons why … and why not. *System*, *41*(3), 587–597.

Cabezas Cabello, J. M. (2010). A SWOT analysis of the Andalusian Plurilingualism Promotion Plan (APPP). In M. L. Pérez Cañado (Ed.), *Proceedings of the 23rd GRETA Convention* (pp. 83–91). Jaén: Joxman.

Casal, S., & Moore, P. (2008). The Andalusian Bilingual Sections Scheme: Evaluation and consultancy. *International CLIL Research Journal*, *1*(1), 36–46.

Casares Fernández, A. (2009). Diccionarios bilingües: Una herramienta, una necesidad. In A. Bueno González, J. M. Nieto García & D. Cobo López (Eds.), *Atención a la diversidad en la enseñanza plurilingüe. I, II y III Jornadas Regionales de Formación del Profesorado* (CD-ROM). Jaén: Delegación Provincial de Educación de Jaén y Universidad de Jaén.

Cenoz, J., Genesee, F., & Gorter, D. (2013). Critical analysis of CLIL: Taking stock and looking forward. *Applied Linguistics*, *35*(3), 243–262.

Clegg, J. (2007). Analyzing the language demands of lessons taught in a second language. *RESLA*, Vol. Extra 1, 113–128.

Cummins, J. (1999). *BICS and CALP: Clarifying the distinction* (Report No. ED438551). Washington, D.C.: ERIC Clearinghouse on Languages and Linguistics.

Del Moral Villalta, M. (2009a). Why wiki now? In A. Bueno González, J. M. Nieto García & D. Cobo López (Eds.), *Atención a la diversidad en la enseñanza plurilingüe. I, II y III Jornadas Regionales de Formación del Profesorado* (CD-ROM). Jaén: Delegación Provincial de Educación de Jaén y Universidad de Jaén.

Del Moral Villalta, M. (2009b). La web 2.0: A teacher's best friend? In A. Bueno González, J. M. Nieto García & D. Cobo López (Eds.), *Atención a la diversidad en la enseñanza plurilingüe. I, II y III Jornadas Regionales de Formación del Profesorado* (CD-ROM). Jaén: Delegación Provincial de Educación de Jaén y Universidad de Jaén.

Espinosa Zafra, I. M. (2009). Recursos para el desarrollo del currículum integrado. In A. Bueno González, J. M. Nieto García & D. Cobo López

(Eds.), *Atención a la diversidad en la enseñanza plurilingüe. I, II y III Jornadas Regionales de Formación del Profesorado* (CD-ROM). Jaén: Delegación Provincial de Educación de Jaén y Universidad de Jaén.

European Commission. (1995). *White paper on education and training. Teaching and learning: Towards the learning society*. Brussels: European Commission.

European Commission. (2012). *Europeans and their languages. Special Eurobarometer 386*. Brussels: European Commission.

European Union. (2000). *The Lisbon Summit: Employment, economic reforms and social cohesion – Towards a Europe based on innovation and knowledge.* Retrieved February 24, 2014 from http://www.cbi.org.uk/ndbs/PositionDoc.nsf/81e68789766d775d8025672a005601aa/3c3c535cf6e6ad468025689e0050af8d/$FILE/EUsummit_statement.pdf.

Fernández, R., & Halbach, A. (2011). Analysing the situation of teachers in the Madrid autonomous community bilingual project. In Y. Ruiz de Zarobe, J. M. Sierra, & F. Gallardo del Puerto (Eds.), *Content and foreign language integrated learning: Contributions to multilingualism in European contexts* (pp. 241–270). Frankfurt-am-Main: Peter Lang.

García Jiménez, F. (2009). El papel de las TIC en AICLE: Openoffice como herramienta de trabajo. In A. Bueno González, J. M. Nieto García & D. Cobo López (Eds.), *Atención a la diversidad en la enseñanza plurilingüe. I, II y III Jornadas Regionales de Formación del Profesorado* (CD-ROM). Jaén: Delegación Provincial de Educación de Jaén y Universidad de Jaén.

García Jiménez, F., & Cobo López, D. (2009). El proyecto bilingüe en infantil y primaria: Reflexiones desde el tercer año. In A. Bueno González, J. M. Nieto García & D. Cobo López (Eds.), *Atención a la diversidad en la enseñanza plurilingüe. I, II y III Jornadas Regionales de Formación del Profesorado* (CD-ROM). Jaén: Delegación Provincial de Educación de Jaén y Universidad de Jaén.

García López, M., & Bruton, A. (2013). Potential drawbacks and actual benefits of CLIL initiatives in public secondary schools. In C. Abello-Contesse, P. M. Chandler, M. D. López-Jiménez & R. Chacón-Beltrán (Eds.), *Bilingual and multilingual education in the 21st century. Building on experience* (pp. 256–272). Bristol: Multilingual Matters.

Gerdes, T. (2009a). CLIL methodology: The SIOP model. In V. Pavón Vázquez & J. Ávila López (Eds.), *Aplicaciones didácticas para la enseñanza integrada de lengua y contenidos* (pp. 153–170). Córdoba: Junta de Andalucía, Universidad de Córdoba, CETA.

Gerdes, T. (2009b). SIOP: Un modelo para AICLE/CLIL. In A. Bueno González, J. M. Nieto García & D. Cobo López (Eds.), *Atención a la diversidad en la enseñanza plurilingüe. I, II y III Jornadas Regionales de Formación del Profesorado* (CD-ROM). Jaén: Delegación Provincial de Educación de Jaén y Universidad de Jaén.

Hornillo Estrella, J. R. (2009). Aplicación del Portfolio Europeo de las Lenguas en la Escuela Oficial de Idiomas de Jaén: Otra forma de aprender. In A. Bueno González, J. M. Nieto García & D. Cobo López (Eds.), *Atención a la diversidad en la enseñanza plurilingüe. I, II y III Jornadas Regionales de Formación del Profesorado* (CD-ROM). Jaén: Delegación Provincial de Educación de Jaén y Universidad de Jaén.

Hughes, S. (2010). The effectiveness of bilingual education: A case study. Paper presented at the *25th GRETA Convention: Celebrating 25 years of teacher inspiration*. University of Granada.

Jáimez Muñoz, S. (2007). Glossary related to the Plurilingualism Promotion Plan: A language policy for Andalusia. *GRETA. Revista para Profesores de Inglés*, *15*(1&2), 67–79.

Julián de Vega, C. (2007). La importancia de la coordinación en la implantación de modelos AICLE. *GRETA. Revista para Profesores de Inglés*, *15*(1&2), 14–19.

Junta de Andalucía. (2005). *Plan de Fomento del Plurilingüismo en Andalucía*. Sevilla: Junta de Andalucía. Retrieved February 24, 2014 from http://www.juntadeandalucia.es/boja/boletines/2005/65/d/5.html.

Junta de Andalucía (2006a). Orden de 24 de julio de 2006, por la que se regulan determinados aspectos sobre la organización y el funcionamiento de los Centros Bilingües. BOJA núm.156 de 11 de agosto de 2006 (pp.11–15). Sevilla: Junta de Andalucía.

Junta de Andalucía (2006b). *Orden de 20 de junio de 2006, por la que se regula la provisión y actividad de los auxiliares de conversación en los centros docentes públicos de la Comunidad Autónoma de Andalucía. Boja núm. 131 de 10 de julio de 2006* (pp. 11–15). Sevilla: Junta de Andalucía.

Junta de Andalucía (2007a). *Orden de 14 de septiembre de 2007, por la que se modifica la de 20 de junio de 2006, por la que se regula la provisión y actividad de los auxiliares de conversación en los centros docentes públicos de la Comunidad Autónoma de Andalucía. BOJA núm. 194 de 2 de octubre de 2007* (pp. 25–26). Sevilla: Junta de Andalucía.

Junta de Andalucía (2007b). *Instrucciones de 21 de septiembre de 2007 de la Dirección General de Ordenación y Evaluación Educativa, por la que se dan orientaciones sobre la organización y funcionamiento de los centros bilingües para el curso 2007/2008*. Sevilla: Junta de Andalucía. Retrieved February 24, 2014 from http://www.csi-csif.es/andalucia/modules/mod_ense/

Normativa_Basica/20070925_andalucia_instrucciones_de_organizacion_y_funcionamiento_de_centros_bilingues.pdf.

Junta de Andalucía (2008a). *Orden de 7 de marzo de 2008, por la que se establecen las bases reguladoras para la concesión de los premios a materiales curriculares relacionados con el fomento del plurilingüismo en los centros educativos públicos dependientes de la Consejería y se efectúa su convocatoria para el año 2008. BOJA núm. 61 de 28 de marzo* (pp. 18–21). Sevilla: Junta de Andalucía.

Junta de Andalucía (2008b). *Instrucciones de 31 de julio de 2008, de la Dirección General de Innovación Educativa sobre la organización y funcionamiento de los centros bilingües para el curso 2008/2009*. Sevilla: Junta de Andalucía. Retrieved February 24, 2014 from http://www.csi-csif.es/andalucia/modules/mod_ense/Normativa_Basica/20080804_andalucia_instrucciones_de_organizacion_y_funcionamiento_de_centros_bilingues.pdf.

Junta de Andalucía (2009a). *Instrucciones de 17 de julio de 2009 de la Dirección General de Participación e Innovación Educativa sobre auxiliares de conversación y otros colaboradores lingüísticos Erasmus para el curso escolar 2009/2010*. Sevilla: Junta de Andalucía. Retrieved February 24, 2014 fromhttps://ieselpalobilingual.wikispaces.com/file/view/assistantteachers0910.pdf.

Junta de Andalucía (2009b). *Instrucciones de 24 de julio de 2009 de la Dirección General de Participación e Innovación Educativa sobre la organización y funcionamiento de los Centros Bilingües para el curso 2009/2010*. Sevilla: Junta de Andalucía. Retrieved February 24, 2014 from http://www.juntadeandalucia.es/educacion/portal/com/bin/Contenidos/OEE/ordenacion/PLURILINGUISMO/instrucciones24julio2009/1248698105682_instrucciones24julio.pdf.

Junta de Andalucía (2010). *Instrucciones de 31 de agosto de 2010 conjuntas de la Dirección General de Participación e Innovación Educativa y de la Dirección General de Formación Profesional y Educación Permanente sobre la organización y funcionamiento de la modalidad de enseñanza bilingüe para el curso 2010–2011*. Sevilla: Junta de Andalucía. Retrieved February 24, 2014 from http://www.juntadeandalucia.es/educacion/portal/com/bin/Contenidos/IEFP/INNOVACION/instrucciones31082010ensenanzabilingue/1283249810674_instruccion31082010educacionbilingue.pdf.

Junta de Andalucía (2011). *Orden de 28 de junio de 2011, por la que se regula la enseñanza bilingüe en los centros docentes dela Comunidad Autónoma de Andalucía. BOJA núm. 135 de 12 de julio de 2011* (pp. 6–17). Sevilla: Junta de Andalucía.

Junta de Andalucía (2013). *Instrucciones de 19 de junio de 2013 conjuntas de la Dirección General de Innovación Educativa y Formación del Profesorado, y de la Dirección General de Formación Profesional Inicial y Educación Permanente sobre la organización y funcionamiento de la enseñanza bilingüe para el curso2013–2014.* Sevilla: Junta de Andalucía. Retrieved February 24, 2014 fromhttp://www.juntadeandalucia.es/educacion/portal/com/bin/Contenidos/IEFP/ProgramasInternacionales/ProgramasEducativos/20130703_InstruccionesEnsenanzaBilingue1314/1372841729096_instrucciones_1314_para_pxgina_web.pdf.

Junta de Andalucía. (2017). *Plan Estratégico de Desarrollo de las Lenguas en Andalucía*. Retrieved March 31, 2017 from http://www.juntadeandalucia.es/educacion/webportal/abaco-portlet/content/462f16e3-c047-479f-a753-1030bf16f822.

Lancaster, N. K. (2016). Stakeholder perspectives on CLIL in a monolingual context. *English Language Teaching, 9*(2), 148–177.

Lasagabaster, D., & Sierra, J. M. (2009). Language attitudes in CLIL and traditional EFL classes. *International CLIL Research Journal, 1*(2), 4–17.

Lasagabaster, D., & Sierra, J. M. (2010). Immersion and CLIL in English: More differences than similarities. *ELT Journal, 64*(4), 367–375.

López Cabrera, E. M. (2009). Cómo abordar la elaboración del currículo integrado de las lenguas y de las áreas no lingüísticas. In V. Pavón Vázquez & J. Ávila López (Eds.), *Aplicaciones didácticas para la enseñanza integrada de lengua y contenidos* (pp. 201–218). Córdoba: Junta de Andalucía, Universidad de Córdoba, CETA.

Lorenzo, F. (2010). CLIL in Andalusia. In D. Lasagabaster & Y. Ruiz de Zarobe (Eds.), *CLIL in Spain: Implementation, results and teacher training* (pp. 2–11). Newcastle upon Tyne: Cambridge Scholars Publishing.

Lorenzo, F. (2019). *Educación bilingüe en Andalucía. Informe de gestión, competencias y organización*. Sevilla: Junta de Andalucía.

Lorenzo, F., Casal, S., & Moore, P. (2009). The effects of Content and Language Integrated Learning in European education: Key findings from the Andalusian Bilingual Sections Evaluation Project. *Applied Linguistics, 31*(3), 418–442.

Lorenzo, F., Casal, S., & Moore, P., & Afonso, Y. M. (2009). *Bilingüismo y educación. Situación de la red de centros bilingües en Andalucía*. Sevilla: Fundación Centro de Estudios Andaluces.

Luque Agulló, G. (2009). Bilingüismo en comunidades monolingües y enseñanza basada en contenidos: Muchas preguntas y algunas respuestas. In A. Bueno González, J. M. Nieto García & D. Cobo López (Eds.), *Atención a la diversidad en la enseñanza plurilingüe. I, II y III Jornadas Regionales de Formación del Profesorado* (CD-ROM). Jaén: Delegación Provincial de Educación de Jaén y Universidad de Jaén.

Lyster, R. (2007). *Learning and teaching languages through content: A counterbalanced approach*. Amsterdam: John Benjamins Publishing Company.

Macaro, E., Curle, S., Pun, J., An, J., & Dearden, J. (2018). A systematic review of English medium instruction in higher education. *Language Teaching, 51*(1), 36–76.

Madrid Fernández, D. (2006). Bilingual and plurilingual education in the European and Andalusian context. *International Journal of Learning, 12*(4), 177–185.

Madrid Fernández, D., & Barrios Espinosa, M. E. (2018). A comparison of students' educational achievement across programmes and school types with and without CLIL provision. *Porta Linguarum, 29*, 29–50.

Madrid Fernández, D., & Hughes, S. (Eds.). (2011). *Studies in bilingual education*. Frankfurt-am-Main: Peter Lang.

Malagón Gallego, A. M., Dunmall Connor, M. J., & Moral Martos, M. (2009). In A. Bueno González, J. M. Nieto García & D. Cobo López (Eds.), *Atención a la diversidad en la enseñanza plurilingüe. I, II y III Jornadas Regionales de Formación del Profesorado* (CD-ROM). Jaén: Delegación Provincial de Educación de Jaén y Universidad de Jaén.

Marsh, D., & Langé, G. (Eds.). (2000). *Using languages to learn and learning to use languages*. Finland: University of Jyväskylä.

Medrano Dorantes, A. M. (2009). AICLE, ÉMILE, CLIL, PEL, ANL, FLE, TIC, MCER, DELF: Hacia un nuevo enfoque metodológico de la enseñanza del francés en Educación Secundaria. In V. Pavón Vázquez & J. Ávila López (Eds.), Aplicaciones didácticas para la enseñanza integrada de lengua y contenidos (pp. 181–200). Córdoba: Junta de Andalucía, Universidad de Córdoba, CETA.

Mehisto, P. (2008). CLIL counterweights: Recognising and decreasing disjuncture in CLIL. *International CLIL Research Journal, 1*(1), 93–119.

Méndez García, M. C. (2009). Educación plurilingüe, educación intercultural. In A. Bueno González, J. M. Nieto García & D. Cobo López (Eds.), *Atención a la diversidad en la enseñanza plurilingüe. I, II y III Jornadas Regionales de Formación del Profesorado* (CD-ROM). Jaén: Delegación Provincial de Educación de Jaén y Universidad de Jaén.

Morilla García, C., & Gallagher, E. (2009). A new CLIL method: AMCO and the practical use of multiple intelligences in the classroom. In V. Pavón

Vázquez & J. Ávila López (Eds.), *Aplicaciones didácticas para la enseñanza integrada de lengua y contenidos* (pp. 131–152). Córdoba: Junta de Andalucía, Universidad de Córdoba, CETA.

Ortega Cebreros, A. M. (2009). El auxiliar de conversación como recurso docente en las aulas de Secundaria y Bachillerato. In A. Bueno González, J. M. Nieto García & D. Cobo López (Eds.), *Atención a la diversidad en la enseñanza plurilingüe. I, II y III Jornadas Regionales de Formación del Profesorado* (CD-ROM). Jaén: Delegación Provincial de Educación de Jaén y Universidad de Jaén.

Pavón Vázquez, V. (2009). La introducción de un programa de enseñanza integrada de lengua y contenidos en la educación superior: Claves para impartir asignaturas a través de una segunda lengua. In V. Pavón Vázquez & J. Ávila López (Eds.), *Aplicaciones didácticas para la enseñanza integrada de lengua y contenidos* (pp. 29–54). Córdoba: Junta de Andalucía, Universidad de Córdoba, CETA.

Pavón Vázquez, V. (2018). Learning outcomes in CLIL programmes: a comparison of results between urban and rural environments. *Porta Linguarum*, *29*, 9–28.

Pérez Cañado, M. L. (2011). The effects of CLIL within the APPP: Lessons learned and ways forward. In R. Crespo Jiménez & M. A. García de Sola (Eds.), *ESP teaching and methodology. English Studies in Honour of Ángeles Linde López* (pp. 13–32). Granada: Editorial Universidad de Granada.

Pérez Cañado, M. L. (2012). CLIL research in Europe: Past, present, and future. *International Journal of Bilingual Education and Bilingualism*, *15*(3), 315–341.

Pérez Cañado, M. L. (2016a). Teacher training needs for bilingual education: In-service teacher perceptions. *International Journal of Bilingual Education and Bilingualism*, *19*(3), 266–295.

Pérez Cañado, M. L. (2016b). Are teachers ready for CLIL? Evidence from the European study NALTT. *European Journal of Teacher Education*, *32*(2), 202–221.

Pérez Cañado, M. L. (2018a). CLIL and educational level: A longitudinal study on the impact of CLIL on language outcomes. *Porta Linguarum*, *29*, 51–70.

Pérez Cañado, M. L. (2018b). The effects of CLIL on L1 and content learning: Updated empirical evidence from monolingual contexts. *Learning and Instruction*, *57*, 18–33.

Pérez Cañado, M. L. (2018c). CLIL and pedagogical innovation: Fact or fiction? *International Journal of Applied Linguistics*, *28*, 369–390.

Pérez Cañado, M. L. (forthcoming). Common CLIL (mis)conceptions: Setting the record straight. In T. Calderón Quindós & N. Barranco Izquierdo (Eds.), *The threefold nature of bilingual education*. Newcastle upon Tyne: Cambridge Scholars Publishing.

Pérez Torres, I. (2009a). Apuntes sobre los principios y características de la metodología AICLE. In V. Pavón Vázquez & J. Ávila López (Eds.), *Aplicaciones didácticas para la enseñanza integrada de lengua y contenidos* (pp. 171–180). Córdoba: Junta de Andalucía, Universidad de Córdoba, CETA.

Pérez Torres, I. (2009b). Las nuevas tecnologías como herramienta para la diversidad en la enseñanza de lengua y contenidos. In A. Bueno González, J. M. Nieto García & D. Cobo López (Eds.), *Atención a la diversidad en la enseñanza plurilingüe. I, II y III Jornadas Regionales de Formación del Profesorado* (CD-ROM). Jaén: Delegación Provincial de Educación de Jaén y Universidad de Jaén.

Rascón Moreno, D., & Bretones Callejas, C. (2018). Socioeconomic status and its impact on language and content attainment in CLIL contexts. *Porta Linguarum*, *29*, 115–136.

Rocha Martín, B. (2009a). La implementación del Portfolio Europeo de las Lenguas en la E.O.I. de Jaén. In A. Bueno González, J. M. Nieto García & D. Cobo López (Eds.), *Atención a la diversidad en la enseñanza plurilingüe. I, II y III Jornadas Regionales de Formación del Profesorado* (CD-ROM). Jaén: Delegación Provincial de Educación de Jaén y Universidad de Jaén.

Rocha Martín, B. (2009b). Pasapalabra del Portafolio Europeo. In A. Bueno González, J. M. Nieto García & D. Cobo López (Eds.), *Atención a la diversidad en la enseñanza plurilingüe. I, II y III Jornadas Regionales de Formación del Profesorado* (CD-ROM). Jaén: Delegación Provincial de Educación de Jaén y Universidad de Jaén.

Roldán Tapia, A. (2005). What do we mean by bilingual education in Andalusia? *GRETA. Revista para Profesores de Inglés*, *13*(1&2), 28–34.

Román Fernández, C., & Moreno Álvarez, J. (2010). Experiencia en la implantación de una sección bilingüe: Do's y dont's. In M. L. Pérez Cañado (Ed.), *Proceedings of the 23rd GRETA Convention* (pp. 77–82). Jaén: Joxman.

Rubio Mostacero, M. D. (2009). *Language teacher training for non-language teachers: Meeting the needs of Andalusian teachers for school plurilingualism projects. Design of a targeted training course.* Jaén: Universidad de Jaén.

Ruiz Gómez, D. A., & Nieto García, J. M. (2009). Las secciones bilingües en Secundaria y Bachillerato. Marco organizativo. Dificultades y propuestas. In A. Bueno González, J. M. Nieto García & D. Cobo López (Eds.), *Atención a la diversidad en la enseñanza plurilingüe. I, II y III Jornadas Regionales de Formación del Profesorado* (CD-ROM). Jaén: Delegación Provincial de Educación de Jaén y Universidad de Jaén.

Salaberri Ramiro, M. S. (2009). Inteligencias múltiples y desarrollo de destrezas orales. In V. Pavón Vázquez & J. Ávila López (Eds.), *Aplicaciones didácticas para la enseñanza integrada de lengua y contenidos* (pp. 113–130). Córdoba: Junta de Andalucía, Universidad de Córdoba, CETA.

Tobin, N. A., & Abello-Contesse, C. (2013). The use of native assistants as language and cultural resources in Andalusia's bilingual schools. In C. Abello-Contesse, P. M. Chandler, M. D. López-Jiménez & R. Chacón-Beltrán (Eds.), *Bilingual and multilingual education in the 21st century. Building on experience* (pp. 231–255). Bristol: Multilingual Matters.

Tomlinson, B., & Masuhara, H. (2009). Engaging learners of English through football. In V. Pavón Vázquez & J. Ávila López (Eds.), *Aplicaciones didácticas para la enseñanza integrada de lengua y contenidos* (pp. 75–90). Córdoba: Junta de Andalucía, Universidad de Córdoba, CETA.

Tudor, I. (2013). From content to competency: Challenge facing higher education language teaching in Europe. In M. L. Pérez Cañado (Ed.), *Competency-based language teaching in higher education* (pp. 21–32). Amsterdam: Springer.

Vez, J. M. (2009). Multilingual education in Europe: Policy developments. *Porta Linguarum, 12*, 7–24.

José Manuel Vez Jeremías

Language policies in Galicia: From bilingual education to trilingual schools[1]

Abstract: This chapter analyses the main language policies developed in a small region in the north-west of Spain: Galicia. Despite the different political measures which have contributed to increasing the social status of the regional language, the number of adolescents who have Galician as their L1 is progressively decreasing. To counteract this tendency, the Galician Government has enacted various educational measures which will be reviewed in the present chapter. These measures have attempted to foster the learning of Galician by incorporating it into the school curriculum, both as a subject and a language of instruction. Over the last years, however, this attempt to increase the use of Galician among teenagers has merged with the implementation of a trilingual model in the Galician school system, which is based on teaching a third of the school subjects in Galician, Spanish and English respectively. The chapter will also examine this trilingual model and canvass the different views on its implementation.

Keywords: Bilingual education, multilingual education, CLIL, minority language

1 Introduction

Multilingual education, as opposed to simply bilingual education, in exceptional environments such as the Autonomous Community of Galicia (hereafter ACG), is particularly important to minority language preservation: competence in English may increase the odds that minority languages will survive, following the evidence that proficiency in more than one language increases the facility in acquiring further languages (Cenoz, 2013a). In order to better understand the role that multilingual education may have for both the preservation of heritage languages and the development of international languages, it is important to analyse language educational policies and the sweeping changes in the current situation in schools. If Galician schools with multilingual curricula succeed in producing individuals with a strong foundation in Galician and Spanish languages/culture as well as the ability, by way of English-language proficiency, to engage in the global marketplace, then they may be the best medium for both

1 This is the result of a research work carried out at the University of Santiago de Compostela during the academic year 2012–2013.

teaching international languages and for strengthening and preserving heritage languages in the long term. But, is this the case?

2 The Galician linguistic landscape

The social reality of Galicia is in the process of transformation, bringing with it sweeping changes in the current situation of education in its schools. One of the most outstanding changes is the increasing diversity in the student body attending rural and urban schools, which shows a great diversity of interests, motivations, abilities as well as cultural and linguistic diversity. As a mirror of the society to which they belong, Galician schools are now becoming more and more multilingual and multicultural centres.

2.1 Within the bilingual framework

At the turn of the 20th century, Galician found itself in a precarious situation. Spanish was enjoying social prestige and was being used in familiar contexts, those in which Galician had traditionally been used, and Galician was undervalued and associated with lack of social mobility. This situation worsened as Galicia became more urbanised and industrialised, and certain areas became economically and socially isolated (Monteagudo, 1999). During Franco's dictatorship (1936–1975), Galician was not explicitly prohibited, but the regime exercised educational, administrative and political practices that supported the use of Spanish only. During this period, the deep-seated stigmas towards Galician and the high/low dichotomy between the two languages became more apparent, leading to the consolidation of the process of linguistic substitution (i.e. Galician being replaced by Spanish) and to a steady increase in bilingualism (Lorenzo Suárez, 2009).

With Franco's death in 1975 came a period of transition, and under the newly established democracy that recognised Spain's multilingualism and people's linguistic rights[2] the ACG was afforded some degree of self-governance, allowing the Galician language to be recognized and established as an official marker of its distinctive identity.

In 1983, the Law of Linguistic Normalization (hereafter LLN) stipulated co-official status of Galician and Castilian, encouraging the use of Galician in all domains of life (Consello da Cultura Galega, 2006). A year earlier, in 1982, the Galician government approved the orthographic and morphological norms of

2 See Article 3:3 of the Spanish Constitution.

the language elaborated by the Institute of Galician Language and the Galician Royal Academy. Those norms were revised in 1995 and later, in 2003[3].

Through this long path, Galician, once a linguistic variety of low prestige associated with lack of education and low socioeconomic status, received the official recognition of 'language' and the ACG was given exclusive control of certain areas, such as education and culture, essential to the defence and promotion of the autochthonous language. These political and structural changes resulted in a process of linguistic normalisation involving the standardisation of Galician, the expansion of its social functions and the creation of public bilingual immersion programmes. All these measures have helped to partially raise the status of Galician, but ironically, they have not prevented the dramatic decline of L1 Galician speakers among adolescents. In fact, as the Galician Secretary of Language Planning recently stated, "*adolescents are the main challenge for the Galician language*"[4].

From a status planning perspective, multiple measures were taken with the aim of changing negative attitudes towards Galician and increasing its presence in formal domains where Spanish had traditionally been the norm, such as public administration and official events (Lorenzo Suárez, 2009: 28–29). As for acquisition planning, the most significant provisions were made in education (O'Rourke, 2011: 75) and involved promoting the acquisition of Galician through its incorporation into the school curriculum, both as subject matter and as language of instruction. In Galicia's bilingual programmes, both Spanish and Galician are used to teach content, and students are never segregated into groups according to their L1 (Fernández Paz, Lorenzo Suárez, & Ramallo, 2008). Because of this approach to language and content teaching, the Galician model has been described as one of 'immersion' (Pérez Vidal, 1998), although in reality, it is an "*additive language learning situation, for the authorities did not envisage the functional replacement of Castilian in all contexts*" (Beswick, 2007: 92).

According to recognized data (González González et al., 1994), the native speakers of Galician feel *self-hatred* in some way because of the low status of their language. Therefore, all the government leaders responsible for this area have seen Galician as an endangered language and have invested, with better or poorer results, in the promotion of the Galician language. Indeed, this tendency of language shift towards the dominant language is present not only in

3 See http://www.edu.xunta.es/web/.

4 See http://www.xunta.es/linguagalega/noticias/2148.

Table 1: Initial and habitual language of Galicians (González González et al., 1994: 39; González González et al., 1995: 94)

Initial language (%)	**Habitual language** (%)
Galician 62.4	Galician 38.7
Both 11.4	More Galician 29.9
Spanish 25.6	More Spanish 20.8
Other 0.6	Spanish 10.6

Spain but in many other countries of the world where minority languages exist (Cenoz & Gorter, 2006), and in some cases efforts are being made to reverse it by means of a specific language policy implemented by the state. However, one can claim that the Galician people's attitude to the linguistic situation (i.e. their linguistic culture) is not always consistent with the government's point of view. It is useful to look at the statistical data on language use in Galicia in the years 1994–1995, obtained by the Galician Royal Academy and reflected in the *Sociolinguistic Map of Galicia* (hereafter MSGa). In Table 1, "*Initial language*" stands for the first language the people learn in their life, and "*Habitual language*", for the language people use in everyday communication. Data from MSGa I were obtained in 1994, and information from MSGa II, in 1995.

The same data have been split according to the informants' age, and data on languages used with family members are given in Table 2 and Table 3:

These data reveal two main tendencies:

- A greater percentage of Spanish as the initial language among younger speakers;
- Predominance of Spanish as the language of habitual use among younger speakers and with children. Among older people and with grandparents and parents, Galician is used more often.

This reality reflects the hierarchy of the languages (Galician subordinated to Spanish) that some consider is implied by the Galician laws, which from a pessimistic perspective has sometimes been interpreted as a sign of shift towards a monolingual tendency into Spanish.

However, in recent years, the *linguistic normalization policy* seems to have influenced people's views on language. More detailed data about the current situation in Galicia are given below. The Galician Culture Council (*Consello da Cultura Galega*) provides statistics on the use of both languages in Galicia on its

Table 2: Initial language by age groups (González González et al., 1994: 71)

Age	Galician (%)	Spanish (%)	Both (%)	Other (%)
16–25	38.9	43.5	16.7	0.9
26–40	53.4	33.0	12.8	0.9
41–65	71.6	18.0	9.9	0.4
+ 65	81.8	11.3	6.6	0.3

Table 3: Language used with different family members (González González et al., 1995: 172, 208)

Age	with grandparents	with parents	with siblings	with partner	with children
16–25	2.88*	2.61	2.40	2.61	2.68
26–40	3.23	3.08	2.94	2.85	2.63
41–65	3.58	3.46	3.40	3.30	3.00
+ 65	3.74	3.65	3.61	3.55	3.39

*On this scale, 4 is "only Galician" and 1, "only Spanish". The central point of the scale is 2.5.

website Loia.org, an open guide to the Galician language[5]. These data are also presented in correlation with the informants' age; however, unlike the data from the MSGa, they are given in the form of graphs. According to these new data, young people predominate among those who learn Castilian first. Consequently, Galician as a first language is more common among older people. In modern times, more and more children have started to speak in both languages.

As it is revealed by these new data[6], in comparison with the above-mentioned data from the 1990s, there is an increase in the number of bilinguals and of the people who learn Spanish first, at the expense of those whose first language is Galician. Compared to the 1990s there are more people who use only Galician in their daily lives. However, it should be mentioned that the total amount of Galicians speaking "*more Spanish*" and "*only Spanish*" has risen from 31.2 % to 36.7 %, while the number of those who use "*more Galician*" fell by 10.9 %. More than 50 % of all people under 25 predominantly use Spanish as their habitual language.

Comparing the above data to the statistics information from 1995, we can see a certain decrease in the use of Galician in the age groups under 45, while older people's language use remained largely the same as 8 years before (see Table 4).

5 These data were first published in 2003.

6 The figures can be taken from the website http://www.loia.org.

Table 4: Language use among family members (data from the CGC, 2003)

Age	with grandparents	with parents	with siblings	with partner	with children
Under16	2.52*	2.4	2.29	-	-
16–25	2.83	2.57	2.39	2.24	2.41
26–35	2.86	2.65	2.48	2.35	2.46
36–45	3.08	2.93	2.8	2.69	2.59
46–55	3.37	3.23	3.14	3	2.79
56–65	3.51	3.4	3.34	3.25	3
+65	3.67	3.58	3.54	3.46	3.3

*On this scale, 4 is "only Galician" and 1, "only Spanish". The central point of the scale is 2.5.

According to the data reflected in the MSGa 2004, the attitude to Galician has improved in present times; if Galician was previously associated with backwardness and provincialism, now there is considerably less prejudice towards it. In a recent sociolinguistic poll, Galicians were asked what language should be taught to Galician children. The results (Universidade de Santiago de Compostela, 2010) are the following: Both languages –72 %; Only Galician –21.4 %. Another question was what language was more useful –Castilian, Galician or both; and the results are as follows: Both –57.3 %; Castilian –31.3 %. Finally, people were asked about the language that Galicians should speak: Galician –57 %; Both –40 %; Castilian –3 %.

As it can be seen from the above data, more than half of Galicians consider the Galician language to be as useful as Spanish, and the loyalty towards Galician, expressed in answer to the question about the language that Galicians should speak, appears to be the same as in 1995.

2.2 Building up the multilingual framework

Since Galicia was declared an autonomous community, the main trend in the official language policy has been the promotion and restoration of the prestige (normalization) of the Galician language. In 2004, when the Partido Popular headed by Manuel Fraga governed the ACG, the General Plan for Galician Language Normalization (hereafter GPGLN) was issued. Its main goals are:

- To guarantee everyone the possibility to communicate in Galician;
- To give the Galician language more social functions and expand the sphere of its use;

- To make rendering services to a client/a citizen (in stores, public institutions, etc.) in Galician the social norm of courtesy;
- To promote the positive image of Galician as a modern and useful language and to eradicate prejudices against it;
- To provide the necessary linguistic and technical resources for the use of Galician in the modern society.

In June 2007, with the regional government ruled by a coalition between the Galician Socialist Party and the Galician Nationalist Bloc, a new education decree was launched (124/2007)[7] requiring that a minimum of 50 % of non-language subjects be taught in Galician, a requirement that was already being met and even exceeded by some schools (such as the rural high school in our study). In another effort to further normalise the use of Galician among the younger generations, this coalition government created the so-called *galescolas*[8], nursery schools for children aged from 0 to 3 years where Galician is the only language used.

In 2009, the Partido Popular won the regional elections and ruled the ACG again. The new President, Núñez Feijóo, declared immediately his solid support for language diversity in Galicia proposing the bases for a "*trilingual decree*" (Decree 79/2010) which implies teaching 1/3 of the school subjects in Spanish, 1/3 in Galician and 1/3 in English (instead of 50 % in Galician and 50 % in Spanish as proposed by the GPGLN). Moreover, parents cannot choose the language of instruction (although Feijóo promised that they would be able to choose the language of the basic subjects, and that students would communicate and write in class in the language that they chose - either Galician or Castilian). With this initiative, Feijóo intended to create a *balance* between languages and help young people to learn English, but also imposed on the people an obligation to receive tuition equally in all three languages. This policy has been denounced as anti-constitutional (because, as it was mentioned before, the Spanish Constitution does not oblige Galicians to know Galician, but only stipulates a right to know it), and since then political parties, language NGOs, trade unions, parents' associations and other groups have been promoting an important number of demonstrations against it (Vilas, 2009).

On May 20, 2010, and despite the strong climate of opposition to its language policies, the Galician government issued the decree 79/2010[9] on education (the

---

7 See http://www.xunta.es/linguagalega/arquivos/Ref.ED_5.pdf.

8 See http://escolasinfantis.net/.

9 See *Decreto 79/2010, do 20 de maio, para o plurilingüismo no ensino non universitario de Galicia (DOG 25-5-2010),* http://www.edu.xunta.es/web/node/939.

formalization of the draft document, called *Bases for a decree on plurilingualism*, first published in 2009). According to its promoters, the Decree is based on a survey carried out among the families of over 330 schoolchildren; they claim that these families' responses demonstrate that modern society supports the equal presence of both official languages in the education system, alongside English, whose knowledge is important as well.

So far, over the last ten years, the emerging changes in Galician linguistic policies have opened a new cycle characterized by a more agreed-upon action in favour of Galician as an underprivileged language. The most remarkable benefits from these linguistic policies would be specified in the following actions:

- The Decree 124/2007 establishes that 50 % of the subjects in compulsory education must be taught in Galician.
- The Association of Language Testers in Europe (ALTE) establishes that the official certification of the knowledge of Galician is now developed according to the reference levels established in the Common European Framework of Reference for Languages, as every other European language.
- A special offer of exclusive schooling in Galician in pre-school stages (0–3 years old) through a network of educational centres similar to Basque *ikastolas*.
- A significant increase in technological and cultural resources in Galician that meet the demands of the present-day ICT society: ICTs, Galician web contents, radio and TV cultural programmes, etc.

However, the most innovative tendency resulting from the linguistic policies applied in recent times is undoubtedly the acceptance of Galicia as a context of additive multilingualism which, according to the new Decree 79/2010, must be planned by its educational system on the basis of a *trilingual formula* (Galician-Spanish-Foreign language), which respects both official languages and, at the same time, progressively incorporates other European languages such as English, French, German, Portuguese, etc.

3 Galician language policies: Bilingual education revisited

The incorporation of Galician into the educational system as a subject and a lingua franca to teach non-linguistic curricular subjects has been (and still is) implicitly aimed at contributing to the social recovery of a language (nowadays official in this Autonomous Community), which went through a large period of abandonment. At the same time, it also has an explicit aim: guaranteeing the bilingual competence of Galician citizens.

The Galician educational system has understood and assumed within the last decades its responsibility in relation to the objective of bilingual competence for all Galicians, as mentioned in article 14.3 of the LLN[10]. Apart from the fact that languages are not only learnt within a formal educational system, it can be inferred from this article that the educational system is ultimately responsible for guaranteeing this universal bilingual competence: an indispensable requirement for the free election of the school language. Thus, it must activate all the necessary curricular mechanisms to compensate for the different prestige, unequal esteem, different environmental presence, and varied resources available for either Galician or Spanish. The regulation approved within the last three decades in relation to bilingualism in Galicia reveals some features representing the model supported by educational authorities. This model is grounded on a co-official statute equal to those in other bilingual autonomous communities in Spain (Pérez-Vidal, Bel, & Garau, 2007). This statute includes the same objective: bilingual competence, yet under slightly different action principles. These principles (with slight variations) were kept in the three decrees which have regulated the school situation of Galician and Spanish so far: Decrees 135/1983, 247/1995, and 124/2007, which is in force until the end of the academic year 2009–2010.

3.1 School linguistic integration

This principle is already considered in the LLN of 1983, which establishes that students cannot be separated into different educational centres due to language reasons. In addition, except in some situations they cannot be separated into different classrooms either. Because of legal hierarchy reasons, this principle applies throughout the whole subsequent legislation. Linguistic integration, therefore, takes priority over segregationist models due to the following reasons:

- The Galician sociolinguistic context, characterized by social permeability in the use of both official languages, does not allow for strictly monolingual population centres;

10 It establishes that Galician educational authorities must guarantee that students know this language, both orally and in writing, on equal terms with the Spanish language, at the end of the cycles in which the Galician language is compulsory.

- The absence of communication barriers between Galician and Spanish facilitates the language learning process regardless of the learner's language;
- The achievement of the common aim of bilingual competence is favoured by the confluence of Galician- and Spanish-speaking students in the classroom.

3.2 First teaching in L1

The LLN acknowledges the right of children to receive their first teaching in their mother tongue. Nevertheless, this right was interpreted slightly differently in consecutive decrees. Thus, the Decree 247/1995 specifies that the predominant language among students is to be used in infant education and the first cycle of primary education, although the other language is to be acquired too. The Decree 124/2007, however, restricts this interpretation of infant education and, to compensate for any social imbalance between both languages, states that Galician should play a similar role to Spanish in Spanish-majority contexts.

For several years this principle informed the positions of the most innovative educational sectors. In educational terms, it can be considered the closest formula to the UNESCO report and the most natural one for the incorporation of children into school life. Nevertheless, it is a scientifically controversial principle, since education through a different language from the students' mother tongue is proven to involve neither serious school difficulties nor problems of knowledge or use of the mother tongue. It is even said to promote the development of bilingual competence.

The co-existence of this principle with non-segregated linguistic practices seems rather difficult. For this reason, Galician school education has been confusing and organizationally complex, also involving the lowest advance of the Galician language:

- *Confusing*: because the concepts used in the Law find no clear correspondence with the official curriculum ('first teaching', 'mother tongue', etc.)
- *Organizational complexity*: because it forces diverging commitments (using the students' mother tongue with no segregation and guaranteeing their learning of the other official language)
- *Lower advance of the Galician language*: because this ambiguity and confusion supports the application of uncontrolled bilingual or monolingual linguistic education.

3.3 Vehicular use of both official languages in the curriculum

Aside from that which the Law calls '*first teaching*', the Galician educational system supports the remaining compulsory education stages and cycles to favour the presence of both official languages as curricular instruments. To apply this function, the procedure followed was a progressive sequence in the vehicular use of languages:

- *Decree 135/1983* establishes the use of any of the two official languages, yet indicating that balance was to be achieved between them.
- *Decree 247/1995* indicates more precisely some subjects which, at least, shall be compulsorily taught in Galician.
- *Decree 124/2007* maintains the same criterion as the previous Decree, although it increases the number of subjects so as to assure a balance (50 %) in the use of Galician and Spanish.

This responds to the obvious situation that legislation on bilingualism, under historical circumstances such as those in Galicia, which leaves linguistic options exclusively in the hands of educational centres or teachers, will never favour the underprivileged language. For this reason, a large section of the Galician society positively valued this progressive specification of the curricular areas to be taught in one of the official languages as a means to advance bilingual education, which seemed to be favoured by the community.

3.4 Linguistic planning in schools

The legislative aspects in the previous section exclusively refer to the areas or subjects in which either Spanish or Galician are used. However, legislation leaves in the hands of educational centres the option of planning and choosing the language contents of non-linguistically-defined subjects. Therefore, educational centres must adapt their linguistic planning to the sociolinguistic context of their students (more Galician in rural areas, and more Spanish in urban areas, etc.). However, the legal horizon that establishes that all students must acquire satisfactory bilingual competence through the period of compulsory education must always be kept in mind.

This principle (present in the three aforementioned decrees) was believed to promote greater teacher and school commitment to the Galician official languages both in their social and academic dimensions. Nevertheless in practice this was not supported by any teacher training measures or monitoring and advising structures. Thus, the result is that linguistic planning in educational centres did not render the expected results. Furthermore, amongst the anarchy in decision-making processes, the fulfilment of the minimum standards legally established for the teaching of Galician or Spanish was the only indicator subjected to some kind of control.

4 Improving language policies: The 'trilingual' trend

The situation of the ACG continues an old tradition: the imposition of Spanish in an originally Galician-speaking territory and society. This situation resulted in a complex co-existence, as proven by sociolinguistic studies. However, this situation of two languages in contact, already subjected to stresses derived from their different status and institutional recognition, must now, within the framework of the rapid transformation that has occurred within recent decades, go hand-in-hand with an accelerating move to incorporate foreign languages (particularly English).

4.1 Improving the teaching of curricular contents through English: Towards a CLIL model

It is important to consider the fact that, in the last few years, the Galician Educational Department has been putting into practice educational curricular reforms regarding foreign languages, in line with existing European guidelines. In relation to early foreign language learning, 90 % of Galician schools are teaching English in infant education. As for language across the curriculum, CLIL is changing educational parameters insofar as it is involving the whole educational community. Galician CLIL pioneering experiences started in 1999 as pilot projects in a few secondary schools. As San Isidro (2009a: 6) remarks: "These pilot projects resulted in the formal regulation of the CLIL provision through several directives". The CLIL Galician model consists in teaching non-linguistic subjects by means of integrating foreign languages (mainly English followed by French) in a progressive way. The name attributed to these classes is *bilingual sections*. So what the Galician educational system provides is a set of subjects taught on a bilingual basis (Foreign Language-Galician or Foreign Language-Spanish) and not bilingual schools with an integrated curriculum, as is the case in other Spanish Communities (Andalusia, etc.). The educational regulation of CLIL teaching in Galicia has run parallel to the gradually increasing number of schools taking part in CLIL programmes - from the initial 12 secondary schools to the present-day 649 centres (primary, secondary, and vocational training levels) with 2,373 bilingual sections. This increase has been brought about by the so-called *Language Learning Promotion Plan in the Context of Galicia*[11] (hereafter

11 An action plan that seeks to foster the learning of official (Galician and Spanish) and foreign languages (English and French) in the ACG. See http://www.xunta.es/c/document_library/get_file?folderId=577713&name=DLFE-17601.pdf.

LLPPGa), with a substantial investment on the part of the central Spanish government that has obviously boosted CLIL implementation. The key actions for improvement of students and teachers rest on the following institutional actions, according to San Isidro (2009a: 7–11):

- *Cuale Programme*: This is a programme aimed at complementing formal additional language teaching and making students and teachers aware of the need to improve their linguistic competence in additional languages. Classes are given by AL (Additional Language) teachers in public secondary schools outside regular school hours. Three main groups are targeted: a) students in secondary education (CUALE-ESO), aiming at complementing curricular AL teaching; b) vocational training students (CUALE-FP), aiming at future mobilisation of workers; and c) teachers (CUALE-PROF), aiming at motivating all kinds of teachers to learn additional languages[12].
- *Language Assistants*: Apart from the Comenius language assistants and the assistants provided by the Spanish Ministry of Education, the Galician Educational Department has signed agreements with the three Galician universities to provide schools with almost 200 Erasmus students from various countries to work as language assistants, thus bringing real multilingualism into the classroom. Schools with bilingual sections are given priority in the distribution of language assistants.
- *Summer Immersion Programmes*: Aiming primarily at motivating students towards foreign language learning, the Galician summer immersion programmes are addressed at students in primary, secondary and post-compulsory secondary education. They consist of stays in bilingual camps in Spain or residential stays abroad. So far, the target countries have been Canada, the United Kingdom, Ireland and France. The increase in the number of scholarships has been as follows: 300 in 2006; 1,500 in 2007; 2,800 in 2008; 2,650 in 2009; 3,077 in 2010; and 3,122 in 2011[13].
- *Teacher Training*: In-service teacher training was considered to be a key aspect, not only regarding linguistic competence but also in terms of methodology update. New training programmes were needed so as to motivate and prepare teachers to face the new challenges of building the multilingual and intercultural identity of present-day Europe. Apart from regional conferences aiming at making CLIL a widespread concept, other training possibilities have been designed[14]. The PIALE teacher training programme consists of three stages (San Isidro, 2009b: 53-54): one month of training focusing on linguistic competence; 3 weeks of training in the United Kingdom and France focusing on language, methodology and job shadowing; and a two-week stage in which teachers are provided with ICT tools in order to adapt and develop materials to use in their classes. The programme targets three main groups of in-service teachers: teachers of English in early language teaching, teachers of English

12 See http://www.edu.xunta.es/pale.

13 See https://www.edu.xunta.es/axudasle/.

14 See http://www.edu.xunta.es/linguasestranxeiras.

and French in primary education and CLIL teachers. The programme has a double benefit: on the one hand, it focuses on teacher training and, on the other hand, it has a real impact on the classroom. Besides the PIALE programme, through which more than 500 in-service teachers had been trained by 2011, there exists another training programme: immersion summer stays, consisting of one-month immersion training in Ireland, Germany, France and Portugal.

- *Attention to Foreign Students*: The Galician Administration favours the incorporation of pupils from foreign countries in the educational system, especially those of compulsory school age, designing a number of interventions of a general nature to provide supplementary attention to immigrant pupils to aid their integration in the system. The Galician Educational Department has committed itself to foster multilingualism:
  - Through the promotion of European Programmes.
  - Through the intercultural LALO Programme, aiming to maintain the linguistic and cultural reference points of the children of Portuguese workers and immigrants, as well as promoting interest and respect among Galician pupils for other cultures. In kindergarten and primary school, the teaching of Portuguese is a part of the normal curriculum, via 'integrated classes' in which Portuguese and Galician teachers teach the whole class together, or in 'simultaneous classes' (in which the Portuguese teacher teaches the members of the group who have chosen to participate in the programme). Furthermore, these schools organise other complementary activities such as exchanges and study visits, cultural weeks and Portuguese Clubs.
  - Through the LACM Programme, which has the following objectives: to teach Moroccan culture and the Arabic language to Moroccan pupils who are being taught in Galician schools; to integrate these pupils into the Galician educational system and to promote intercultural education. There are two systems: in schools with few Moroccan pupils, teaching is provided outside school time; there is one Moroccan teacher for several schools; when schools have a large number of Moroccan students, teaching is provided during school time and there is usually one teacher for each school.
- *Leaves and Awards:* Besides all the aforementioned actions, two more motivating strategies have been designed: a) 2-month paid leaves for AL and CLIL teachers to design their own training abroad (20 per year); and b) CLIL materials design awards to boost creation and sharing of CLIL curricular materials (10 per year).

As noted by San Isidro from his deep knowledge of the situation of foreign language education in the ACG,

> Effort, involvement and investment on the part of the Galician Educational Department, the '*Plan Linguas*' has made it possible to see the first successful results regarding CLIL implementation and the revitalisation of additional language learning. (San Isidro, 2009a: 12)

In fact we are facing a process of taking on a new multilingual reality which is making its way through the educational system of the ACG. And so far we can say that the CLIL model is not only changing teachers' profile but also posing new challenges in the treatment of languages and language teacher education.

4.2 The Decree 79/2010 on 'plurilingualism'

The Decree 79/2010 on '*plurilingualism*' (see footnote 9) marks the beginning of a new path in the development of Galician educational language policies. The trigger for this change must be seen in the discontent shown by certain parts of the Galician population with the current situation of bilingualism in compulsory education: too much Galician and insufficient Spanish for some; and the contrary for others. This discontent was manifested through the citizen platform '*Galicia Bilingüe*'[15], which, throughout the election campaign to the Galician Regional Government, had shown great belligerence regarding the linguistic conflict.

The bases of the initial draft for this new Decree are the unprecedented linguistic share in the Galician and Spanish educational system which attempts to settle trilingual learning (the integration of three languages in the teaching of curricular contents in all compulsory education stages: 33 % of the curricular areas to be taught in Galician, 33 % to be taught in Spanish, and the remaining 33 % to be taught in English). This trilingual model, compulsory for all students since the first year of primary education[16], is justified on the basis of experiences in some European multilingual regions where several languages co-exist in their societies and schools. The documentary study which informed the Galician Educational Department (to which the GPLP belongs as a promoter of the trilingual model), focuses on an exhaustive analysis of how languages are shared in the classroom in model European countries with more than one official language (Finland, Luxembourg, Val D'Aosta (Italy), Frisia (Holland) or

15 See its website: http://www.galiciabilingue.es.

16 The Basque Autonomous Community proposed in March 2010 an experimental program at the Parliament within the Framework of Trilingual Education for the promotion of Euskera, the consolidation of bilingualism, and the activation of English. Unlike the Galician proposal, the Basque measure shall be applied in the 2010-11 academic year in the fourth year of primary education and the first year of secondary education, and the participation of students and educational centres is voluntary. After analysing the results of this pilot experience applied in 40 primary and secondary education centres (which shall also be accompanied by a plan for the linguistic and didactic training of the participating teachers, as well as a more general plan aimed at foreign language teacher training), the measures for the elaboration of a definitive proposal shall be studied.

Ireland). Communities such as Catalonia, the Basque Country, or Valencia were also studied in the Spanish context.

Replicas of this model are developed by Galician official institutions and university researchers, who agree that a fully trilingual model (i.e., with three active languages spoken by the citizens of a community and reflected in their educational system), can only be found in four instances - Finland, Italy, Switzerland, and Luxembourg. Thus, some experts believe these replicas are in fact bilingual models, incorporating the study of a modern language (i.e. a 2+1 language model, as the foreign language has not the same status as the other two). The remaining differences, bilingualism experts argue, can only be considered as *bilingual* models with the incorporation (at most) of English (i.e., a 2+1 language model, as the foreign language has not the same status as the other two).

The months between the presentation of this trilingual draft (end of December 2009) and the day the new Decree was published in the ACG Official Gazette (May 25th 2010) are marked by profound and continuous discontent, reaching high public confrontation levels unprecedented in Galicia (Vilas, 2009) or any of the other three official bilingual communities in Spain. The draft of the Decree was subjected to the public consideration of educational agents, trade unions, political parties, and public institutions, all of which are legally bound to publicly express their opinion on a measure of this kind. This is a summary of the results of their evaluation:

- *Royal Academy of Galicia*: the RAG receives the referential document on December 30th 2009 and officially expresses its opinion on January 16th 2010. Its collegial position, through academic analysis, shows up global rejection of the document. The section 8 in its pronouncement (titled "*The Issue of Foreign Languages*") is worth quoting:

> Indeed plurilingualism is an old aim of the whole society, just because it is a lack. There is an old Latin saying *Tot linguas calles, tot homines vales* ("The more languages you speak, the more human you are"). Languages multiply our own competence: a person commanding three languages multiplies by three his/her job opportunities. It is true that nowadays-wealthy parents send their children to the UK for cultural and linguistic immersion, that working parents cannot always afford this, and that the in-house immersion proposed in this Decree project would equal the different social classes regarding this issue. It is also true that teaching contents in a foreign language multiplies the students' expressive fluency in this language. Everything so far seems perfect. However, this plurilingualism should not be presented as an innovation to compensate now the sacrifice of reducing the presence of Galician through the approval of these *Bases*.

- *Galician Culture Council*: The GCC is another official institution consulted on the adoption of measures of this kind. Like in the RAG pronouncement, the GCC declared itself completely against the *Bases* document proposed by the Galician Regional Government. On February 1st 2010 the GCC made a pronouncement, stating that "in no case measures involving a drawback in the normalization process should be taken", that the discourse on language should not be formulated "in terms of a problem", and that that agreed upon in the GPGLN, unanimously approved by the Galician Autonomic Parliament in 2004, must be obeyed. The main arguments in the negative GCC pronouncement concerning *foreign languages* were summarized in this way:

- The introduction of a foreign language as a lingua franca in 33 % of school weekly time is, on the one hand, a hasty measure and, on the other hand, should not be introduced in a decree aimed at regulating the use of official languages.

The vehicular use of a foreign language should be in any case voluntary.

More precisely and categorically, the GCC pronouncement devotes a particular section to the *teaching of curricular subjects in a foreign language*, expressing that its objections are formulated with an acknowledgement that the attainment of a satisfactory level of proficiency in a foreign language (English) by Galician students constitutes one of the most important objectives of the educational system. However, as stated by this pronouncement:

> The achievement of this aim shall demand great efforts to the Administration and the educational community (teachers in particular) and force the Galician Regional Government to elaborate a carefully studied and ambitious program to continue those already functioning, which have rendered noticeable results (the badly-called "bilingual sections", which are actually "trilingual sections"). Nevertheless, regarding the use of English (or any other foreign language) as the language of instruction, we must point out that:
>
> a) From a formal viewpoint, this issue should not be tackled in a norm aimed at regulating the use of both official languages in Galicia in the educational system. A foreign language, no matter its importance, has a dramatically different legal status to both official languages: the official status of the latter is established by the Constitution and the Regional Statute, while the status of the former corresponds to the field of public policies. In any case, the objective of improving and extending the English (or any other foreign language of international projection such as Portuguese) competence through its introduction as a language of instruction can be mentioned in the norm, referring to a different specific regulation, and with a general indication that this introduction should not be detrimental to the use of any of the two official languages.
> b) The general and uniform use of a foreign language as the language of instruction along 33 % of the school time from primary to high school education is not recommendable from a pedagogical perspective and practically unfeasible, at least within a short-to-medium term. Undoubtedly, several EU reports recommend the use of a foreign language in formal education (particularly English) as the language of

> instruction to assure substantial advance in foreign language competence[17]. This recommendation is applied to both monolingual and bilingual regions such as Galicia. In any case, due to important reasons, efforts in this issue in most European countries focus, at least in the initial stages of foreign language introduction, on university teaching. This is what the GCC precisely recommends: in the first stage efforts favouring plurilingualism should focus on university teaching (by the way, plurilingualism should include the use of Galician). Regarding non-university levels, EU-member countries (including Spain) generally introduce English as a lingua franca voluntarily and gradually, and inexcusably accompanied by a set of reinforcement measures aimed at both teachers and students. The progressive introduction of the foreign language as a lingua franca demands previous substantial advance in the methods, resources and results used in the learning-teaching of English as a subject. Focusing efforts in these stages precisely on this seems rather logical. No reason recommends the segregation of professional training, or artistic and sports subjects from foreign language reinforcement.

> To sum up, advance in the students' command of foreign languages (English) is a highly important challenge faced by our educational system, constitutes a substantially-different issue from that tackled in the *Bases* document, and, as such, should be carefully studied, analysed and debated. Besides, all this should be put forward in specific regulations and governmental action. The foresights in the *Bases* shall mainly lead to easily avoidable confusion.

The result of the prescriptive consultations to these collegial bodies should have forced the Galician Regional Government to correct important aspects in the *Bases* draft. However, the Government did not renounce its immediate official publication to enforce its measures and so they were applied in the academic year 2010–11. As already indicated, this decree was approved on May 20th 2010 under the title (*Decree for Plurilingualism in Galician Non-University Teaching*)[18] including some modifications on the initial draft *Bases* document. The ways in which the new approach to catering for multilingual education in Galicia differs from pervious approaches can be summarized in the following ways:

- While the Decree 124/2007 established that at least 50 % of the subjects are to be taught in Galician (establishing no maximum), the new regulation establishes equilibrium between both official languages in primary

17 The pronouncement refers, in this point, to European documents such as the *Fourth General Objectives of the White Paper on Education and Training —Teaching and Learning: Towards the Learning Society. European Commission* [DG XXII & DG V], 1995) and the reports titled *Trilingual Primary Education in Europe* (2001) and *CLIL/EMILE: The European Dimension. Actions, Trends and Foresight Potential* (2002).

18 See footnote 9 above.

(Maths is taught in Spanish and Natural Sciences in Galician) and secondary (Social Sciences, Geography and History, Natural Sciences, and Biology and Geology are taught in Galician, whereas Maths, Technology, and Physics and Chemistry are taught in Spanish) education. The language for the remaining subjects was selected by each educational centre.

- Another difference deals with the language students should use. This new regulation allows students to choose the official language they prefer (except in subjects specifically taught in Galician, Spanish or a foreign language, in which both the students and the teacher must use the respective language).
- Educational centres shall elaborate a language strategy every four years with an annual addendum reporting changes on the four-year project.
- This Decree devotes a particular chapter to foreign language teaching, indicating the promotion of the CLIL approach (mainly in English), so as to enable educational centres to offer (progressively and voluntarily) up to a maximum of 33 % of the weekly lessons in a foreign language.
- When a centre opts for one or several English-taught subjects, it should adapt its language strategy to guarantee maximum equilibrium between Galician- and Spanish-taught hours a week.
- The most controversial issue was eliminated from the Decree: consultation to parents on the official language they want their children to study in. This option is only kept for pre-school education and would not be applied in primary and secondary education within the current legal framework.

4.3 Trilingual school centres: Improving the private educational sector?

Multilingualism, on the one hand, and CLIL, on the other, have been defined in many different ways (Cenoz, 2013b; Cenoz, Genesee, & Gorter, 2014) but never on the basis of funding criteria or taking into account public/private educational interests. However, discussion of the particular issue of language policies in the ACG cannot be completed without a reference to such questions. In fact, the data collected after the first three years of implementing the trilingual model (a kind of CLIL model) in Galician schools reveal what this policy, consciously or not, is hiding. The question we would like to pose here is: to what extent does the current network of "*plurilingual centres*"[19] maintain the real proportionality of the existing typology of school centres in the Galician educational system?

19 The provision of "*plurilingual centres*" for the academic year 2013-2014 is about 183 schools. This is a 23 % more than the previous academic year.

Table 5: Typology of '*plurilingual centres*' (Academic 2010–2011/2012–2013)

2010–2011	No. of centres (total 58)	No. of curricular subjects offered	- Although there is some provision for secondary school, most of the subjects being offered are placed in 1st year of primary education. - 'Crafts' is the predominant area.
Public sector	33	1–2 (only 1 offers FR in 1st ESO)	
Private sector	25 (= 43 %)	4–5 (all of them in EN)	
2011–2012	No. of centres (total 52)	No. of curricular subjects offered	- The provision for secondary school comes down; the offer of subjects is mainly in primary education. - 'Crafts' is the predominant area.
Public sector	24	1–2 (all of them in EN)	
Private sector	28 (= 54 %)	2–3 (all of them in EN)	
2012–2013	No. of centres (total 39)	No. of curricular subjects offered	- The offer of plurilingual centres at secondary level is reduced to 6 schools (5 private/1 public). - 97 % of the subjects are 'Crafts'.
Public sector	19	1–2 (all of them in EN)	
Private sector	20 (= 51 %)	1–5 (all of them in EN)	

At the end of the academic year 2012–2013, the number of "*plurilingual centres*" was exactly 149 schools: 76 belonging to the public system and 73 being private schools. Table 5 shows the distribution (public/private) of the "*plurilingual centres*", since their creation in the academic year 2010–2011, and the predominance of the curricular area being offered in a foreign language.

According to the data of Table 5, we can see that:

- There is a progressive decrease in the total number of school centres, which are enrolled within the Galician '*plurilingual network*' through the first three years of implementation (58-52-39).
- Except for one secondary school (IES X. Neira Vilas), which offered in 2010–2011 two non-linguistic subjects in the French language ('Interdisciplinary project and Social Sciences'), the whole provision of curricular subjects taught in a foreign language has been conducted in English (both in public and private schools).
- The difference between the number of curricular subjects offered through English in public and private schools is large: while the average number of subjects taught in English in public centres is one or two, the private offer reaches a number between four and five.

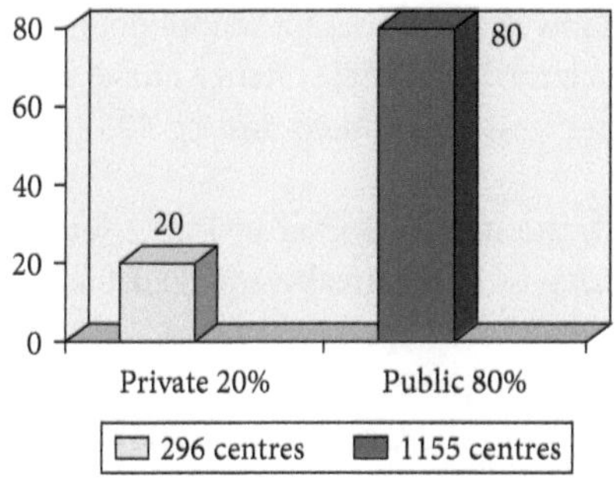

Fig. 1: Distribution 1,447 schools of the Galician general framework (2012–2013)

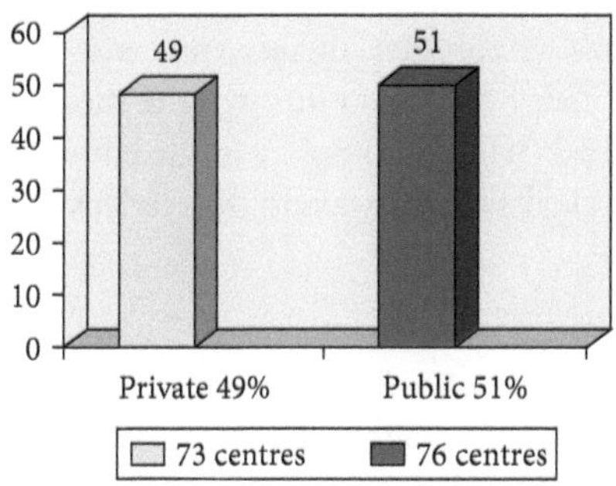

Fig. 2: Distribution of the 149 '*plurilingual schools*' (2012–2013)

- The provision for the primary education level is much bigger than the provision of 'plurilingual' schools for the secondary level.
- The main provision of non-linguistic subjects offered in English is the curricular area of Arts and Crafts (basically Crafts).
- Out of a total of 149 plurilingual centres by the end of 2012–2013, 73 schools belong to the private educational sector. That is, almost half of the Galician plurilingual schools (49 %) are in the private sector (with most of them under the 'educational agreement' protocol).

This last point perhaps deserves special attention. If 49 % of the recently created 'plurilingual schools' in Galicia are in the private sector of the educational system, up to which point does this percentage remain in line with the proportional distribution of schools within the general framework of the Galician educational system? An analysis of the data in Fig. 1 and 2 will be helpful:

The data in Fig. 1 show that the present school population within the general framework of the Galician educational system - nursery, primary and secondary levels (lower and upper) - is distributed among 296 private centres and 1,155 public centres[20].

On the other hand, the data collected in Fig. 2 reveals that the number of private '*plurilingual schools*' is practically equal to the number of '*plurilingual schools*' in the public sector.

This, without any doubt, represents a serious distortion of the real map of distribution of school centres in the Galician educational system, which is divided proportionally 80/20 between the public and private educational sectors. If we consider the fact that the selected centres which become '*plurilingual schools*' receive an additional budget from the administration in relation to "operational costs", is it possible to think that the trilingual school-net system is improving the private educational sector in Galicia? And, is it possible to believe that teaching 'Crafts' in primary education through the medium of English becomes an authentic plurilingual (trilingual) policy in the educational system? We pose the questions here and leave the answers to the reader's own perception.

References

Beswick, J. (2007). *Regional nationalism in Spain: Language use and ethnic identity in Galicia linguistic diversity and language rights*. Clevedon: Multilingual Matters.

Cenoz, J. (2013a). The influence of bilingualism on third language acquisition: Focus on multilingualism. *Language Teaching, 46*(1), 71–86.

Cenoz, J. (2013b). Defining multilingualism. *Annual Review of Applied Linguistics, 33*, 3–18.

Cenoz, J., & Gorter, G. (2006). Linguistic landscape and minority languages. *International Journal of Multilingualism, 3*(1), 67–80.

Cenoz, J., Genesee, F., & Gorter, D. (2014). Critical analysis of CLIL: Taking stock and looking forward. *Applied Linguistics, 35*(3), 243–262.

Consello da Cultura Galega. (2006). Loia.org: Open guide to Galician language. Retrieved December 20, 2013 from http://www.consellodacultura.org/arquivos/cdsg/loia/?idioma=2.

---

20 These data have been collected from CCEOU (*Secretaría Xeral Técnica. Subdirección Xeral de Sistemas Informáticos. Subárea de Estatísticas Educativas*). See Xunta de Galicia (2012: 21).

Fernández Paz, A., Lorenzo Suárez, A., & Ramallo, F. (2008). *A planificación lingüística nos centros educativos*. Santiago de Compostela: Xunta de Galicia.

González González, M., Fernández Rodríguez, M., Rodríguez Neira, M. A., Domínguez-Seco, L., Fernández Ferreiro, M., Fernández Ramallo, F., Recalde Fernández, M., & Rei Doval, G. (1994). *Lingua inicial e competencia lingüística en Galicia. Compendio do I volume do mapa sociolingüístico de Galicia* [Mother tongue and linguistic competence in Galicia. A compendium of the first volume of the sociolinguistic map of Galicia]. A Coruña: Real Academia Galega.

González González, M., Fernández Rodríguez, M., Rodríguez Neira, M. A., Domínguez-Seco, L., Fernández Ferreiro, M., Fernández Ramallo, F., Recalde Fernández, M., & Rei Doval, G. (1995). *Usos lingüísticos en Galicia. Compendio do II volume do mapa sociolingüístico de Galicia* [Linguistic uses in Galicia. A compendium of the second volume of the sociolinguistic map of Galicia]. A Coruña: Real Academia Galega.

Lorenzo Suárez, A. M. (2009). A situación actual da lingua galega: Unha ollada desde a sociolingüística e a política lingüística. *Galicia 21*, *A*, 20–39.

Monteagudo, H. (1999). *Historia social da lingua galega. Idioma, sociedade e cultura a través do tempo*. Vigo: Galaxia.

O'Rourke, B. (2011). *Galician and Irish in the European context: Attitudes towards weak and strong minority languages*. Basingstoke: Palgrave Macmillan.

Pérez Vidal, C. (1998). *Language teacher training and bilingual education in Spain. ELC report on teacher training for bilingual education*. Jyväskylä: University of Jyväskylä.

Perez-Vidal, C., Bel, A. & Garau, M. J. (Eds.). (2007). *A portrait of the young in the new multilingual Spain*. Clevedon: Multilingual Matters.

San Isidro, X. (2009a). Galicia, CLIL success in a bilingual community. In D. Marsh & P. Mehisto (Eds.), *CLIL practice: Perspectives from the field* (pp. 5–13). Jyväskylä: CCN-University of Jyväskylä.

San Isidro, X. (2009b). CLIL, un nuevo horizonte en la formación del profesorado. *Latin American Journal of Content & Language Integrated Learning*, *2*(1), 51–54.

Universidade de Santiago de Compostela. (2010). *O galego na docencia: Datos*. Retrieved January 8, 2014 from http://www.usc.es/snl/dinamiza/xeral2009-2010.pdf.

Vilas, R. (2009). Feijóo cambia la libertad de elección de lengua por un "modelo trilingüe". *Libertad Digital*. Retrieved May

5, 2010 from http://www.libertaddigital.com/portada/feijoocambia-la-libertad-de-eleccion-por-un-modelo-trilingue-1276380284/.

Xunta de Galicia. (2012). *Datos e cifras do ensino non universitario. Curso 2012-2013*. Santiago de Compostela: Consellería de Cultura, Educación e Ordenación Universitaria.

Borja Manzano Vázquez

From bilingualism to multilingualism in the Basque Autonomous Community: An overview of language policies and research outcomes

Abstract: The present chapter analyses the different language policies and initiatives implemented to promote language education in the Basque Autonomous Community (a small region in the north of Spain), focusing on the shift from bilingualism to multilingualism due to the implementation of CLIL (Content and Language Integrated Learning) methodology in Basque schools. The chapter begins by examining the development of bilingual education (Basque-Spanish) in the region and it then discusses how CLIL has been implemented in the Basque school system. Next, it explores the findings of the main studies conducted in the Basque Autonomous Community on the impact of CLIL on learners' language learning, pointing out potential flaws and shortcomings in these studies so as to address them in future research. The chapter concludes by suggesting different courses of action which should be adopted in the near future in order to improve multilingual education and the implementation of CLIL methodology in this Spanish region.

Keywords: Bilingual education, multilingual education, CLIL, CLIL research

1 Introduction

These days, we are witnesses to how our world is becoming more and more connected. With globalisation contributing to reducing barriers between countries and encouraging closer economic and social interaction, new professional and personal opportunities are opening up to people living anywhere in the world. These opportunities include the possibility of travelling, working and studying abroad. To benefit from and participate effectively in these activities it is essential that individuals develop *multilingual competence* or, in other words, "the capacity to use several languages appropriately and effectively for communication in oral and written language" (Cenoz & Genesee, 1998: 17). The importance of developing multilingual competence is reflected in the different documents issued at European level in recent decades to promote linguistic diversity and multilingualism in education: the *White Paper on Education and Training* (European Commission, 1995), which establishes the 1 + 2 principle, that is, all European citizens should develop communicative competence in at least two foreign languages as well as their mother tongue; the *Action Plan*

"Promoting Language Learning and Linguistic Diversity" (European Commission, 2004); *"A New Framework Strategy for Multilingualism"* (European Commission, 2005); and *"Multilingualism - An Asset for Europe and a Shared Commitment"* (European Commission, 2008). This advocacy of multilingualism has promoted the search for new teaching approaches which support the learning of foreign languages. One of these approaches is CLIL (Content and Language Integrated Learning), which consists of teaching content subjects, or parts of these subjects, through the medium of a foreign language. Nowadays, CLIL instruction is gaining more and more prominence within the European educational landscape and Spain is no exception in this respect.

When it comes to language knowledge, Spain is often depicted on "the bottom rung of the foreign-language-knowledge ladder" (Lasagabaster & Sierra, 2009: 7). The Spanish population has long been characterised by having a monoglot mentality and low levels of foreign language knowledge. This fact has been corroborated by the last Eurobarometer surveys "Europeans and their languages" (European Commission, 2006, 2012), two extensive surveys carried out by the European Commission to assess European citizens' language skills. The results yielded by both surveys reveal that Spain is clearly below the average for the European Union as regards command of foreign languages. With the aim of reducing this foreign language deficit as well as complying with European language policies and regulations, the Spanish educational authorities have strongly committed themselves to the promotion of multilingual education and, to this end, CLIL methodology has been adopted as a promising tool for improving learners' foreign language skills.

Today CLIL is an established teaching approach in Spanish primary and secondary education, being also implemented in different higher education contexts. The major aim of the present chapter is to examine the implementation of CLIL in a Spanish bilingual community (the Basque Autonomous Community [henceforth BAC]) where education was already conducted in two different languages: Spanish and the official regional language (Basque). On the one hand, the chapter will describe the language policies and initiatives developed to foster language education in the Basque school system. It will begin by examining the development of bilingual education. Next, it will discuss how CLIL has been implemented in Basque schools. The chapter will then explore the findings of the main studies conducted in the BAC on the impact of CLIL on learners' language learning. In doing so, it will identify potential flaws and shortcomings in these studies to be addressed in future research. To conclude, the chapter will propose various courses of action which can be adopted in the future so as to enhance multilingual education and the implementation of CLIL in this region.

2 Language education in the Basque Autonomous Community

Spain comprises 17 autonomous communities as well as two autonomous cities. Although education is regulated at national level by the LOMCE or *Ley Orgánica para la Mejora de la Calidad Educativa* (Organic Law for the Improvement of the Quality of Education), the different autonomous communities have the power to regulate and adapt this law to their local characteristics. One consequence of the transfer of competences and decision-making to the communities is the wide variety of CLIL initiatives which have been implemented in Spain thus far (bilingual primary and secondary schools, bilingual sections, bilingual programmes/projects, etc.). In bilingual communities like the BAC, Catalonia and Galicia, for example, the implementation of CLIL has brought about the introduction of trilingual programmes since in these regions the teaching of curricular contents by means of an L2 (the corresponding regional language) has been a common practice for more than three decades[1]. In what follows, I will focus on the example of the BAC. I will examine the language policy of this region, paying special attention to how bilingual education was originally conceived of and how CLIL instruction has been incorporated into the school curriculum.

2.1 The development of bilingual education in the Basque school system

The BAC (*País Vasco* in Spanish; *Euskadi* in Basque) is a region located in the north of Spain, bordering on France in the north-east. It comprises three provinces: Álava, Guipúzcoa and Vizcaya. Although it is a relatively small region (covering an area of approximately 7,300 km^2), it has a population of more than two million. As noted above, the BAC is a bilingual region in which Spanish coexists with Basque, the official regional language. This language is considered to be one of the oldest living languages in Europe and, unlike most European languages (e.g. Spanish), it is a non-Indo-European language. Thus, Basque bears no resemblance to the official language of the whole nation[2].

Nowadays, the teaching of the Basque language is accommodated in the Basque educational system, but it has not always been like this. During the military dictatorships set up, first, by Primo de Rivera (1923–1930) and, later,

1 See Escobar Urmeneta and Unamuno (2008) and Vez Jeremías (in this volume) for a review of language education in Catalonia and Galicia, respectively.

2 This lack of resemblance can clearly be seen, for example, when comparing the translation of the sentence '*Do you work here?*' in both languages: '*¿Tú trabajas aquí?*' (Spanish) vs. '*Hemen lan egiten duzu?*' (Basque) (Cenoz, 2008: 14).

by Franco (1939–1975), the rights of the Basque population were repressed, including their regional language. Basque was excluded from the public domain, namely the local media, public administration and education. Its teaching was forbidden in schools, where children were severely punished for using this language (see Erize, 2003: 33). This repression led Basque people to speak in Spanish more frequently and lose their proficiency in Basque. With the passing of time, Basque progressively became a minority language, being replaced by the dominant language (i.e. Spanish). Despite these restrictions on Basque, there were different attempts to keep the language as well as Basque culture alive. One of them was the reopening in the 1960s of private schools run by groups of parents and teachers. These schools were known as *ikastolas* and provided children with the opportunity to receive tuition in Basque.

In 1978, the Spanish Constitution acknowledged the right to autonomy of the different regions of Spain and its enactment opened up the possibility of restoring the social status of Basque, which was subsequently declared an official language in the BAC by means of the Statute of Autonomy for the Basque Country (BOE, 1979) and the Basic Law for the Normalisation of the Use of Basque (BOE, 1982). These documents recognised the right of Basque people to learn and use Basque. The reality, however, was that in 1981 only 21.9 % of the Basque population were bilingual (i.e. they were able to use both Spanish and Basque fluently) and 12.21 % were passive bilinguals (i.e. they could understand Basque but they were unable to produce it either in oral or written form) (Eustat, 2015). For this reason, the Basque Government developed a firm language policy to foster the knowledge and use of the Basque language. The result was the development and implementation of three different linguistic models in the public and private schools of the Basque educational system (Gobierno Vasco, 1983): Model A, Model B and Model D[3]. These models have been in operation ever since, despite the initial obstacles encountered in their implementation (e.g. the lack of teachers qualified to teach in Basque).

In Model A, Spanish is the main language of instruction while Basque is taught only as a school subject for four to five hours a week. Among its main objectives is helping learners develop a good understanding of Basque, communicative competence to cope with daily routines, and a positive attitude

3 A fourth model (Model X) was later developed. This model was targeted at learners who were temporarily living in the BAC. In it, Spanish was the only language learned by learners. Nowadays, this model is almost non-existent in the Basque educational system.

towards the language (Cobarrubias, 2008: 147). This model is implemented mainly in schools located in areas where Spanish is the most predominant language. Model B and Model D are examples of bilingual education. They share similarities to the language immersion programmes implemented in Canada since the mid-1960s. In this case, learners learn content (either partially or totally) through their L2 (i.e. Basque). In Model B, both Spanish and Basque[4] are used as languages of instruction. Approximately 50 % of the curricular subjects are taught through each language (e.g. arts and social and natural sciences in Basque; mathematics in Spanish). This model was for many years implemented only in primary and compulsory secondary education. It was in 2015 that the Basque Government began to offer Model B also in post-compulsory secondary education. Finally, in Model D, Basque is the medium of instruction for all the subjects whereas Spanish is taught as another school subject for four to five hours per week. As noted by Cenoz (2009), the implementation of these models in schools is not homogeneous since there are variations within each model (e.g. versions of Model A in which learners have greater exposure to Basque or Basque is the language of instruction in one subject). The models are complemented by the *NOLEGA* programme whose aim is to contribute to the normalisation of Basque by means of activities organised to encourage language use and knowledge (plays, literary contests, short stays in residential centres, and visits to schools by Basque authors, among others).

Enrolling on any of the three linguistic models is voluntary, being subject in most cases to parental choice. Although Model A was originally the most popular one, the number of learners enrolled on this model has progressively declined over the last decades, whilst Basque-medium instruction has grown. In the academic year 2017–2018, 65.9 % of the Basque learners followed Model D; 18.9 %, Model B; and only 15.1 %, Model A. Despite this preference for Basque as the language of learning and its official status, it still remains a minority language. According to the *Fifth Sociolinguistic Survey* conducted by the Department of Education, Language Policy and Culture of the Basque Government (Gobierno Vasco, 2013), Spanish is the predominant language in everyday communication for all the age groups surveyed (see Fig. 1). The figures, however, show that this

4 Since 1983, the Department of Education of the Basque Government runs the *EIMA* (*Euskal IkasMaterialgintzA*) programme whereby it funds the production of printed and audiovisual learning materials as well as educational software in Basque.

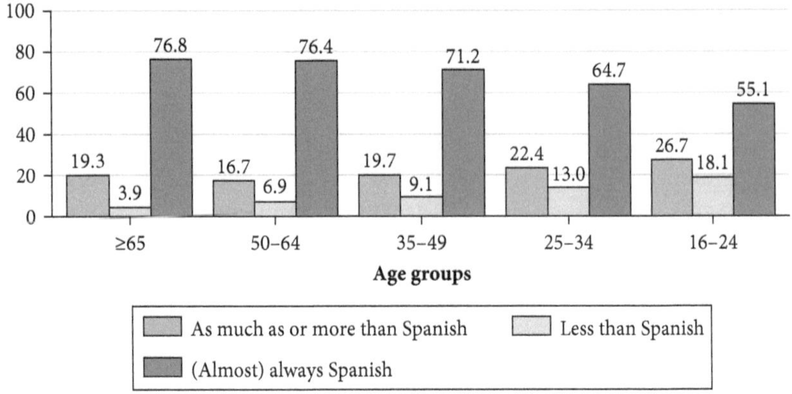

Fig. 1: Basque and Spanish language use according to age group. (Source: Fifth Sociolinguistic Survey [Gobierno Vasco, 2013: 104])

predominance decreases with lower age groups, suggesting that the situation may change in the future.

The Basque Institute for Research and Evaluation in Education (ISEI-IVEI) plays a key role in assessing education in the BAC. Since its establishment in 2001, this institution has evaluated the impact of the linguistic models on learners' competence in different areas (Basque, Spanish and non-linguistic subjects such as mathematics and science). To illustrate the general trend of the results obtained so far, I will draw on the evaluation carried out in 2015 (ISEI-IVEI, 2015a, 2015b), which involved more than 41,300 learners in the fourth year of primary education and the second year of secondary education. The results of this evaluation confirm that the number of hours of exposure to Basque at school correlates with the proficiency developed in this language. Thus, those learners enrolled on Model D are more proficient in Basque than learners in Model B who, in turn, are more proficient than learners in Model A. The evaluation furthermore highlights that using Basque as the language of instruction does not negatively affect learners' proficiency in Spanish. In fact, learners in Model D get better scores than learners following the two other linguistic models available. Finally, the results also indicate that Basque-medium teaching is not detrimental to learners' academic development in other subjects. While the levels of achievement in science are similar irrespective of the linguistic model followed, learners in Model D obtain better scores in mathematics than learners taught through Spanish, especially learners in Model A who get the lowest scores.

2.2 The implementation of CLIL in Basque schools

With the aim of preparing its citizens for greater economic and social interaction at an international level, the Spanish Government introduced the learning of a foreign language as a compulsory subject in the school curriculum. In the BAC, French was originally the most common foreign language taught at schools due to the proximity of the region to France. However, the rise of English as the global language of communication led most Basque schools to replace French with English as the first option for foreign language teaching. Today French is offered as a second foreign language in secondary education. Initially, the foreign language began to be taught in the sixth year of primary education (age 11). However, the Educational Reform of the Spanish school system in 1993 advanced the introduction of the foreign language three years, beginning in the third year of primary education (age 8). Based on the idea that more years of exposure to the foreign language would result in higher levels of proficiency, the BAC went a step further and in 1996 it established foreign language instruction in the second cycle of infant education (ages 4–5) and the first cycle of primary education (ages 6–7). This was done by means of a pilot programme known as *Early Start to English* which was implemented in 13 schools and which allowed learners to receive three sessions of English instruction a week. Its aims were to promote a positive attitude towards English among learners, to work on phonology and oral comprehension, and to use the foreign language as a tool for basic communication.

The programme *Early Start to English* represented one of the first steps towards CLIL instruction in the Basque educational system. As part of this pilot experience, some teachers implemented a content-based approach whereby learners worked on English through contents covering different subjects (e.g. mathematics, music, social sciences, etc.) and materials developed following a CLIL approach (García Gurrutxaga et al., 2011: 275). This content-based approach was progressively extended to the rest of compulsory schooling by means of the programmes *INEBI* (Basque acronym for English through Content, *INgelesa Edukien Bidez*) in the second and third cycle of primary education (ages 8–11) and *BHINEBI* (Basque acronym meaning English through Content in Secondary Education, *Bigarren Hezkuntza INgelesa Edukien Bidez*) at secondary level (ages 12–16). The major aim of these programmes was to give continuity to the learning of curricular content from other subjects in the English language classes. In the private domain, the network of *ikastolas* created the *Eleanitz* ('Multilingual') project[5]. This project promoted a multilingual approach encompassing the

5 See https://www.eleanitz.org/.

learning of the region's official languages (by means of the Model D) and two foreign languages (English and French). Like the previous programmes, it adopted a content-based approach in English instruction. Thus, in primary education and the first cycle of secondary education, learners learned English through dramatised stories, tasks and projects which were linked to other subjects of the school curriculum. The project, in turn, was a pioneer in introducing the learning of a whole school subject through a foreign language. In the second cycle of secondary education, a CLIL project called *SSLIC* (Social Sciences and Language Integrated Curriculum) was implemented. It consisted of teaching social sciences in English for three hours per week as well as designing materials for the English syllabus which contributed to acquiring the specific concepts of this subject area. For French classes, a similar content-based approach (known as *En Français Aussi*, 'In French too') was developed in secondary education. Today all these programmes are still operative in the Basque educational system.

After these educational experiences, CLIL began to emerge as the dominant approach in the new initiatives undertaken to promote multilingual education in the BAC. In 2003, the Basque Government initiated an experimental project known as *Plurilingual Experience* to be implemented in compulsory and post-compulsory secondary education. It was initially set up in 12 secondary schools, although this was then extended to other schools. This initiative establishes that during the four years of compulsory secondary education at least seven hours per week must be devoted to teaching part of the curriculum in the foreign language (namely English). In post-compulsory secondary education, 20 % to 25 % of the curricular subjects are to be taught through the foreign language. These subjects can vary from school to school depending on teachers' availability but they often encompass arts, music, physical education, history, and biology. Another experimental project on CLIL implementation was the *Framework for Trilingual Education* (Gobierno Vasco, 2010), which was carried out from 2010 to 2013 in 40 schools and from 2011 to 2014 in 112 schools (including both public and private schools). The aim of this initiative was to maintain the trilingual approach which gave learners the opportunity to study the curriculum in three different languages (Basque, Spanish and the foreign language) but introducing it in primary education as well. Thus, it began being implemented from the fourth year of primary education and the first year of secondary education. In both educational levels, a minimum of five to six hours of the school timetable was to be taught in each of the three languages. To improve learners' proficiency in the target language, the framework was also supplemented by the following actions: language immersion stays in camps for primary school learners where they could spend one week learning English; English courses during the summer term for secondary school learners; the assignment of native language assistants to the participating schools; and training in language teaching for content teachers (Aliaga, 2010: 5–6).

Since 2014, by means of the *Eleaniztasunerantz* ('Towards multilingualism') programme, the Department of Education of the Basque Government has provided grants for schools to elaborate their own multilingual projects in which at least one content subject should be taught through the foreign language (typically English). This measure has resulted in a wide range of schools offering alternative CLIL curricula. In 2016, for example, 315 schools[6] of the BAC had their own multilingual project. In general, learners' enrolment on these multilingual initiatives is voluntary, although some schools may have their own selection criteria. Content teachers, in turn, are required to hold a B2 level in the target language to participate in CLIL teaching. One of the main shortcomings for the implementation of CLIL is the availability of teachers who fulfil this requirement. In the academic year 2015–2016, only 13.3 % of the teaching staff in the public school system (i.e. 2,800 teachers out of 22,000) held this level of proficiency in English (Gobierno Vasco, 2016). Other important shortcomings are the lack of CLIL materials (Alonso, Grisaleña, & Campo, 2008; Merino & Lasagabaster, 2018) or the notable lacunae in CLIL teacher education (Ruiz de Zarobe & Lasagabaster, 2010). It must be noted that, apart from these shortcomings, there are some critical voices (e.g. Etxeberria, 2004; Etxeberria & Ruiz Bikandi, 2002) who question the increasing role of English in Basque education as they regard it as a potential threat to the revitalisation and normalisation of the Basque language. In many cases, the CLIL initiatives developed have been implemented at the expense of reducing the number of hours of instruction in Basque (especially in Model D).

3 Research on the effects of CLIL in the Basque Autonomous Community

In general, the research conducted in the BAC on the effects of CLIL instruction has yielded positive findings in favour of this type of programme[7]. One example

6 One hundred of these schools belonged to the public sector. The rest were charter schools.

7 Various studies on CLIL have been jointly conducted in the BAC and other Spanish communities such as Catalonia (see Celaya & Ruiz de Zarobe, 2010; Ruiz de Zarobe & Celaya, 2011) or La Rioja (see Agustín Llach, 2009; Jiménez Catalán & Ruiz de Zarobe, 2009; Jiménez Catalán, Ruiz de Zarobe, & Cenoz, 2006; Moreno Espinosa, 2009; Ojeda

is the study by Lasagabaster (2008), who compared the foreign language competence of CLIL and non-CLIL learners in terms of grammar, listening, speaking and writing. The sample for the research consisted of a CLIL group and a non-CLIL group in the fourth year of secondary education and another CLIL group in the third year of secondary education. The findings showed that the CLIL learners significantly outstripped their non-CLIL counterparts in every single test taken and in the overall English competence score. Although they were a year younger, the CLIL cohort in the third grade not only caught up with the non-CLIL cohort but they also outscored them in all the tests but the listening one, with significant differences in grammar and overall foreign language competence. Three years later, Lasagabaster (2011) conducted a similar study and obtained similar positive linguistic outcomes in favour of CLIL learners.

While the studies undertaken by Lasagabaster were of a cross-sectional nature, other studies have adopted a longitudinal approach to investigating language proficiency development. One of these studies was the study by Alonso, Grisaleña, and Campo (2008). This research was conducted in six out of the 12 secondary schools which initially participated in the project *Plurilingual Experience*. By means of different Cambridge English tests administered in October 2004 and May 2006, the authors analysed the foreign language competence of CLIL and non-CLIL learners enrolled on the first and third year of secondary education and the first year of post-compulsory secondary education. The results showed that over the three grades the initial between-group differences in favour of the CLIL participants increased in the post-tests, confirming "the educational value and effectiveness of the Plurilingual Experience" (p. 47). However, it must be taken into account that no statistical analyses were performed to determine whether or not these differences were significant. Alonso, Grisaleña and Campo also investigated the learners' level of subject matter knowledge. They found that "the level obtained by the students taking the subjects in English [was] similar to that of those who learn[ed] in their usual language of instruction" (i.e. Basque or Spanish) (p. 44), concluding that studying a subject in the foreign language does not have any negative effect on subject matter knowledge. This finding, however, was based on teachers' perspectives collected through a questionnaire rather than a test taken by the learners.

Over a one-year period, Merino and Lasagabaster (2018) examined the impact of CLIL on learners' general English competence and the different language skills

Alba, 2009). This review, however, will only include those studies which have been entirely conducted in the BAC.

which make up this faculty. The sample comprised CLIL and non-CLIL learners at lower secondary level from eight Basque schools. The results showed that the CLIL learners performed significantly better than the non-CLIL learners in the post-tests. This finding is not surprising if we take into account that the CLIL group already surpassed the non-CLIL group at the beginning of the research and that their exposure to English was almost twice that of the control group. The most relevant finding for the authors in this respect was to observe that, as regards the longitudinal evaluation of the results, both groups had a similar linguistic development, concluding that "the success of CLIL programmes revolves around the number of years and the intensity of such programmes, as a significant proficiency enhancement is not observable in a one-year period when compared to non-CLIL programmes" (p. 88). In response to previous literature regarding CLIL and the increasing presence of English in the curriculum as a threat to the learning of the Basque language (cf. Etxeberria, 2004; Etxeberria & Ruiz Bikandi, 2002), Merino and Lasagabaster also analysed the development of learners' L1 and L2 (Spanish and Basque). They found that over the year, in which the research was undertaken, the participants' competence in both languages was not adversely affected by the programme they followed.

Particular aspects of foreign language competence like oral and written production have also been explored by means of cross-sectional and longitudinal studies. Gallardo del Puerto and Gómez Lacabex (2013) examined the oral production of two secondary education groups with similar characteristics (same age of onset of foreign language learning, same level of motivation, and no extramural exposure to the foreign language) but differing in the methodological approach followed (a CLIL programme vs. a conventional English as a foreign language programme). The participants' productions were assessed by two Spanish postgraduates in English Studies who had experience as language judges. The study showed that the oral production of the CLIL cohort exhibited better grammar and fluency than that of the non-CLIL cohort whereas no significant differences between both groups were found with regard to content, pronunciation and vocabulary. On the other hand, although the non-CLIL learners' oral productions were found to be longer in duration and greater in quantity, the CLIL learners displayed denser speech as well as lesser reliance on their L1 and the interviewer's help or clarifications. Ruiz de Zarobe (2008) also compared CLIL and non-CLIL learners as regards their oral competence but in this case this was analysed longitudinally in the third and fourth year of secondary education and the second year of post-compulsory secondary education. The data gathered revealed that in the third year of secondary education the CLIL learners significantly outperformed the non-CLIL learners in every single category analysed (pronunciation, vocabulary, grammar, fluency and content). However, although they continued scoring higher than their non-CLIL counterparts, there was not a significant increase in proficiency throughout the different grades. The differences between both groups remained significant in four categories in the fourth year of secondary education and only in two categories in post-compulsory secondary education. Using the same sample and longitudinal approach, Ruiz de Zarobe (2010) analysed the participants' written competence based on five categories: content, vocabulary, language usage, organisation and mechanics. In this case, the CLIL and non-CLIL learners were compared in the fourth year of secondary education and the second year of post-compulsory secondary education. Unlike the results obtained concerning oral competence, the differences in written competence between the CLIL and non-CLIL strand – favourable to the former – were significant in three of the categories (mechanics, language usage and vocabulary) at the end of secondary education and in the five categories at the end of post-compulsory secondary education.

Another area of interest in CLIL research has been analysing the impact of CLIL instruction on phonetics and morphosyntax. Like previous studies, this research has been conducted in the context of secondary education. Gallardo del Puerto, Gómez Lacabex and García Lecumberri (2009) analysed the pronunciation of CLIL and non-CLIL learners through the judgements made by five native English speakers. They observed that the CLIL participants had a more intelligible and less irritating foreign accent than the non-CLIL participants. Nevertheless, as regards the degree of foreign accent, the authors did not find any statistically significant difference between the two groups, attributing this finding to the fact that, although they had greater exposure to the foreign language, the CLIL learners were also taught by non-native teachers and, consequently, "authentic input was for the most part missing" (p. 74) in their tuition. Villarreal Olaizola and García Mayo (2009) compared the oral production of CLIL and non-CLIL learners as regards their production of tense and agreement markers. Data analysis revealed that the CLIL group significantly outperformed the non-CLIL group in the production of affixal morphemes (3rd person singular -s and past tense -ed) but not in the production of suppletive forms (auxiliary and copula *be*), which were supplied in a parallel fashion. In a subsequent longitudinal study spanning from the third year of secondary education to the second year of post-compulsory secondary education, García Mayo and Villarreal Olaizola (2010) found no significant differences between the CLIL and non-CLIL cohorts tested concerning the development of both suppletive and affixal morphemes. The study by Martínez Adrián and Gutiérrez

Mangado (2009) also focused on investigating morphosyntactic features in oral production. The focus in this case was on null subjects, null objects, negation and placeholders. As observed in the two previous studies, CLIL did not offer substantial gains regarding the morphosyntactic features analysed since only in the use of placeholders was the difference between the CLIL and non-CLIL group statistically significant.

Other studies have focused on investigating non-linguistic aspects. This is the case of the studies undertaken by Lasagabaster (2009) and Lasagabaster and Sierra (2009) on the language attitudes of CLIL and non-CLIL learners in secondary education. Lasagabaster (2009) analysed learners' general attitude towards trilingualism according to five factors: 1) attitude towards trilingualism regarding knowledge, job opportunities, and age of onset; 2) attitude towards the social presence of trilingualism; 3) attitude towards the cognitive and economic benefits of trilingualism; 4) attitude towards the learning of three languages; and 5) attitude towards the social benefits of trilingualism. He observed that the CLIL learners obtained significantly higher scores in all the factors. They attached more importance to trilingualism and to its spread amongst the Basque population and were more positive about the effects of trilingualism. The data, however, revealed that both groups of learners found the learning of three languages difficult, which highlighted, according to the author (p. 38), the "urgent need to improve the language teaching methodology". Lasagabaster and Sierra (2009), in turn, examined learners' specific attitudes towards each of the three languages they studied: Basque, Spanish and English. The outcomes revealed that the learners enrolled on the CLIL programme not only showed a more positive attitude towards the foreign language but also towards the two other languages of the curriculum.

These studies represent valuable approaches to the study of CLIL instruction and its effects on language learning in the BAC. Nevertheless, there are certain shortcomings in their methodology and design which may call their results into question. One of these shortcomings is the lack of matching in the CLIL and non-CLIL samples used. Except for the age of onset of foreign language learning, the participants are not usually matched for intervening variables such as motivation, language proficiency, socioeconomic status, or extramural exposure to the foreign language. In this sense, one variable which can be highly influential upon the results obtained is the amount of exposure to the target language. When analysing the impact of CLIL, the studies conducted have been based on comparing groups of CLIL and non-CLIL learners who differed in the number of hours of exposure to the foreign language, with CLIL groups having greater exposure. In some cases (see, for example, Gallardo del Puerto & Gómez Lacabex, 2013;

Ruiz de Zarobe, 2008, 2010; Villarreal Olaizola & García Mayo, 2009)[8], the CLIL learners had received more than 200 hours of additional exposure to the target language. This fact raises two questions about the findings reported: Are the positive results in favour of CLIL attributable to this methodological approach? Or are they just the result of a greater exposure to the target language on the part of CLIL learners?

The study by Iglesias Diéguez and Martínez Adrián (2017) seems to tip the scales in favour of the second interpretation. The sample for this research was made up of four groups[9]: a CLIL and a non-CLIL group in the first year of secondary education plus a CLIL and a non-CLIL group in the third year of secondary education. In both cases, the CLIL groups had had more hours of exposure to the foreign language than the non-CLIL groups (144 more hours in the first grade and 278 in the third grade). The aim of the study was to measure these groups' general proficiency and receptive lexical knowledge. To this end, the authors used the Quick Placement Test and two vocabulary tests including the 1,000 and 2,000 most frequent words in English. The analysis of between-group differences revealed that the CLIL learners significantly outperformed their non-CLIL counterparts in the same grade regarding general proficiency and receptive vocabulary, the only exception being the 1,000 word vocabulary test in the third-grade groups. This finding was in line with previous research, underlining the positive effect of CLIL instruction on language learning. However, the results changed drastically when the participants were matched for time of target language exposure. In a second analysis, Iglesias Diéguez and Martínez Adrián compared the results obtained by the CLIL group in the first grade and the non-CLIL group in the third grade, who had a similar number of hours of exposure to the foreign language (1,116 and 1,173 hours respectively). In this case, no significant differences were found between the two groups in the three tests administered; that is, with a similar amount of target language exposure, the CLIL learners did not perform better than the non-CLIL learners. They even got slightly lower scores in the placement test and the 2,000 word vocabulary test. For this reason, it is essential to control the extent of target language exposure in future research. Unless experimental and control groups are matched for this variable, we cannot confirm that it is

8 Some studies (Alonso, Grisaleña, & Campo, 2008; Lasagabaster, 2008, 2011) do not provide information about the participants' amount of exposure to the target language.

9 The participants were matched for socioeconomic status and extramural exposure to the target language.

the CLIL approach (and not just a longer amount of exposure to the language) which is responsible for the outcomes obtained.

Most of the studies reviewed here are cross-sectional. They lack a longitudinal approach including a pre-testing phase which could guarantee that the participants' competence in the linguistic aspects analysed is similar before the implementation of the CLIL approach, since those learners who enroll on CLIL tend to have a higher level of proficiency in the foreign language (San Isidro & Lasagabaster, 2018)[10]. This longitudinal focus is essential when researching the impact of CLIL not only on linguistic aspects but also on affective factors such as motivation and language attitudes. As we have seen, the studies by Lasagabaster (2009) and Lasagabaster and Sierra (2009) indicated that CLIL learners have a more positive attitude towards trilingualism than non-CLIL learners. This finding led the authors to conclude that the implementation of CLIL has a substantial impact on language attitudes. However, the main flaw in these studies was that no pre-test was conducted. Therefore, we do not know whether the CLIL learners already had a more positive language attitude than their non-CLIL counterparts when they began CLIL instruction. As noted in section 2.2, enrolling on CLIL is voluntary, so we can assume that those learners who follow this type of programme may be more motivated and interested in language learning (Bruton, 2011). In order to confirm that CLIL has a positive effect on learners' language attitudes, it is necessary to guarantee the homogeneity of the groups at the outset of the research and analyse possible differences between CLIL and non-CLIL learners in a post-test.

Another shortcoming with respect to the methodology is the reduced size, both numerically and geographically, of the samples used. On the one hand, there are studies (Gallardo del Puerto & Gómez Lacabex, 2013; Gallardo del Puerto, Gómez Lacabex & García Lecumberri, 2009; Martínez Adrián & Gutiérrez Mangado, 2009) in which the total sample size is less than 30 participants. On the other hand, most of the studies conducted include participants from just three or four schools of the BAC, thus offering a small picture of the outcomes of CLIL programmes in the region. In this respect, there are variables related to the school context which need to be factored in in future research such as the type of school (public or private) and the setting (urban or rural).

10 See the longitudinal studies by Alonso, Grisaleña and Campo (2008) and Merino and Lasagabaster (2018) where initial differences between CLIL and non-CLIL learners were already found in favour of the former.

4 Concluding remarks and future avenues

The present chapter has offered an overview of how during the past two decades the emphasis in Basque education has shifted from bilingualism to multilingualism with the implementation of CLIL. This has led the BAC to position itself as one of the most active communities in terms of multilingual education in Spain, becoming a leader in CLIL practice and research. Despite these advances, there are still certain aspects which can be improved. In this section, I will suggest what could be done in the future to enhance multilingual education and the implementation of CLIL in this region and I will discuss possible avenues for further research on its effectiveness.

First of all, it has become clear throughout this review that, as observed in other Spanish communities (see Lozano-Martínez, 2017; Manzano Vázquez, 2015; Nieto Moreno de Diezmas, 2016), CLIL in the BAC is a synonym for English-medium instruction. This foreign language is clearly the predominant one when we talk about teaching content subjects through a language which is not Spanish or Basque. To accommodate to the multilingual principle established by the European Union (European Commission, 1995), Basque education authorities should provide greater support to the teaching and learning of other foreign languages by giving them equal priority and opportunities in the CLIL initiatives developed. By means of measures like the *Eleaniztasunerantz* programme, the BAC is experiencing a marked increase in the number of schools offering various CLIL initiatives. As pointed out by Cenoz, Genesee and Gorter (2014: 246), this diversity of CLIL formats can result in a state of conceptual confusion and ambiguity. To avoid this, it would be necessary to homogenise the CLIL initiatives set up across Basque schools. Teacher education is vital if we want CLIL to be successfully implemented at classroom level. For this reason, it is necessary to ensure that CLIL teachers acquire the professional knowledge and competences which enable them to integrate content and language instruction in their teaching practice. One of these competences is teachers' level of proficiency in the target language. As we have seen, content teachers in the BAC must have a B2 level to take part in CLIL instruction. Nevertheless, there are still many teachers who do not meet this requirement (Gobierno Vasco, 2016). Promoting language courses which assist teachers in achieving not only this language level but an even higher one (at least a C1 level) is a compelling need. Finally, it is also essential to address the lack of CLIL materials. One measure to overcome this shortcoming could be developing an initiative, similar to the *EIMA* programme, which promotes the creation of this type of materials.

Empirically-driven research can play a pivotal role in determining future courses of action in the development of CLIL. This chapter has made a critical appraisal of the main studies conducted in the BAC on the effects of CLIL. Although there are areas where clear gains are not observed yet (morphosyntax or pronunciation), previous studies have reported positive results in favour of this type of instruction vis-à-vis both linguistic and non-linguistic aspects. These findings, however, must be interpreted with caution due to some flaws present in the existing research. As has been noted above, these flaws include the lack of a pre-testing phase prior to the implementation of CLIL, the small size of the samples used, and the lack of homogeneity of the participants. In fact, given the differences between CLIL and non-CLIL learners in research, the results in favour of CLIL are not really significant. For this reason, there is the need for future research to remedy these shortcomings, putting special emphasis on the development of longitudinal studies into the long-term effects of CLIL. Research will also need to focus on areas which remain almost unexplored, such as the impact of CLIL on receptive and productive vocabulary, subject matter knowledge, or L1 and L2 development. The studies undertaken thus far have been framed exclusively in the context of secondary education. Therefore, research on the initial effects of CLIL in primary education is necessary. On the other hand, research outcomes are largely dependent upon classroom practice. In this sense, one important avenue for future CLIL research is to analyse the effectiveness of the methodological practices implemented and the quality of language instruction CLIL learners receive. Studies need to be further complemented by a qualitative approach, which probes the attitudes towards CLIL of the main participants involved in its development, that is, teachers and learners.

References

Agustín Llach, M. P. (2009). The role of Spanish L1 in the vocabulary use of CLIL and non-CLIL learners. In Y. Ruiz de Zarobe & R. M. Jiménez Catalán (Eds.), *Content and Language Integrated Learning: Evidence from research in Europe* (pp. 112–129). Bristol: Multilingual Matters.

Aliaga, R. (2010). La enseñanza de las lenguas extranjeras en Euskadi. *Avances en Supervisión Educativa*, *13*, 1–6.

Alonso, E., Grisaleña, J., & Campo, A. (2008). Plurilingual education in secondary schools: Analysis of results. *International CLIL Research Journal*, *1*(1), 36–49.

BOE. (1979). *Ley Orgánica 3/1979, de 18 de diciembre, de Estatuto de Autonomía para el País Vasco*. Retrieved June 22, 2018 from https://www.boe.es/buscar/pdf/1979/BOE-A-1979-30177-consolidado.pdf.

BOE. (1982). *Ley 10/1982, de 24 de noviembre, básica de normalización del uso del Euskera*. Retrieved June 22, 2018 from https://www.boe.es/boe/dias/2012/04/26/pdfs/BOE-A-2012-5539.pdf.

Bruton, A. (2011). Is CLIL so beneficial, or just selective? Re-evaluating some of the research. *System*, *39*(4), 1–10.

Celaya, M. L., & Ruiz de Zarobe, Y. (2010). First languages and age in CLIL and non-CLIL contexts. *International CLIL Research Journal*, *1*(3), 60–66.

Cenoz, J. (2008). Achievements and challenges in bilingual and multilingual education in the Basque Country. *AILA Review*, *21*, 13–30.

Cenoz, J. (2009). *Towards multilingual education: Basque educational research from an international perspective*. Bristol: Multilingual Matters.

Cenoz, J., & Genesee, F. (1998). Psycholinguistic perspectives on multilingualism and multilingual education. In J. Cenoz & F. Genessee (Eds.), *Beyond bilingualism: multilingualism and multilingual education* (pp. 16–32). Clevedon: Multilingual Matters.

Cenoz, J., Genesee, F., & Gorter, D. (2014). Critical analysis of CLIL: Taking stock and looking forward. *Applied Linguistics*, *35*(3), 243–262.

Cobarrubias, J. (2008). History of the "normalization" of Basque in the public administration sphere. In G. Totoricagüena & I. Urrutia (Eds.), *The legal status of the Basque language today: One language, three administrations, seven different geographies and a diaspora* (pp. 135–164). Donostia-San Sebastián: Eusko Ikaskuntza.

Erize, X. (2003). History of the Basque language: From the discourse of its death to its maintenance. In M. J. Azumendi & I. Martínez de Luna (Eds.), *The case of Basque: Past, present and future* (pp. 19–41). Donostia-San Sebastián: Soziolinguistika Klusterra.

Escobar Urmeneta, C., & Unamuno, V. (2008). Languages and language learning in Catalan schools: From the bilingual to the multilingual challenge. In C. Hélot & A. de Mejía (Eds.), *Forging multilingual spaces: Integrated perspectives on majority and minority bilingual education* (pp. 228–255). Bristol: Multilingual Matters.

Etxeberria, F. (2004). 40 años de educación bilingüe en el país del Euskera. *Revista de Educación*, *334*, 281–313.

Etxeberria, F., & Ruiz Bikandi, U. (2002). *¿Trilingües a los 4 Años? [Trilingual at the age of 4?]*. Donostia-San Sebastián: Universidad del País Vasco.

European Commission. (1995). *White paper on education and training. Teaching and learning: Towards the learning society*. Brussels: European Commission.

European Commission. (2004). *Promoting language learning and linguistic diversity: An action plan 2004-2006*. Brussels: European Commission.

European Commission. (2005). *A new framework strategy for multilingualism*. Brussels: Commission of the European Communities.

European Commission. (2006). *Europeans and their languages. Special Eurobarometer 243*. Brussels: European Commission.

European Commission. (2008). *Multilingualism: An asset for Europe and a shared commitment*. Brussels: European Commission.

European Commission. (2012). *Europeans and their languages. Special Eurobarometer 386*. Brussels: European Commission.

Eustat. (2015). *Population aged 5 and over of the Basque Country by province and age group according to language skills. 1981-2011*. Retrieved June 25, 2018 from http://en.eustat.eus/elementos/ele0009500/Population_aged_5_and_over_of_the_Basque_Country_by_province_and_age_group_according_to__language_skills/tbl0009563_i.html.

Gallardo del Puerto, F., & Gómez Lacabex, E. (2013). The impact of additional CLIL exposure on oral English pronunciation. *Journal of English Studies, 13*, 113–131.

Gallardo del Puerto, F., Gómez Lacabex, E., & García Lecumberri, M. L. (2009). Testing the effectiveness of Content and Language Integrated Learning in foreign language contexts: The assessment of English pronunciation. In Y. Ruiz de Zarobe & R. M. Jiménez Catalán (Eds.), *Content and Language Integrated Learning: Evidence from research in Europe* (pp. 63–80). Bristol: Multilingual Matters.

García Gurrutxaga, M. L., del Nozal, M., Villa, M., & Aliaga, R. (2011). Teaching-learning foreign languages in the Basque state schools: the INEB and BHINEBI projects, a practical example for CLIL and competence-based learning. In Y. Ruiz de Zarobe, J. M. Sierra & F. Gallardo del Puerto (Eds.), *Content and Language Integrated Learning: Contributions to multilingualism in European contexts* (pp. 271–292). Frankfurt am Main: Peter Lang.

García Mayo, M. P., & Villareal Olaizola, I. (2010). The development of suppletive and affixal tense and agreement morphemes in the L3 English of Basque-Spanish bilinguals. *Second Language Research, 27*(1), 129–149.

Gobierno Vasco. (1983). *Decreto 138/1983, de 11 de Julio, del Departamento de Educación y Cultura, por el que se regula el uso de las lenguas oficiales en la enseñanza no universitaria en el País Vasco*. Vitoria-Gasteiz: Departamento de Educación y Cultura. Retrieved June 26, 2018 from https://www.euskadi.eus/y22-bopv/es/bopv2/datos/1983/07/8301433a.pdf.

Gobierno Vasco. (2010). *Proceso de experimentación del marco de educación trilingüe*. Vitoria-Gasteiz: Departamento de Educación, Universidades e Investigación. Retrieved July 5, 2018 from http://www.euskadi.eus/

contenidos/libro/dig_publicaciones_lenguas/es_def/adjuntos/500013c_Pub_EJ_experimentacion_MET_c.pdf.

Gobierno Vasco. (2013). *Fifth sociolinguistic survey 2011*. Vitoria-Gasteiz: Servicio Central de Publicaciones del Gobierno Vasco.

Gobierno Vasco. (2016). *Plan de mejora del sistema educativo de la CAPV: Basado en la equidad hacia la excelencia*. Retrieved July 6, 2018 from http://www.euskadi.eus/contenidos/informacion/heziberri_2020/es_dokument/adjuntos/Plan_Mejora_marzo_2016_c.pdf.

Iglesias Diéguez, K., & Martínez Adrián, M. (2017). The influence of CLIL on receptive vocabulary: A preliminary study. *Journal of English Studies*, *15*, 107–134.

ISEI-IVEI. (2015a). *Evaluación de diagnóstico 2015. Informe ejecutivo. 4º Educación Primaria*. Retrieved July 10, 2018 from https://www.berrigasteiz.com/site_argitalpenak/docs/311_evaluacion_diagnostico/3112016004c_Pub_ISEI_ED_2015_txosten_exekutiboa_4lh_c.pdf.

ISEI-IVEI. (2015b). *Evaluación de diagnóstico 2015. Informe ejecutivo. 2º Educación Secundaria Obligatoria*. Retrieved July 10, 2018 from https://www.berrigasteiz.com/site_argitalpenak/docs/311_evaluacion_diagnostico/3112016004c_Pub_ISEI_ED_2015_txosten_exekutiboa_4lh_c.pdf.

Jiménez Catalán, R. M., & Ruiz de Zarobe, Y. (2009). Receptive vocabulary of EFL learners in two instructional contexts. In Y. Ruiz de Zarobe & R. M. Jiménez Catalán (Eds.), *Content and Language Integrated Learning: Evidence from research in Europe* (pp. 81–92). Bristol: Multilingual Matters.

Jiménez Catalán, R. M., Ruiz de Zarobe, Y., & Cenoz, J. (2006). Vocabulary profiles of English foreign language learners in English as a subject and as a vehicular language. *Vienna English Working Papers (VIEWS)*, *15*(3), 23–27.

Lasagabaster, D. (2008). Foreign language competence in content and language integrated courses. *The Open Applied Linguistics Journal*, *1*, 31–42.

Lasagabaster, D. (2009). The implementation of CLIL and attitudes towards trilingualism. *International Journal of Applied Linguistics*, *157*, 23–43.

Lasagabaster, D. (2011). English achievement and student motivation in CLIL and EFL settings. *Innovation in Language Learning and Teaching*, *5*(1), 3–18.

Lasagabaster, D., & Sierra, J. M. (2009). Language attitudes in CLIL and traditional EFL classes. *International CLIL Research Journal*, *1*(2), 4–17.

Lozano-Martínez, L. (2017). Los docentes en los programas de educación bilingüe en Cantabria. *ELIA*, *17*, 93–123.

Manzano Vázquez, B. (2015). CLIL in three monolingual communities: The examples of Extremadura, Madrid and La Rioja. *ELIA*, *15*, 135–158.

Martínez Adrián, M., & Gutiérrez Mangado, M. J. (2009). The acquisition of English syntax by CLIL learners in the Basque Country. In Y. Ruiz de Zarobe & R. M. Jiménez Catalán (Eds.), *Content and Language Integrated Learning: Evidence from research in Europe* (pp. 176–196). Bristol: Multilingual Matters.

Merino, J. A., & Lasagabaster, D. (2018). CLIL as a way to multilingualism. *International Journal of Bilingual Education and Bilingualism*, *21*(1), 79–92.

Moreno Espinosa, S. (2009). Young learners' L2 word association responses in two different learning contexts. In Y. Ruiz de Zarobe & R. M. Jiménez Catalán (Eds.), *Content and Language Integrated Learning: Evidence from research in Europe* (pp. 93–111). Bristol: Multilingual Matters.

Nieto Moreno de Diezmas, E. (2016). The impact of CLIL on the acquisition of the learning to learn competence in secondary school education in the bilingual programmes of Castilla-La Mancha. *Porta Linguarum*, *25*, 21–34.

Ojeda Alba, J. (2009). Themes and Vocabulary in CLIL and non-CLIL Instruction. In Y. Ruiz de Zarobe & R. M. Jiménez Catalán (Eds.), *Content and Language Integrated Learning: Evidence from research in Europe* (pp. 130–156). Bristol: Multilingual Matters.

Ruiz de Zarobe, Y. (2008). CLIL and foreign language learning: A longitudinal study in the Basque Country. *International CLIL Research Journal*, *1*(1), 60–73.

Ruiz de Zarobe, Y. (2010). Written production and CLIL: An empirical study. In C. Dalton-Puffer, J. Nikula & U. Smit (Eds.), *Language use and language learning in CLIL classrooms* (pp. 191–210). Amsterdam: John Benjamins.

Ruiz de Zarobe, Y., & Celaya, M. L. (2011). CLIL across languages: Research outcomes in two bilingual communities. *TESI*, *12*(3), 200–214.

Ruiz de Zarobe, Y., & Lasagabaster, D. (2010). The emergence of CLIL in Spain: An educational challenge. In Y. Ruiz de Zarobe & D. Lasagabaster (Eds.), *CLIL in Spain: Implementation, results and teacher training* (pp. ix–xvii). Newcastle upon Tyne: Cambridge Scholars Publishing.

San Isidro, X., & Lasagabaster, D. (2018). The impact of CLIL on pluriliteracy development and content learning in a rural multilingual setting: A longitudinal study. *Language Teaching Research*, *23*(5), 584–602.

Villarreal Olaizola, I., & García Mayo, M. P. (2009). Tense and agreement morphology in the interlanguage of Basque/Spanish bilinguals: CLIL vs. non-CLIL. In Y. Ruiz de Zarobe & R. M. Jiménez Catalán (Eds.), *Content and Language Integrated Learning: Evidence from research in Europe* (pp. 157–175). Bristol: Multilingual Matters.

François Victor Tochon

Language education policy in the United States: A hesitation waltz

"Americans will be consigned to being linguistically retarded."

(Fishman, 2005: 127)

Abstract: Using the Hesitation Waltz as a metaphor, this chapter describes the back and forth movements characterising language education policies in the United States, that is, how language education has moved from restriction to expediency, from tolerance to repression, from absence of support to promotion or the other way round. The chapter begins by discussing two examples of the current situation of the United States regarding language education policies targeted at Native Americans and the Ebonics controversy. Next, it analyses modern language education policies after 9/11, the progressive opening to measures assisting Hispanic heritage learners, the detrimental effect of the No Child Left Behind Act on foreign language education, and the 'Hesitation Waltz' experienced in higher education. The chapter concludes by discussing the influence of both dialectical and cultural substrates on language education policies.

Keywords: Native Americans, Ebonics, Hispanic heritage learners, No Child Left Behind, higher education

Hesitation Waltz, a variation of the Boston and Valse, was defined as a dance based on a pause and glide, with steps moving back and forth demonstrating the uncertainty of male birds, both attracted by and rejecting the moves of their partner. This back and forth movement characterizes Language Education Policy in the United States quite well. There were periods of likes and dislikes, attractions and rejections, which led to contradictory moves, back and forth, with no apparent consistency nor real assertiveness. This lack of certainty has led to the situation of today, in which monolingual speakers are more and more unemployed or limited to providing low status services, as globalization develops increasingly not towards English as the world language (it is only shared by 15 % of the planet) but to a multiplicity of exchanges in the various world tongues, about ten of them, that count more than a hundred million speakers.

1 A two-century-old hesitation waltz

History provides evidence that language education policies in the United States were used as tolls to eliminate populations that were not welcome for various political and ideological reasons. Wiley (2002) provides an overview of education policies that have affected the language rights of minorities in the United States. When the Europeans arrived on the American continent, around two million Native Americans were living north of present-day Mexico. Soon, in addition to their three hundred or so languages, numerous African languages were shared among slaves, and various European languages were spoken, including English, Dutch, French, German, Spanish, etc. The Hesitation Waltz begins around 1740 with the compulsory ignorance laws installed under colonial rule that were retained in the slave codes of Southern States: slaves were barred from becoming literate until 1865. Mission schools were established in 1819 under the Civilization Fund Act that promoted and imposed English and Anglo values to Native American peoples (see Harrison, in this volume). Mission schools would "make the whole tribe English in their language, civilized in their habits and Christian in their religion" (Del Valle, 2003: 281). However, German Bilingual Schools were thriving in Wisconsin, and laws were passed in Pennsylvania (1837) and Ohio (1840) authorizing the creation of German-English public schools. Between 1845 and 1905, the integration of peoples then residing in Mexican territory was subject to U.S. territorial and State laws.

Thus bilingual schools of German and English were accepted even though Native American languages had been prohibited from being spoken or written in American schools. One step forward, one step back, and turn around. The first Boarding School was established in 1889 with compulsory English, even in Cherokee, Choctaw, Creek and Seminole regions where Native American writing systems had been developed in independent schools from 1822 to 1852. With the flood of German immigrants in the 1880s, English-only laws were passed and then repealed in Illinois and Wisconsin. German instruction declined from 1905 to 1923; it was banned in most States during the First World War (Wiley, 2004). Laws designating English as the official language were passed in a majority of States and the use of 'foreign languages' was restricted. The Supreme Court nevertheless repealed a few laws such as the prohibition of Japanese in Hawaiian private schools. The 1930s then witnessed a Tribal Restoration, during which deculturation language policies targeting Native Americans were relaxed, a trend which lasted until the 1950s, at which time Native American Termination policies renewed restrictions on indigenous peoples. In Navajo-speaking homes, children tended to respond to their parents in English. Even before they had entered school, those children had internalized the silencing messages of the English-dominant society (McCarthy, 2013: 302). Thus not only did schools affect language use and the perception of lack of status of these languages: it was also conveyed in the family, which later led to the study of family language policy.

The post-war geopolitical climate mandated a need for international expertise, particularly in less commonly taught languages, which motivated the Title VI National Defense Education Act of 1958 (Tochon & Harrison, 2017). Its purpose was to ensure quality to meet national needs: "Prior to the passage of the act, few of the languages spoken by more than three-fourths of the world's population were being offered in the United States and not enough scholars were available to perform research in such languages or to teach them... Hindi, for example, was being studied by only twenty-three students in the United States in 1958" (Hines, 2011: 6–7). During the sixties and the seventies a number of civil rights cases were won leading to better legal protections from discrimination. The Supreme Court imposed on School Districts the duty to accommodate language minority children. Bilingual education was prescribed in certain contexts. Jurisprudence established criteria for bilingual program accountability (García, 2009). Yet during the same years a wave of restrictionism returned with the English Only Movement and lack of investment from the Reagan administration (Lee & Marshall, 2001). Immigrant rights were restricted and propositions against bilingual education were put forward in California and Arizona. The designation of English as an official language in some States was accompanied by restrictions applied to the use of foreign or indigenous languages (Crawford, 1995, 2000).

The attrition of non-English languages was not a uniform process. Their "recurring rise and fall" (Fishman, 2005: 118) varied from State to State in both rate and degree. Young settlers may bring years of upswing due to proximity and clustering in neighborhoods; some small groups like the Dutch in Pennsylvania, the French speakers in Maine and Vermont, the Germans and the Norwegians in Wisconsin, or the Yiddish ultra-Orthodox communities have succeeded in keeping their language for many generations until recently, with peaks in the middle of the 20th century.

In the early 1900s, immigrants often had a high level of education and would keep the language spoken in their household, a phenomenon that almost disappeared after World War II. Even during the Vietnam War there was a willingness to keep sound and thorough knowledge of the languages of the countries with which the U.S. was interacting. However, the U.S. "began to lose the edge of the depth of our knowledge" in a "New World Disorder" expresses Admiral Inman (2003: 7), reflecting on the critical role of language education.

In the 1980s and the 1990s, the number of elementary school language programs increased, which was perceived as a time of expansion favored by a number of federal initiatives; for example, the expansion of Title VI University Centers that had as part of their function to support the teaching of their language and culture in K-12 school settings (now functioning with half of their budgets and on their way to being closed); the Foreign Language Assistance Program (FLAP) that supported innovative language programs in schools from 1988 (a program terminated 20 years later); and STARTALK student and teacher language programs in a large variety of languages.

Since then things have not evolved in the direction of tolerance or expediency, negatively affecting the possible promotion of indigenous languages and foreign languages, even though the David L. Boren National Security Education Act of 1991 (NSEA, Title VIII) was an attempt at reestablishing the importance of cultural and language learning. This Act funded international education and foreign language studies by higher education students. One step forward, one step back, and turn around. In 1997, David Rothkopf, a professor of international relations and former manager of Kissinger Associates, published in his journal, *Foreign Policy* #107, the advice to encourage the promotion of English abroad. It led to a policy of outsourcing English development abroad rather than cultivating foreign languages at home. His argument, presented in the section "Toward a Global Culture" and abundantly discussed by Phillipson (2008) in *The linguistic imperialism of neoliberal empire*, was that:

> It is in the general interest of the United States to encourage the development of a world in which the fault lines separating nations are bridged by shared interests. And it is in the economic and political interests of the United States to ensure that if the world is moving toward a common language, it be English. (Rothkopf, 1997: 5)

Nonetheless, the 1990s witnessed an increasing concern for teaching modern languages in schools. Modern language teaching in elementary schools increased by 9 %, from 22 % in 1987 (one in five) to 31 % in 1997 (almost one in three) (Branaman & Rhodes, 1999). Language classes for native speakers increased in number, Japanese and Russian as well as other less commonly taught languages were more frequently taught, and computer language learning was more common.

At the end of the 1990s, new efforts to improve foreign language education marked the creation of educational standards by the American Council for the Teaching of Foreign Languages (ACTFL, 1996). The Center for Applied Linguistics in Washington DC conducted a study on modern language teaching, collecting data from 22 educators in 19 countries (Pufahl, Rhodes, & Christian,

2001). The study described what works in various countries that could be implemented in the U.S. Among the characteristics of model programs were the following aspects:

- An early start with widespread compulsory education in modern languages by age 8.
- Well-articulated frameworks to guide program development, such as the Common European Framework of Reference for Languages (Council of Europe, 2001).
- Effective teaching strategies integrating languages and content learning, communicative methods and intercultural learning with innovative technologies supporting interactions with native speakers, information and entertainment in the target language (policies for learner autonomy).
- Rigorous teacher education was one of the most cited factors to reach excellence, with at least one year of thorough teaching methods associated with intensive reflective practice. "A crucial factor in teacher quality is the status of the teaching profession, because it directly impacts the quality of candidates who go into teaching." (ibid., online)

Sound teacher education with critical reflection on the role of language status and language ideologies is a way to respond to various types of social injustice related to language education policies (Osborn, 2007; Reagan, 2005). Here are two brief examples of the current U.S. situation regarding Amerindian and African-American populations.

1.1 Language education policies related to Amerindian populations

The Indigenous or Amerindian population in the U.S. consists of less than 2 million citizens. Out of around two hundred languages that survive, some 20 Amerindian languages have child speakers, and less than ten are relatively large. Many among these languages struggle to survive and some communities are engaged in revitalization, as documented in Harrison (2013). Like in Canada, these languages had been targeted for elimination in the late 19th century through boarding school education. Young children were forcefully taken from their families to schools far from their homes. Their languages and traditions were considered inferior. However, when struggles for educational sovereignty succeeded in their language reclamation, and the Native American Languages Act (1990/1992) and Esther Martinez Act (2006) were passed, educational achievement became acknowledged as linked to mother tongue and heritage language development. Speakers of aboriginal languages are nevertheless very few in number, just as the number of Americans who learn another language to a proficient level is low. Fishman (2005: 115) qualifies multilingualism in the U.S. as an exotic phenomenon:

> While English is widely regarded as the language of mainstream USA, the relegating of other languages spoken by immigrants and their native-born offspring, those languages even of world communities [...] are not recognized as great natural and national resources [...] In most cases, immigrant languages and those of Native Americans endure not even benign neglect but aggressive discouragement and disparagement.

Problems of identity and self-esteem, poverty, crime, drugs, and educational failure make language revitalization difficult. After two centuries of racism and forced assimilation, the trauma inherited from centuries of oppression has led young Native Americans to be the lowest achieving students in school (McCarty, 2008). These students are often placed in English Language Learner classes, even though English is most often their mother tongue. Locally, community efforts to develop adapted schooling, for instance through immersion, involve family and school integrative planning to renew the social bond.

1.2 The Ebonics controversy: The case of the Oakland California School Board

In December 1996, a Californian school board passed a resolution acknowledging the existence of the African-American vernacular named Ebonics and proposed to teach in that language as a legitimate bridge to standard English. The resolution triggered mass media criticisms and ignited a national debate. According to the UNESCO principles, the Oakland resolution mandated early instruction in that dialect "to facilitate [...] the mastery of English language skills" (Morgan, 1999: 173). The controversy was born from considering Ebonics as a distinct language with an African origin, and proposing funding to help bridge the gap with standard English, teaching young children of Ebonic heritage in their own language (Wolfram, 1998). What was often misunderstood by opponents of the Oakland resolution is that they were not "trying to teach Black English as a standard language. They're looking for tools to teach children standard English so they might be competitive." (Davidson, 1996, A5).

Various associations of linguistics and applied linguists acknowledged the legitimacy of African-American Vernacular English as a language system with a specific grammar: "There is evidence from Sweden, the U.S., and other countries that speakers of other varieties can be aided in their learning of the standard variety by pedagogical approaches which recognize the legitimacy of the other varieties of a language. From this perspective, the Oakland School Board's decision to recognize the vernacular of African-American students in teaching them Standard English is linguistically and pedagogically sound", acknowledged the Linguistic Society of America (1997) membership after a mail ballot. When the controversy had settled somewhat, Wolfram (1998) noted the intensity of people's beliefs about languages, the widespread misinformation about language variation and the need for better informed knowledge about language diversity and its place in education policy.

2 Modern language education policies after 9/11

In order to keep up with the rest of the world in providing quality foreign language teaching, the federal government issued policies, guidelines or recommendations to promote foreign language education from the primary school to colleges. Examples include: recognition of foreign languages as part of the core curriculum in the Goals 2000: Educate America Act, referred to in Branaman and Rhodes (1999); the No Child Left Behind Act categorizing foreign languages in the core curriculum; and the Homeland Security Strategy Act of 2001 with its determination of critical languages necessary for national security.

Starting in 2002, the National Flagship Language Initiative targeting critical languages reinforced this shift in strategy. A Human Capital Approach to foreign languages was defined to improve proficiency and increase the number of foreign language speakers in various government agencies[1]. Its goals, relating to national order, were obviously different from the goals of emancipation related to a focus on linguistic human rights. Inspired by Wiley (2002) who reviewed the implications of language policies for language rights, Fig. 1 maps the steps of the Hesitation Waltz that characterized Language Education Policies in the United States of America, at various degrees and paces in different States, moving from tolerance to repression, from restriction to expediency, and from absence of support to promotion or the opposite.

In 2003, the House of Representatives introduced the National Security Language Act (HR3676), a piece of legislation significantly expanding U.S. investment in foreign language education at the primary, secondary, and post-secondary level. The Act emphasized the need to start learning foreign languages at an earlier age, promoting quality language education and following the language markets and needs. The International and Foreign Language Studies Act and Intelligence Reform and Terrorism Protection Act of 2004

1 See Congressional Bills here: http://www.gpo.gov/fdsys/browse/collection.action?collectionCode=BILLS.

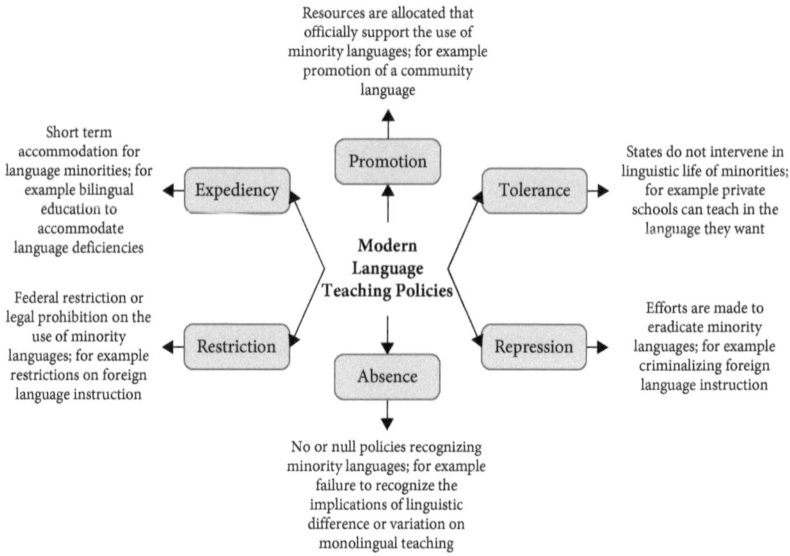

Fig. 1: The various steps of U.S. Language Education Policies (inspired by Wiley, 2002)

prolonged the previous efforts at funding less commonly taught languages. The following years were characterized by a recrudescence of legislations supporting the study of languages: the 2005 Call to Action for National Foreign Language Capabilities, the National Security Education Program, the Year of Study Abroad, the National Security Language Initiative in 2006 and the National Security Language, Foreign Language Education Expansion, and Access to Language Education Acts in 2007, followed by the Intelligence Authorization Act in 2008, along with the Keys to Securing America's Future based on international education and the International Education Leadership and National Security Culture and Language Training Acts.

In 2008, a representative sample of modern language teachers, department chairs and principals were surveyed by the Washington DC National Resource Center in more than 5,000 private and public schools to provide an accurate account of modern language teaching in U.S. schools (Rhodes & Pufahl, 2010). The results of the surveys indicated a significant decrease since the previous survey of 1997: down from 31 % to 25 % in Elementary Schools, and from 75 % to 58 % in Middle Schools. Such a substantial decrease may be explained by the decrease in funding, the increased attention to STEM disciplines (i.e. Science, Technology,

Engineering and Mathematics), and the propaganda related to the misleading scope of English worldwide, which led many Americans to believe that they do not need to learn other languages (Tochon, 2009). Still there was a slight, positive trend towards encouraging immersion, and Arabic and Chinese classes. The field of Language Education Policy witnessed applications of the Law of Darwin: in the linguistic jungle, the strong will survive and the weak die off.

It is difficult in the space of a single chapter to explore a number of important issues deriving from accountability rationales, standardized testing, and a simplification in the definition of teacher quality reducing it to quantitative measures: the situation is complex and encompasses the narrow expansion of a select few critical languages for the sake of national security, the rejection of Ebonics in California, the thundering English Only movement, the death of indigenous languages, the progressive opening of measures to help Hispanic heritage learners, the crisis of foreign language teacher education and the higher levels of central control that decreased education funding in the name of efficacy. In the following sections just a few are briefly examined.

2.1 Opening to Hispanic heritage learners

The Ethnologue[2] estimates that Spanish is spoken by 332 million people worldwide, which would make it the second most spoken language in the world. One of the official working languages of the United Nations, it is the official language of twenty-one countries and territories. While the U.S. is not part of this group, it is the 5th largest Spanish-speaking country in the world. Zentella (2002) even posits that the USA is the 4th Spanish-speaking country in the world since the post-Katrina immigration[3]. The role of Spanish in this country has become more and more prominent. The U.S. Census Bureau (2012), for example, noted that 53 million U.S. residents over the age of 5 speak Spanish at home, and this seems to be a conservative number, which roughly represents some 17 % of the population, with an increase of some 2 % per year. The projected Hispanic population for 2060 in the U.S. may approach 129 million, more than Mexico. Due to the size of the Spanish-speaking population, the U.S. has a chapter of the Royal Academy founded in 1973: *La Academia Norteamericana de la Lengua Española*. Despite this situation, Spanish is usually lost by the third generation of immigrants,

---

2 https://www.ethnologue.com.

3 After the hurricane Katrina hit Louisiana, 1.5 million 18-month green cards were provided to bring helpers from Latin-American countries; many decided to stay and moved to different states.

such as in the case of Puerto Rican populations coming to the United States. It might sound surprising when in many locations Spanish speakers could live their lives comfortably without speaking any word of English, as there are large Hispanic neighborhoods in many U.S. cities. However, they are pushed away from speaking their language and pulled by English in many ways, such as the "pressure to assimilate to the monolingual norm of the host country" (Milroy, 2002: 560). Attrition is both psychological and sociolinguistic. It leads to a situation in which speakers are unable "to produce, perceive or recognize particular rules, lexical items, concepts, or categorical distinctions due to L2 influence" (Ben-Rafael, 2004: 47). A common issue among heritage learners is their feeling of guilt vis-à-vis their low mastery of the mother tongue and the sense of superiority of the host language in which they are immersed daily (de Avila, 2012). Recognition that this so-called language superiority is not a scientifically validated notion, that discrimination is arbitrary, and that its focus, linked to power relations, varies from place to place, needs to be nurtured. The value of multilingual cities in which spaces are created to challenge monolingual hegemonies, valuing more inclusive cross-cultural sharing and plurilingualism, has been proposed by Lamb (2015).

Bilingual education has as its purpose to challenge the superiority notions associated with English so that children think positively about their cultural heritage; however, it is often perceived that bilingualism poses long-term dangers to the fabric of our nation (Abolish bilingual education, 2007). This explains once again the back and forth movements that characterize language education policy vis-à-vis heritage learners, another illustration of the Hesitation Waltz. Many such bilingual immersion programs are transitional: children are taught in their mother tongue for as long as it takes them to learn English. Maintaining the mother tongue is not the main objective. Indeed, the push in favor of immersion programs for heritage learners created a demand on the part of the English-speaking families for dual immersion, the morning being taught in the target languages and the afternoon in English. Thus this system of schooling is largely used by monolingual Anglophone families.

Despite this situation, post-Katrina immigration may somehow slow the assimilationist, gravedigger trend. After the Katrina hurricane, it was decided to open the borders to Mexican help, and one and a half million Hispanic workers were accepted with a temporary, 18-month green card. After 18 months, when the border closed again, many of these Hispanic workers stayed in the U.S. as illegal immigrants and moved to various different States. This Chicano diaspora was also enlarged at a time when television networks noticed that they could benefit from the number of Spanish speakers by opening TV Channels in the

Spanish language. Thus it became possible for this large minority to maintain their language at home while watching the news and entertainment. There are some indications that the post-Katrina diaspora may have led to the formation of Hispanic neighborhoods in various States, which might enable them to keep their language across generations.

Such immigration waves tend to reinforce the ideological arguments of the proponents of the "English-Only" movement, whose prohibitions may affect State-level legislation until judged unconstitutional, as the United States has no official language in its constitution. As noted by Fishman (2005), such prohibitions are impossible to enforce, but create a climate of hassle and suspicion, divide populations and reinforce negative attitudes across groups.

2.2 No Child Left Behind: A policy detrimental to foreign language education

The No Child Left Behind Act of 2001 (NCLB) established measurable standards to reform education and control student-, teacher-, and school-achievement in core disciplines. Federal funding was dependent upon the assessment of all students at specific grade levels. Under-achieving schools would be closed. Students from these 'failed schools' would then have to migrate to the nearest school or district. Even if a foreign language was listed as a core discipline in NCLB, it was not associated with standardized tests. Therefore, the discipline of foreign languages was neglected in favor of the common core disciplines, which resulted in a decrease in teaching time for foreign languages in schools, with higher impact on minority schools (Harmon Rosenbusch, 2005). A foreign language is required for access to most higher education settings, therefore NCLB created *de facto* a discriminatory situation in which schools in poor neighborhoods had to over-emphasize STEM disciplines to survive, which prevented the students from low income settings from accessing higher education.

Vuksanovich (2009) studied the perceptions of foreign language elementary school (FLES) teachers under the NCLB legislation, at the time of the reauthorization of this Act, giving voice to a traditionally under-researched group of teachers. Interviews were analyzed to identify patterns in the ways in which FLES teachers were influenced by NCLB. Classroom observations were also conducted. The study uncovered two critical issues in the climate of NCLB: (1) FLES teachers faced increased challenges in integrating students from NCLB failed (i.e. closed) schools into their language curriculum; and (2) FLES teachers perceived increased workloads and increased use of school resources, including greater interaction with the school's special education staff, as a result of mainstreaming students with cognitive and behavioral disabilities into their programs under NCLB.

2.3 Hesitation waltz in higher education

Despite post-9/11 (and earlier) efforts to reinforce foreign language education in the U.S., attention to the importance of languages for a better understanding of the world has steadily decreased since the beginning of the 1900s. Nonetheless, there has been some new vitality in universities, as mentioned in the 2007 report of the Modern Language Association: "With a 6.6 per cent increase from 2006 to 2009, foreign language course enrollment at U.S. universities is at an all-time high, continuing a steady rise (47.8 per cent) since 1995. However […] enrollment in graduate language courses has fallen to 1995 levels" (p. 1).

In 2010, the *Chronicle of Higher Education* published an article entitled: "Deficiency in Foreign Language Competency: What Is Wrong with the U.S. Educational System?". The author notes:

> It doesn't take much to realize that the U.S. trails far behind other countries on the second language issue. Moreover, we constantly receive clear signals of the need to more seriously discuss the appropriateness and feasibility of implementing a second-language education policy. At the same time, we hear voices telling us that such an idea is just another unnecessary notion. The rationale used by many who justify this widespread second-language deficiency is that English is today's lingua franca. (Marmolejo, 2010)

However, 2005 data from the British Council suggest that, by 2050, the most widely spoken language in the world will still be Mandarin, followed by Spanish. The number of people speaking English will tie with Arabic as the third largest language group, followed by Hindi/Urdu. These languages are rarely mastered on U.S. soil, apart from by people who themselves immigrated.

"Culture defines not only what its members should think or learn but also what they should ignore or treat as irrelevant" (Armour-Thomas & Gopaul-McNicol, 1998: 56). Here is an example. Wisconsin is a State that has the reputation of being strong in languages and active for their cause. This is attested by the presence of a foreign language consultant in the Department of Public Instruction, an active association of foreign languages teachers and various forms of support for study abroad and international relations. However, only two universities (Madison and Milwaukee) belonging to the State Universities network demand at least two years of foreign language courses as a compulsory requirement. The 118.33-1am law of the Department of Public Instruction in Wisconsin expresses that the state superintendent shall encourage school boards to require an additional 8.5 credits selected from any combination of vocational education, foreign languages, fine arts and other courses. However, no high school *must* require students to enroll in any foreign language courses. While the Wisconsin Association of Foreign Language Teachers (WAFLT) is one of the most active in the U.S., the perception that English mastery is all what counts still prevails. What is the history behind such preconceptions? The following section presents a hypothesis according to which language education policies are linked to ideologies that are represented by dialectal and cultural substrates, which are underlying layers of prior linguistic and cultural influence. Indeed, when a new language and culture are brought to a region through colonization, migration or displacement, it is influenced by the previously dominant language and culture in that particular region, which may impact accent, vocabulary, and syntax, behavior and attitudes arising from their contact.

3 Dialectal and cultural substrates may influence language education policies

Everyday language is 'tinged' with contextual and cultural information. The very act of talking implies social and cultural roles, which are entrenched in thought processes and most often go unnoticed. An interesting demonstration, sketched by Labov (2006) in a lecture, is that language dialectal substrates in the United States cover belief and political differences that impact policies, of which language education policies would be a particular case. The dialectal substrate of specific regions in the U.S. is related to specific belief systems that direct policy reforms.

To study the cracks in the building of social equality policy, dialectal variation provides interesting clues. In terms of both American dialects and policies, the Inland North corresponds to what has been designated as 'Blue States', attesting the diaspora of Yankee culture at the time of the Northern cities' shift due to mass immigration from the East Coast. The term 'Yankee' refers to Northern Americans who fought for the regions on the Union side of the Civil War, and those with New England cultural ties, descendants from colonial English settlers (Schell, 1963). Their speech dialect is referred to as "Yankee dialect" (Hendrickson, 2002: 326). According to Morain (1988: 45), Yankees shared similar convictions that informed their policies: for example, "The righteous are responsible for the welfare of the community. It (is) sometimes necessary to use the legal authority of the state by making immoral activities illegal."

The dialect regions of the United States are described in the Atlas of North American English (Labov, Ash, & Boberg, 2005). Mass migrations seemed congenial to the Puritan tradition: whole parishes, including the parson and all inhabitants sometimes migrated from England to the Inland North in the U.S. Power (1953: 14) mentions 22 colonies in Illinois alone, originating in New England or in New York State, which moved to the Inland North between 1830 and 1840. Such massive exodus indicates there was at the time vast community movements and migrations from New England. The result was that a certain dialectal variation of English, which came from the New England Yankees, was considered the best form of English around, and this landed in the Upper Mid-West as well as part of the North East Coast. Yankee politics differentiates the North and the South in terms of votes against and for slavery and the death penalty, as well as the presidential elections from 1856 (Buchanan) to 1924 (Coolidge) and from 1988 (Ford) to 2004 (Bush). The dialectal variation correlated with the votes of these populations, for example in 2004, when Americans had to vote in favor or against John Kerry as President. Hence the hypothesis advanced in this section that there was a Yankee *cultural* as well as linguistic substrate. There is ample evidence of the pre-existing linguistic substrate of New England in the Northern Midwestern United States; however, this is to my knowledge the first time that an author brings some evidence of the pre-existing influence of a cultural substrate which, spreading from New England to Midwest, was key in the dissemination of Yankee ideologies, from anti-slavery stands to global neoliberalism. The hypothesis is that a form of messianic globalization would be born from that substrate, having started with New England Parish migration in search of the Promised Land.

This migration led to the establishment of Inland Northern in the Great Lakes region as the prestige dialect (Frazer, 1993). "Yankee cultural imperialism" led to specific language education policies that favored the internationalization of English and contributed to a century of corporate expansion and American intervention in the Philippines, Central America, the Caribbean, Vietnam, and the Middle East (Harper, 2011). Linguistic pride was paired with a high attention to language quality in schools. One indication of this influence is the high quality of education and schooling in the Inland North. In Wisconsin, for example, public schools performed better than private schools until the son of a Baptist minister from Colorado, Tea Party extremist was elected as Governor of Wisconsin in 2010.

4 Conclusion: U.S. assimilationism 'sidestreams' world languages

While the U.S. may count between 27 and 32 million multilingual people having a non-English mother tongue, the loss of the mother tongue dominates the scene, as assimilationism is part of the mindset of 'becoming an American'. After two or three generations, the children of immigration inevitably become monolingual English speakers. Proficiency in the heritage language is usually wiped out across generations. However, as noted by Fishman, cultural memories as well as deep resentment for past and present discrimination against their language and culture as well as the sense of being marginalized do not disappear.

The Hesitation Waltz of language education policies has come to an apparent end, as it is moving backwards and in slow motion. While foreign language education is a top priority for many professions, it is neglected in U.S. education on the whole. Experienced language educators know that you cannot understand a language without having a good grasp of its culture because of cross-cultural pragmatics (Wierzbicka, 1999). Thus any short-term solution will be a bad fit. Decision-makers may know about this but may not want to invest money in the long term. They need some serious convincing about it.

While some States promote 21st century capabilities to prepare students to become global citizens and be able to converse with people around the planet (North Carolina State Board of Education, 2013), the downturn in the economy coupled with the negative impacts of the NCLB legislation led many early language programs to close in Elementary schools around the U.S. Most language educators recognize that the current focus should be to bring to the fore a thorough approach to languages and cultures from elementary fourth grade (age 9). Learning a second language early will help people learn a third language later. Regarding the neglect of less commonly taught languages, there are different issues at stake. The first issue is creating a new culture that values language pedagogy in Literature Departments and increasing collaboration across schools (MLA, 2007). It is only by gathering interest in including the many 'smaller' language areas in education, and enabling them to expand their niche, audience, and outreach, that a new and broader approach can be proposed in language teacher education. Another issue is to initiate policies for learner autonomy (Lamb, 2008; Tochon, 2015).

In the pendulum swing, we are currently remote from the idea of a society that would invest in reason, knowledge, and wisdom.

> It is as scandalous and injurious to waste "native" language resources as to waste our air, water, mineral, animal, and non-linguistic human resources. *How long must languages and cultures be trivialized when they are learned at home, in infancy and childhood, and respected only when they are acquired during adulthood, where they are usually learned less well and at much greater cost in time and money?* (Fishman, 2005: 124)

The analyses and the brief overview presented in this chapter suggest that the goals of the American Empire have interfered with the goals of building language and cultural competencies for its population. As Phillipson (2008) emphasizes in reference to Hardt and Negri's work on how deterritorialized networks contribute to power: "The communications industries integrate the imaginary and the symbolic within the biopolitical fabric, not merely putting them at the service of power but actually integrating them into its very functioning" (Hardt & Negri, 2001: 33).

The English language, having become a commodity producing neoliberal elitist subjectivities, gave to partners of outer circles the instruments through which they could place the empire on its knees. The lack of depth of foreign language education in the United States, not to speak of the neglect for indigenous and minority languages, has created a language deficit in this country such that now it can barely compete on the world markets, in which multilingualism is the rule. In addition, the invasive policies of Americanization of foreigners have created a situation in which English monolinguals are at a disadvantage on the international scene, because they do not have the intercultural perception and subtlety that allows them to sense foreign cultures. Thus, in addition to the language deficit, a vast cross-cultural communication deficit characterizes the American scene, which is paradoxical since this was initially a nation of immigrants from all over the world, but one whose languages and cultures have been proscribed, ostracized, regimented, restricted, and devalued in favor of English.

Deliberate ignorance of other cultures has isolated the U.S. and its status seems to be changing worldwide. Inappropriate foreign policies may create a boomerang effect. The United States seems to be losing their voice in the community of nations. At a time when we face rapid world changes and such a radicalization of discourse that diplomacy seems part of history, foreign language education can bring a new mindset.

References

Abolish Bilingual Education (2007, March 31). CNN on the Web. Retrieved February 10, 2014 from http://www.firehouse.com/forums/t89396/.

ACTFL (1996). *Standards for foreign language learning: Preparing for the 21st century*. Lawrence: Allen.

Armour-Thomas, E., & Gopaul-McNicol, S. A. (1998). *Assessing intelligence: Applying a bio-cultural model. Racial and ethnic minority psychology* (Vol. 1). Thousand Oaks: Sage.

Ben-Rafael, M. (2004). Language contact and attrition. In M. S. Schmid, B. Köpke, M. Keijzer & L. Weilemar (Eds.), *First language attrition: Interdisciplinary perspectives on methodological issues* (pp. 165–188). Philadelphia: Benjamins.

Branaman, L., & Rhodes N. (1999). *A national survey of foreign language instruction in elementary and secondary schools*. Washington, DC: National Resource Center. Retrieved February 2, 2014 from http://webdev.cal.org/development/topics/fl/flsurvey97execsummary.pdf.

Council of Europe (2001). *Common European framework of reference for languages: Learning, teaching, assessment*. Cambridge: Cambridge University Press.

Crawford, J. (1995). *Bilingual education: History, politics, theory and practice* (3rd Ed.). Los Angeles: Bilingual Education Services.

Crawford, J. (2000). Language politics in the U.S.A.: The paradox of bilingual education. In C. Ovando & P. McLaren (Eds.), *The politics of multiculturalism and bilingual education: Students and teachers caught in the cross-fire*. New York: McGraw-Hill.

Davidson, R. (1996, December). Jackson supports Oakland Ebonics: In reviser, he says School Board Action was misunderstood. Pittsburgh Post – Gazette. December 3. Retrieved January 10, 2014 from http://news.google.com/newspapers?id=2OQxAAAAIBAJ&sjid=mW8DAAAAIBAJ&pg=6455,8926366.

De Avila, M. C. (2012). *Zacatecanos and Spanish in Chicago* (Unpublished dissertation). Madison: University of Wisconsin-Madison.

Del Valle, J. (2003). *Language rights and the law in the United States*. Clevedon: Multilingual Matters.

Fishman, J. (2005). Multilingualism and non-English mother tongues. In E. Finegan & J. R. Rickford (Eds.), *Language in the USA. Themes for the twenty-first century* (pp. 115–132). New York: Cambridge University Press.

Frazer, T. (1993). *Heartland English*. Tuscaloosa: University of Alabama Press.

García, O. (2009). *Bilingual education in the 21st century: A global perspective*. Malden: Wiley-Blackwell.

Hardt, M., & Negri, A. (2001). *Empire*. Cambridge: Harvard University Press.

Harmon Rosenbusch, M. (2005). The No Child Left Behind Act and teaching and learning languages in U.S. schools. *Modern Language Journal*, *89*(2), 250–261.

Harper, S. M. (2011). Counting the costs of a global Anglophonic hegemony: Examining the impact of U.S. language education policy on linguistic minorities worldwide. *Indiana Journal of Global Legal Studies*, *18*(1), 515–538.

Harrison, K. M. (2013). U.S. Native Americans. In F. V. Tochon (Ed.), *Language education policy studies* (online). Madison: University of Wisconsin—Madison. Retrieved February 2, 2014 from http://www.languageeducationpolicy.org.

Hendrickson, R. (2002). *Yankee talk: A dictionary of New England expressions.* New York: Booksales.

Hines, R. (2011). *An overview of title VI.* In P. O'Meara, H. D. Mehlinger & R. M. Newman (Eds.), *Changing perspectives on international education* (pp. 6–10). Bloomington: Indiana University Press.

Inman, B. R. (2003). Coping with a turbulent world: The critical role of education. Conference on global challenges and U.S. higher education. Duke University, January 23-25, 2003. Retrieved February 11, 2014 from http://ducis.jhfc.duke.edu/archives/globalchallenges/pdf/inman.pdf

Labov, W. (2006). Yankee Cultural Imperialism and the Northern Cities Shift. Presentation made at Yale University, October 20, 2008.

Labov, W., Ash, S., & Boberg, C. (2005). *Atlas of North American English: Phonetics, phonology and sound change.* New York: Mouton de Gruyter.

Lamb, T. E. (2008). Learner autonomy in eight European countries: Opportunities and tensions in education reform and language teaching policy. In M. Jiménez Raya & T. E. Lamb (Eds.), *Pedagogy for autonomy in modern languages education: Theory, practice, and teacher education* (pp. 36–57). Dublin: Authentik.

Lamb, T. E. (2015). Towards a plurilingual habitus: Engendering interlinguality in urban spaces. *International Journal of Pedagogies and Learning, 10*(2), 151–165.

Lee, R. H., & Marshall, D. F. (2001). "Shooting themselves in the foot": Consequences of English only supporters "going to law". In R. Duenas Gonzalez & I. Melis (Eds.), *Language ideologies. Critical perspectives of the official English movement. Vol. 2. History, theory, and policy* (pp. 171–190). Mahwah: Lawrence Erlbaum.

Linguistic Society of America (1997). Resolution on the Oakland Ebonics debate. Retrieved February 6, 2014 from http://www-personal.umich.edu/~jlawler/ebonics.lsa.html.

Marmolejo, F. (2010). Deficiency in foreign language competency: What is wrong with the U.S. educational system? *The Chronicle of Higher Education*, November 9th, 2010. Retrieved February 4, 2014 from http://chronicle.com/blogs/worldwise/deficiency-in-foreign-language-competency-what-is-wrong-with-the-u-s-educational-system/27558.

McCarthy, C. (2013). *Language planning and policy in native America: History, theory, praxis.* Tonawanda: Multilingual Matters.

McCarty, T. L. (2008). American Indian, Alaska Native, and Native Hawaiian education in the era of standardization and NCLB- An introduction. *Journal of American Indian Education, 47*(1), 1–8.

Milroy, L. (2002). Social networks. In J. K. Chambers, P. Trudgill & N. Schiling-Estes (Eds.), *The handbook of language variation and change* (pp. 549–572). Malden: Blackwell.

MLA, Modern Language Association (2007). *Foreign languages and higher education: New structures for a changed world.* Retrieved February 2, 2014 from http://www.mla.org/flreport.

Morain, T. J. (1988). *Prairie grass roots: An Iowa small town in the early twentieth century.* Ames: Iowa State University Press.

Morgan, M. (1999). US language planning and policies for social dialect speakers. In K. A. Davis & T. Huebner (Eds.), *Sociopolitical perspectives on language policy and planning in the USA* (pp. 243–266). Philadelphia: John Benjamins.

North Carolina State Board of Education (2013). *Preparing students for the world: Final report of the state board of education's task force on global education.* Retrieved February 9, 2014 from http://www.ncpublicschools.org/docs/globaled/final-report.pdf.

Osborn, T. A. (2007). *Teaching world languages for social justice. A sourcebook of principles and practices.* Mahwah: Lawrence Erlbaum.

Phillipson, R. (2008). The linguistic imperialism of neoliberal empire. *Critical Inquiry in Language Studies, 5*(1), 1–43.

Power, R. L. (1953). *Planting Corn Belt culture: The impress of the upland southerner and Yankee in the old northwest.* Bloomington: Indiana Historical Society.

Pufahl, I., Rhodes, N. C., & Christian D. (2001). *Foreign language teaching: What the United States can learn from other countries.* ERIC Clearinghouse on languages and linguistics. Washington DC: National Resource Center. September 2001. Retrieved February 6, 2014 from http://webdev.cal.org/development/resources/digest/digest_pdfs/0106-pufahl.pdf.

Reagan, T. (2005). *Critical questions, critical perspectives: Languages and the second language educator.* Greenwich: Information Age, Contemporary Language Studies in Education.

Rhodes, N. C., & Pufahl, I. (2010). *Foreign language teaching in U.S. schools.* Washington DC: National Resource Center. Retrieved February 6, 2014 from http://webdev.cal.org/development/projects/executive-summary-08-09-10.pdf.

Rothkopf, D. (1997). In praise of cultural imperialism? Effects of globalization on culture. *Foreign Policy, 107*, Summer. Retrieved February 9, 2014 from http://www.globalpolicy.org/globaliz/cultural/globcult.htm.

Schell, R. (1963). Swamp Yankee. *American Speech, 38*(2), 121–123.

Tochon, F. V. (2009). The key to global understanding: World languages education – Why schools need to adapt. *Review of Educational Research, 79*(2), 650–682.

Tochon, F. V. (2015). *Language education policies unlimited: Global perspectives and local practices.* Blue Mounds: Deep University Press.

Tochon, F. V., & Harrison, K. M. (2017). *Policy for peace: Language education unlimited.* Blue Mounds: Deep University Press.

U.S. Census Bureau (2012). Hispanic Americans by the numbers. Retrieved February 6, 2014 from http://www.infoplease.com/spot/hhmcensus1.html.

Vuksanovich, M. L. (2009). *The FLES teacher's voice: A case study examining the impact of the No Child Left Behind Act on elementary school foreign language teachers* (Unpublished doctoral dissertation). Iowa City: University of Iowa.

Wierzbicka, A. (1999). *Emotions across languages and cultures.* Cambridge: Cambridge University Press.

Wiley, T. G. (2002). Accessing language rights in education: A brief history of the U.S. context. In J. W. Tollefson (Ed.), *Language policies in education* (pp. 39–64). Mahwah: Lawrence Erlbaum.

Wiley, T. G. (2004). Language planning, language policy, and the English-Only movement. In E. Finegan & J. R. Rickford (Eds.), *Language in the USA. Themes for the twenty-first century.* New York: Cambridge University Press.

Wolfram, W. (1998). Language ideology and dialect: Understanding the Ebonics controversy. *Journal of English Linguistics, 26*(2), 108–121.

Zentella, A. C. (2002). Latin@ languages and identities. In M. M. Suárez-Orozco & M. M. Páez (Eds.), *Latinos remaking America* (pp. 321–337). Berkeley and Los Angeles: University of California Press.

Kristine M. Harrison

Toward empathetic multilingual language education policy (LEP) in the U.S. and the world: An indigenous view of linguistic autonomy through the Native American Languages Act

There is not an Indian pupil...who is permitted to study any other language than our own

(Commissioner of Indian Affairs John D.C. Atkins, 1887, quoted in McCarty, 2013: 54)

Abstract: This chapter presents an interpretive policy analysis of the NALA (Native American Languages Act) of the United States, a law promoted to revitalise endangered languages. This Act included precepts about language which will be analysed as regards their implications in school for global English Language teaching. Even before English as a Global Lingua Franca gained ground worldwide, 'English-only' was the language education policy for Native Americans and immigrants in the United States. For Native Americans, this meant forced education in boarding schools and language shift to English. For immigrants, it implied a process of first language attrition. The result of the English-only policy in the United States has been an institutionally monolingual society, and it has had strong implications for identity formation: continued assimilation is disguised as integration for those students already displaced from home cultures and languages. The chapter concludes by describing the MEMES (Making Empathetic Multilingual Environments in School) project, a nascent initiative promoting teacher support, training and policy change for multilingual education.

Keywords: Native Americans, Native American Languages Act, English-only language policy, English language teaching

1 Introduction

Displacements and migrations were the norm in the rapidly changing world of the 20th century and have increased in the 21st (UNHCR, 2018), creating super-diverse societies, albeit with borders and institutions that govern people's lives. The term 'super-diversity' refers to the last two decades' "dynamic interplay of variables among [...] small and scattered, multiple-origin, transnationally connected, socio-economically differentiated" displaced peoples (Vertovec, 2007: 1024). Some of these people are (im)migrants, others undocumented, or their children and grandchildren, who straddle cultures and languages. Among the many challenging variables of super-diversity and its institutional governance, language education is central. Except for perhaps a few grandparents, most displaced persons must go to school or work and join a new society using a new language, i.e. they have to 'integrate', and language is a key factor.

Societal linguistic landscapes and norms can reveal a spectrum between dynamic multilingualism or an official monolingualism. The former allows for cultural and linguistic rights, and contributes to intercultural harmony and a respectful exchange of goods and services. In a few places, this is still the norm; multiple languages are present even at a family level, often with a lingua franca, and used fluidly in domains such as work or family. Of course language shifts have always been common, through migrations, political upheavals, or conflicts. However, in today's world of displacements, these often become heritage languages that slowly die off across generations when language shift occurs, due to forces such as language education policy (LEP). By the third generation, displaced students often shift to monolingualism in an official language. National language policies, global education initiatives, and school accountability measures like tests construct institutional linguistic norms that enforce the official language as *de-facto* language education policy (Menken, 2017). I start the chapter with two premises. First, schools should not be the main predator of linguistic diversity, since language education policy (LEP) contributes to a Darwinian evolution of languages in linguistic jungles where only the strong survive (Tochon, this volume). The second premise is empathy and the possibilities of a moral education that may bring sensitivity and harmony between peoples, seeing ourselves in relation to those around us, especially those who are displaced. Empathy, sentiments, passions, and new social skills, which are fundamental to social harmony (Tochon, 2018), may emerge through a commitment to those near us. Teacher practices can support this emotional education by encouraging plurilingual classroom practices (Celic & Seltzer, 2012/3; Harrison, 2018a) that may extend into communities (Harrison & Tochon, in press; Harrison, 2018c).

Worldwide, multilingualism in the institutional realm – school, university, or government – often includes bilingualism – second language acquisition with English or another colonial or national language. The situation in the United States, however, has tended to be monolingual at the institutional level. Over the course of the 16th to 19th centuries, and without downplaying the brutal treatment towards the Native American or Indigenous peoples, many languages co-existed in North America, but immigrants from numerous language groups arrived and by the end of the 19th century built schools where English was part of the educational practice, without room for the Native American or immigrant languages. Progressive ideology in education required schools to solve social issues and develop the child according to notions of citizenship, certain social practices, or religion (Popkewitz, 2008). Some immigrants had bilingual schools for their own heritage languages for a time, such as the Germans and Norwegians in Wisconsin, maintaining the languages there or at home into the 20th century. Some even debated allowing children to go to school at all for fear of losing their culture, language, and religious beliefs, such as the Norwegians in Wisconsin (Nelson, n/d). Yet progressive education practices for Native American children meant forced displacement from their families into boarding schools, eventually joining the immigrant children in English-only public schools and an English-speaking society. In sum, although LEP in the U.S. from the 1700s to today has been a waltz with back and forth movements for and against multilingual education (Tochon, this volume), the U.S. system remains monolingual. Despite recent policy recommendations tied largely to global demands, national security, and economic competition, today U.S. students are actually at a disadvantage as monolinguals, and not on a par with the world in terms of multilingualism or cultural sensitivity. The next section explains indigenous conceptual parameters in approach to language education. The rest of the chapter describes what happened to the indigenous languages of the U.S. through the legacy of instruction during the boarding school years, a result of U.S. progressive education principles. Then it analyzes the role of English and education as it spread in the U.S. and the world through global educational initiatives like Education for All by UNESCO. Then I turn to the Native American Languages Act of 1990, which serves as an alternative view of education and language that, by advocating linguistic autonomy, would support multilingual and empathetic relations between peoples at local and global levels. Finally, I discuss the implications of applying these parameters to all students, especially the displaced students/indigenous children as well as immigrants and refugees.

2 Method and conceptual frame

Policy plays a key role in current experiences and realities as "part of the unique legal and political status of Native peoples in the United States" (McCarty, 2013: 2). Thus the chapter's theoretical argument stems from an interpretive policy analysis (Schwartz-Shea & Yanow, 2012; Yanow, 2000), which has been used by Cherubini (2010) and Warhol (2011) for similar studies of policies in

Canada and the U.S. respectively, and which has been extended to be used for LEPs (Harrison & Tochon, 2015) and for questions related to Indigenous identity (Harrison, 2016). I analyze the principles in the Native American Languages Act of 1990, and discuss Education for All by UNESCO from the perspective of indigenous notions of education and language.

Languages shift and evolve, and many have disappeared in the past 150 years at an accelerated rate (Sallabank, 2010) or are endangered (UNESCO, 2019). Languages represent worldviews and contain various types of knowledge and practices: place-based, cultural, historical, medicinal, and folkloric (Maffi, 2001). Multilingual education (MLE) research shows the positive achievements tied to language learning in terms of academic, social, and identity realms (Cummins, 2009; Harrison, 2018b; Hornberger, 2009; Skutnabb-Kangas et al., 2009; Trudell, 2014); it also describes mother tongue education (MTE) as a right, even a linguistic human right (Skutnabb-Kangas, 2012a, 2012b). This perspective is more meaningful when the *nature or conceptual view* of language and education is explicated. In this chapter, I use the indigenous approach.

Smith (1999) defines 'Indigenous peoples' as an umbrella term that, although a collective term for peoples worldwide, gives many different groups of people voice, united in an experience as peoples who have had their land and culture colonized, and who struggle for self-determination even after the colonizers may have left. The Indigenous worldview is a cosmology, a unified ecology between humans and all things in the universe with a relational view of parts to whole (Cajete, 1994; Chilisa, 2012). The Indigenous approach is a 'flow of life', part of a divinized conception of nature that is unfolding rather than fixed by laws (Cajete, 1994). People are parts of communities in living and sacred cosmos, together constituting balanced familiar relations. The single whole does not allow separation of the many parts or binary organization (i.e. dead vs. living, earth vs. people).

To answer the question "what are the rules that govern our human perceptions?" (Wynter, 1992: 12), it is important to consider how worldview relates to categories of thought and representation. At the time Indigenous peoples met the colonizers, western thought had become a binary organization of sign and signifier, or separation between the subject and the object. However, a previous (past) 'categorization' of western categories would have divined a visible mark (such as cave drawings) for its invisible force, and the task of the viewer would have been to figure out its message. This mode of thought was still available in the West before the 17th century, which is Foucault's second episteme (Foucault, 1970). In this episteme, the object had the animus; and the humans tuned into the pre-existing message to draw out the meaning. Even in this formative period of the 'West', language was implicated: all things had a soul, and different levels existed in the hierarchy of ontology. This formation includes changes in representative categories:

> ... he appears in his existence immediately interwoven with others; lastly he has a language, he can constitute a whole symbolic universe for himself, within which he has a relation to his past, to things, to other men, and on the basis of which he is able equally to build something like a body of knowledge (in particular, that knowledge of himself, of which the human sciences outline one of the possible forms). (p. 351)

The first statement is similar to the indigenous view of interrelations, but the 'universe' through language and western science became a focus on the written word and the material science. Oral knowledge and memory were devalued. The Indigenous way of knowing is similar to Foucault's second episteme.

Knowledge and education are intertwined. Haig-Brown (2008) defines Indigenous knowledge as what arises from "innumerable generations of people living in relation to a specific land and seeing it as the source of all their relations. And by land, I reach beyond any simple material notion to the spiritual, intellectual and emotional dimensions thereof" (p. 12). Knowledge includes histories, reclassified as 'oral tradition' by western thought (Smith, 1999). 'Knowing' and 'being' are not dependent on material criteria, but intricately related to language and place. Education is part of all aspects of life, holistic and well developed; knowledge and history and a vision of the world were passed through the generations orally, depending on memory (Warrior, 2005). The link between the spoken word and oral tradition is integral (McCarty, 2013). Educational reproduction is via narrative, song, oral traditions, and petroglyphs. Indigenous education is inseparable from life and the language, and is included in the Indigenous historical narratives that existed for millennia before Europeans came (Miller, 2008).

The western view of Indigenous knowledge dismisses it as primitive (Smith, 1999). What is learned in school counts as education usually without questioning the meaning of 'education' which, since the European enlightenment, has steadily evolved to be almost synonymous with the word 'schooling' (Illich, 1971). Indigenous—non-western—forms of knowing have been excluded from school education. In fact, there could be no more fundamental cultural conflict than when 17th-century Europeans began to confront Native Americans (R. M. Adams, 1995: 5):

> For tribal elders who had witnessed the catastrophic developments of the nineteenth century-- the bloody warfare, the near-extinction of the bison, the scourge of disease and starvation, the shrinking of the tribal land base, the indignities of reservation life, the invasion of missionaries and white settlers--there seemed to be no end to the cruelties perpetrated by whites. And after all this, the schools ...They were coming for the children. (D. W. Adams, 1995: 336-337)

Native Americans are the Indigenous peoples[1] of North America, so the description of the Indigenous approach in this section applies. While many tribes exist belonging to distinct culture groups and linguistic families, all the languages in the U.S. are endangered and spoken by very few. The next section discusses the late 19th-early 20th century boarding schooling experience that lasted until the 1970s in some places and how LEP expressly sought to rewrite Native American histories, their world view or way of 'knowing', 'being', and 'doing' by erasing their heritage and languages and forcing language shift to English, enacting a de-evolution of traditional knowledge through schools.

3 Native American children's experience of knowledge devolution in U.S. schools

The de-evolution of what was common Indigenous knowledge for the Native Americans of the U.S.—knowledge that had evolved over centuries or millennia in relation to the land—began with the loss of ancestral lands for some groups. Many groups were forcibly relocated or their resources taken or destroyed, and had to create new ties to the land. Progressive education principles also provided a new tool to conquer the native peoples and their histories. Native American children were forced into boarding schools and taught their own inferiority, learning to distrust their own heritage, knowledge base and language—considered inferior by the Europeans. 'Devolution' also included eliminating the spiritual or unseen realm from what was considered possible to know or even exist as described in the previous section. Thus, a student's - the youngest generation's - traditional learning of the oral histories, ways of life, and culture was eroded. The goal was the complete and rapid transformation of Native Americans to 'civilised' beings by breaking all tribal relations and losing all their Indigenous ways.

Henry Richard Pratt was "the great apostle of eradicating from students every available trace of native identity and replacing it with a facsimile of whiteness" (Warrior, 2005: 112). His educational ideologies were the turning point in the U.S. war against Native Americans, bringing the war to the classroom or school. In the 1870s, he took a group of prisoners east, surprised when they learned English, the basics of western education, and eventually went to a vocational college. From this experience he concluded that removing them from their natural and cultural environment, they would learn the ways of white people. Boarding schools began, but academic learning was in fact minimal. Much of the day was

1 I use 'indigenous' and Native American interchangeably, except when describing the concepts.

hard work to keep the school running—cooking, gardening, washing clothes, sewing, tending animals, cleaning. Children often did not see their families for years, and were beaten and punished, even for speaking their own language. One year in this environment was considered more effective than ten years among their people; i.e. "kill the Indian and save the man" (ibid.). Pratt argued for a cultural, not racial environment and opposed keeping them on reservations with paternalistic governance and allotments of food (Warrior, 2005). By attending boarding schools, "…Indian youth, stripped bare of their tribal heritage, (could) take to heart the inspiring lessons of white civilization" (D. W. Adams, 1995: 52–53).

A first step in these assimilation efforts focused on erasing the languages. The schools were English only and native languages were prohibited. Pratt's famous educational philosophy was to create a linguistic distance from students' home communities (Warrior, 2005). The dominant curricular ideology was that of manual training, equally deemed fit for African Americans, Puerto Ricans, and other colonized groups. Often textbooks taught things like shoe repair, filling the tank, being a good waitress, or being a good citizen (McCarty, 2013).

The previous section showed how Native Americans inherit wisdom from the experience of those who have gone before, and this section has shown how the boarding schools enacted a journey of devolution: from traditional tribal forms of education that included spiritual realms, many interconnections, relationship to the land; to western and monolingual English education, disrupting intergenerational knowledge transmission, robbing many of their languages and even identity. The oral tradition had been "irrevocably altered by the European intrusion - principally by the practice of taking kids from the tellers who had in all past generations told the children an entire culture, an entire identity of a people" (Warrior, 2005: 130). In sum, the role of schools was to change their identity through language and knowledge, teaching them who and what they were and should be; in other words, they experienced educational imperialism (Harrison, 2016) and many became monolingual English speakers.

4 English as a lingua franca worldwide, Education for All, and the lack of multilingual education

> *But I do not see why we should not try to spread our common language even more widely throughout the globe … an international language capable of a very wide transaction of practical business and interchange of ideas. (Winston Churchill, 1943)*

The enactment of English as the only language for immigrants in the U.S. is beyond the scope of this chapter, but unfortunately for Native Americans, many became monolingual in what would become a global force. English became not only the dominant language of the U.S., but also a powerful world language. By the time most Native Americans were speaking English and many Native children had become English monolinguals, the *world* English (and education) project had begun. Many young Native American men had fought in both world wars (even though they were not even U.S. citizens until 1924) and, after WWI, education and the English language began to be spread 'beneficently', with projects at the government, corporate, and business level to promote policies, textbooks, and tests, creating an ideology around English. The same happened with education projects: schools and education principles were built and spread beneficently by disparate groups such as NGOs until 1990 when Education for All (by UNESCO) was born, consolidating and governing a global education initiative. Education became part of a country's development and investment in human capital. By ten years later, sustainable development goals (SDGs) and a plan were set for 2015 but despite progress, largely deemed failures. Perhaps aided by the radical increase in displacements and migrations in the 21st century, the education initiative was transformed into the Education 2030: Incheon Declaration—the framework for action took on a focus on the implementation of Sustainable Development Goal 4 "towards inclusive and equitable quality education and lifelong learning for all" (UNESCO, 2016). In addition, since 2016, Global Education Monitoring Reports are published annually.

However, this approach is unrealistic on a global scale in terms of thousands of cultures and languages (Baker & Wiseman, 2007; Harrison, 2009; Mundy, 2007). The shift to a common school language and especially the spread of English has been devastating in terms of the world's linguistic diversity. Many languages, often with rich oral histories and knowledge, are endangered (Skutnabb-Kangas, Maffi, & Harmon, 2006; UNESCO, 2019) by schools and/or English, a language that Churchill described in the following way: "The whole of it is comprised in about 650 nouns and 200 verbs or other parts of speech – no more indeed than can be written on one side of a single sheet of paper" (Churchill, 1943). The history of the spread of English shows its ties to the corporate and political interests of Great Britain and the United States. English (like education) has become a global business, the language of neoliberalism or market imperialism (Phillipson, 2008, 2019). English is used for business and diplomacy despite diminishing and even erasing cultural and linguistic human rights. Phillipson (2008: 47) describes the hegemonic position of English with this definition: "Linguistic imperialism is the process by which the dominance of English is asserted and maintained by the establishment and continuous reconstitution of structural and cultural inequalities between English and other languages." Furthermore, economic globalization seemingly ties languages to the global political economy creating a hierarchy of 'useful' languages such as English, Spanish or Chinese. The hierarchy positions English hegemonically as a global communication metanarrative that policymakers treat as a 'lingua nullius', or a language that belongs to no one, claiming English is therefore culturally neutral (Phillipson, 2014). Yet English also dominates academia, air control, and many international organizations.

While linguistic human rights include the right to mother tongue instruction (Skutnab-Kangas, 2012b), hegemonic and linguistically dominant ideologies are embedded in LEPs, including standards for teaching practice and assessments, proficiency and competence requirements. Schools (more specifically LEPs) often ignore MLE and MTE, despite research showing that they are positive and possible (see Skutnabb-Kangas, Phillipson, Mohanty, & Panda, 2009). Global English language learning is tied to schooling and LEPs. Phillipson's theory of linguistic imperialism entails structures, exploitation, ideologies, hegemony, and unequal rights, all related to language, in addition to subtractive language learning and *linguicism* (Phillipson, 1992, 2008; Phillipson & Skutnabb-Kangas, 2013). Despite the fact that most of the world does not speak English, English is called a 'basic skill' and linked to educational rankings. In countries where it is not the mother tongue or an official language, it is becoming the medium of instruction at an ever-younger age rather than it simply being taught as a school subject (Phillipson, 2012), and it is increasingly being used in higher education, including in much of academia. It also continues to be taught as a foreign language, not only in schools, especially private ones, but in language centers and online. Unsurprisingly, since the 1990 advent of global education standards, the field of English Language Teaching (ELT) has grown with many educational reforms pushing English. The ELT industry is a business endeavor that targets students of many first languages, some of whom will become non-native English teachers, though facing discrimination in hiring practices as well (Phillipson, 2019). From pre-schools to language schools to universities, it is a veritable industry from teacher education to textbooks. The inequality between first languages, dominant school languages and English is a real phenomenon, written into national language policies and LEPs, with many consequences, even to the level of identity. However, as I will describe next, in 1990 the Native Americans of the U.S. won a major victory in the area of first languages.

5 Native American Languages Act and implications for English

> *There is convincing evidence that student achievement and performance, community and school pride, and educational opportunity is clearly and directly tied to respect for, and support of, the first language of the child or student. (Native American Languages Act, 1990, Section 102, Article 6)*

The usual discourses of language for multilingual students invoke 1) the alleged interference of a first language (which is not the language of instruction in school) with academic progress, as well as 2) the alleged need to start English at a young age. Both points position students in terms of having a language deficit rather than having a beneficial ability. This language deficit view (MacSwan, 2000) contrasts with the additive view I presented earlier. After over a century of early U.S. settlers' land conquests and wars, and the subsequent treaties to establish reservations, the U.S. government policy shifted to education, profoundly disrupting the "concrete and ideological connections between language, people and place that Europeans systematically sought to destroy and replace with English and Christian values" (McCarty, 2013: 47). About one hundred years after the boarding schools began and after many decades of activism, the NALA was passed in 1990 by a Republican Congress, "overturning more than two centuries of federal Indian policy" (Warhol, 2011: 279). This section turns to the NALA, perhaps enacted too late. It begins by considering the significance of a few of its bold statements.

Significantly, the NALA addresses past wrongs that have "often resulted in acts of suppression and extermination of Native American languages and cultures" (Sec. 102, Article 5). This is a clear reference to the boarding school period where schools forced linguistic assimilation to English. It goes further and recognizes that Indigenous languages exist in the present, by stating that "... there is a widespread practice of treating Native American languages as if they were anachronisms" (Sec. 102, article 4), when, in fact, many of the people and a few of the languages are still living. Next, the NALA states that "there is convincing evidence that student achievement and performance, community and school pride, and educational opportunity is clearly and directly tied to respect for, and support of, the first language of the child or student" (Section 102, Article 6). This statement addresses the importance of the individual, the community and the group while maintaining the intrinsic worth of a language. The principles of mother tongue and multilingual education are common sense from a perspective of cultural and linguistic rights. In addition, it states the 'clear and direct' relation to school achievement. If a child knows his or her first language well, he or she acquires the school language more easily.

In sum, the Act's express purpose is to "preserve, protect, and promote the rights and freedom of Native Americans to use, practice, and develop Native American languages" (Section 104, article 1), giving "special status [...] (that) recognizes distinct cultural and political rights, including the right to continue separate identities" (Sec. 102, Article 2). The main points of the NALA are summed up here:

- Language (i.e. first language, mother tongue) is a right
- Languages have intrinsic value
- Languages and cultures are connected and political rights have an effect
- Languages and cultures lead to higher school achievement
- Heritage languages are not anachronisms
- Languages should be used, developed, and preserved
- Community and individual identity and pride are strengthened and supported by the first language

The complete evolution of policy is beyond my scope here, but these bold goals and statements taken from the NALA had finally emerged after a century of policies that aimed at removing livelihoods and eradicating the language, culture, and sovereignty of Native Americans. At least two or three generations of children had gone through the boarding schools and had become mostly monolingual English speakers.

By 2002, the NALA had "sponsored some of the boldest efforts in language revitalization to date" (McCarty, 2002: 296). Between 1990 and 2014 the number of language immersion schools with Indigenous languages as medium of instruction grew from three to thirty-one (National Alliance, 2019). In 2006, after frustrations over funding and No Child Left Behind requirements, the Esther Martinez Native American Languages Preservation Act was passed. This act is a law and therefore much more specific than the NALA with specific provisions to ensure language survival and continuing vitality by establishing language nests and site-based educational programs where the dominant medium of instruction would be the Native language, specifying hours and authorizing funds for such purposes. Lessons had to be learned about how and where to revitalize languages and the role of communities in this process, given the intergenerational differences in language experiences resulting from the destructive boarding school period. The NALA enabled ideological shifts and motivation that initially were used to develop Indigenous language immersion programs such as summer camps, and other activism (Warhol, 2012). Despite the challenges from standardized testing and lack of funding, an energized and invigorated community awakened in many tribal governments regarding the urgent need to take action (Beaulieu, 2008). According to Harper and Rawlin (2016), the current federal policy has provisions for assessments in other languages, but a single set of standards based on English for teaching and assessment. This does not work because there are not enough speakers left to teach the languages, train new teachers, and develop curricular materials as well as assessments (ibid.). Furthermore, funding has been threatened.

However, McCarty (2012) describes the history of Native American languages and policies with a 'safety zone theory'. This theory posits the perceived threat of the culture and languages as what guides the policies that now support the preservation and revitalization of languages. This means that when Native American people and cultures were a threat to U.S. unity and cultural and material dominance of their lands, the languages were forbidden through schools. Once the languages were almost completely erased, policy could promote languages as integral (ibid.). This amounts to languages being purposefully eliminated and optionally revitalized, despite the bold rhetoric of the NALA. Thus, many cultural and language groups are faced with the challenging task of learning and rediscovering languages that involves corpus, acquisition, and prestige planning in a context of many other compelling issues and problems they face such as poverty, health issues, discrimination, and environmental racism.

Nevertheless, a paradigm shift had occurred, from school laws compelling the adoption of English to recognition of past errors and support for first languages. In sum, the NALA represents a radical change in policy that even immigrants have never enjoyed in the U.S. and reflects the main principles of multilingual education. Such efforts, however, faced another set of challenges - that of standardized testing and the prospect of how to reverse not only language but identity assimilation and shifts.

6 Discussion: Implications for NALA principles in terms of linguistic genocide and identity

Cultural identities may be stereotyped and essentialized into a static past representation of what it means to be Ojibwe, Navajo, Mexican, and so on, especially in cases where the groups of people have faced assimilation or displacement. Native Americans faced this displacement in their own land. There was widespread language shift and a diminished number of mother tongue speakers, but some of the languages have remained. In the case where the original language may have disappeared, it could still be an integral part of the cultural identity

- one does not have to know the language to identify with it (Skutnabb-Kangas, 2000). Therefore, the NALA early on highlights the fault in the ideology that treats Native American languages as if they only existed in the past, by pointing out that living speakers are still present. The same is the case for heritage language speakers—those who are beyond the second or third generation and no longer speak the language as a first language. This section turns to the implications of multilingual education for heritage and other multilingual students who want to maintain or revitalize their language in a context of educational standardization and language shift, especially in the context of massive worldwide displacements occurring on a larger scale than ever before (UNHCR, 2018).

The NALA is an example of a policy that is a multilingual education initiative, a move that could have implications for multilingual students worldwide, despite the situation getting worse with ongoing displacement and its legacy. It has the assumption of language for culture, identity and education, and the imperative of community support and motivation. This leads us to question why the same principles do not apply to immigrant languages, or worldwide to initiatives like UNESCO's Incheon Declaration of Education 2030 or the ELT phenomenon.

Today across the world students face an educational context that has evolved into standardized content and testing, and often curriculum in one dominant language. This view plays a key role in the assimilation efforts through education. The students of non-dominant languages who would benefit from the principles in the NALA are immigrants, refugees, Indigenous peoples. Yet few of these students in the United States - perhaps with the exception of those in the few immersion schools or homeschools - and very few worldwide enjoy the link between mother tongue and education, a link that is well-known to be a positive factor in school achievement and life and would benefit communities and societies. Globally, education policy defines educational success according to standardized tests, and virtually cancels out any initiative like the NALA that supports multilingual education. The NALA gives the right and support for language revitalization, while most school systems demand proficiency in a dominant language and/or English, compelling accountability through tests and restricting teaching that would allow for other first languages.

Displaced students of different ages are usually displaced twice: some from their homes to a new country and otherwise again from their language. From their home to the school culture often means learning a dominant language and specific content knowledge, where the first language is considered a deficit (MacSwan, 2000). Then, using Schmidt's (2000) notions of identity, these students learn to understand the self in relation to the group or community. This politics of group identity 1) constitutes the self, 2) builds the relationship with others, and 3) is used for the allocation of goods. Yet while people construct their own identities "in dialectically intertwined relationships with others" (p. 48), some may be deeply attached to ethno-national groups at the level of personal identity. Language importance is a variable: a person can experience language as fundamental and constitutive of core identity, especially the mother tongue; some may easily give it up while others resist and defend it. This experience affects the next generation as well through family care.

Therefore, when LEPs cause language shifts they contribute to identity negotiation and assimilation. Thus, second and third generations are more European or American than their parents and grandparents. Along with policies are knowledge and attitudes and school practices, which result in ignorance of cultures as well as the conflicts that caused the displacement; in addition to hate crimes, discrimination, and bullying. The process may extend into the workplace. Skutnabb-Kangas and McCarty (2008: 6) define the process as *linguicide* or linguistic genocide:

> The deliberate elimination of a language, without killing its speakers; forcing speakers to give up a mother tongue through "forcibly transferring children of the group to another group"; "causing serious bodily or mental harm to members of the group" (United Nations International Convention on the Prevention and Punishment of the Crime of Genocide 1948, E 793, Articles 2e and 2b); or "prohibiting the use of the [mother tongue] in daily intercourse, or in schools..." (from the 1948 Final Draft of the above, not part of the Convention)

Similar to these notions, when a group of people is deprived of their linguistic, cultural, economic and political infrastructure, it may cease to exist (Dawson & Farber, 2012). Stemming from work on the United Nations International Criminal Tribunal for the former Yugoslavia and elsewhere, and the crime of forcible displacement and refugee law, the issue becomes *proof of intent to destroy the group*. An international criminal and human rights law specialist and world expert on the law of genocide concludes that forcible displacement seriously disrupts and destroys cultural identity, even when the group survives and carries on, because the group does not exist as it did before displacement (Schabas, 2001, quoted in Dawson & Farber, 2012: 124).

Schools have similar effects when they destroy a cultural group through the child by forcibly transferring the children to the dominant language. Ethnic cleansing relates to language shift: People are displaced by wars or economic situations to an often-unwelcoming society where children are sent to school. A few well-meaning people may welcome them, yet cultures and languages remain at home. Success depends on integration into the new society- learning the language and behavior, for children the school's content of knowledge according to standards of 21st-century western schooling and language requirements. Thus, *integration is another displacement.* LEPs would thus be proof of intent to destroy the group, in cultural and linguistic terms. Furthermore, the new environment (school or society) is often hostile and micro-aggressions, cultural misunderstandings, and discrimination are common. Teachers have little recourse in the classroom to learn about the students and plan creative activities to *give them space to develop and share their language.* With these conditions, as is often the case, people cannot exist as they did before in terms of cultural identity (or they must negotiate it); and each generation and each individual shapeshifts or negotiates to their own degree. Thus assimilation and integration are also on a continuum relative to the displacement (Harrison, 2018a).

In sum, as Harrison (2016) maintains, a form of educational imperialism affects identity: students, displaced physically and then culturally from their home, learn who and what they are from the receiving or dominant society's eyes via a new language and body of knowledge in school. Then their language becomes an anachronism. Expected to learn the dominant language and school material, their own history and culture, even if it is acknowledged in textbooks, teaching, and exams, is often taught in a discriminatory way through misrepresentation of their identity (ibid.). How can groups of people, more likely individuals, reverse language assimilation that also becomes an identity assimilation? The next section discusses an initiative to reverse the legacy and effects of language shifts and monolingual schooling.

7 The MEMES project

The chapter's argument demonstrates the urgency for the MEMES[2] (Making Empathetic Multilingual Environments in School) project, a nascent ideological movement and online research platform and support space. In it teachers and policymakers may connect and gather resources in an effort to create harmonious societies where multilingual education is the norm for indigenous and other world languages. The dynamic multilingualism with which I began the chapter has two directions: one towards the indigenous heritage languages that largely need to be recovered and revitalized, and the other towards the newcomers (the immigrants, refugees, and youth born to parents who speak languages other than English) whose languages will likely become heritage languages if nothing changes. Both directions point to physical or cultural and

2 https://memes.education.wisc.edu.

linguistic displacement, as occurred with our great-grandfathers (in the U.S.) who came as immigrants, bearing progeny who at some point shifted to English, leaving us without our heritage, or the Native Americans who were moved onto reservations. It is time to reverse the results where school systems fail in terms of creating monolingual speakers by eliminating multilingualism.

The MEMES project has two facets. The first facet includes (1) resources and classroom strategies (such as valuing mother tongues and translanguaging) that are introduced to participating teachers to show them how to allow languages to be heard in the classroom. These support the acquisition of languages and maintenance of mother tongues/first languages, and connect teachers and learners. The second facet of the project asks (2) 'what are the results of valuing a multilingual classroom approach by changing strategies?' with a goal toward a radical re-visioning of language education. The goal is to help teachers and all language learners benefit from self- and peer-created multilingual support spaces, and the resources of the research and support platform. By disseminating approaches and strategies such as translanguaging and *pluri*lingualism (drawing on the whole linguistic repertoire to make meaning) and principles of MLE, teachers (and eventually policymakers) will see how these may benefit *all* students—monolingual, heritage learners who wish to recover a language, multilingual—in their identity formation, achievement, and community-building. Thus, shared research result will benefit all types of language speakers either displaced (immigrant, refugee), indigenous communities, or monolinguals (Harrison, 2018b). This endeavor calls for future research to develop teacher training and practical classroom strategies.

The theoretical and conceptual bases of MEMES are embedded in the acronym - Making Empathetic Multilingual Environments in Schools - and include the goal of dynamic multilingualism with the principles of MLE, in addition to empathy which includes commonalities and seeing ourselves in relation to those around us. The entire ideological movement goes against the teaching of English as a Lingua Franca or monolingual schooling in any form. The MEMES project supports and serves the value of MLE. It begins with *Making* something different: education systems and schools were built according to western knowledge systems that isolated variables such as one's language, the knowledge taught in schools, and one's identity, family, and culture. This approach is still the superstructure for education and language policies, which the MEMES project seeks to change. The postmodern approach of researchers deconstructs these variables, but in practical terms the MEMES approach supports community and bottom-up movements. *Empathetic* highlights the 'we' instead of the 'I', seeing the other in the self. Empathy is not sympathy but emotional education and common ground with our classmates and neighbors, conducive to a peaceful and functioning society. The research in *Multilingual* Language Education (MLE) (see Skutnabb-Kangas et al, 2009) suggests the implementation of policies requiring second language learning beginning in grade 3 or 4, with a third language in high school. The preceding aspects are in sum making a new *Environment*. The movement I posit to launch will be through the education system (MLE) in *Schools*, since multilingualism in today's education system cannot thrive without support structures in schools. The environments I want to 'make' in schools are empathetic and multilingual, and very near the indigenous approach. We may establish a myriad of perspectives, and even alliances between groups.

8 Conclusion

This chapter has explored the Indigenous approach and included a focus on the Native American Languages Act (NALA) of 1990. The goal is to change the status quo, given that most western education systems today have standardized content and language and present culturally and linguistically external ideas that erase knowledge, cultures and languages. It has been developed under the theoretical umbrella that embracing the precepts of the NALA that support languages and linguistic autonomy would be beneficial to other students who face language shift through school, such as immigrants and refugees; and even to later-generation immigrants who are now monolingual.

The previous sections described how language is fundamental to the clash in education systems. The chapter showed the value of MLE and how language policies that began in an educational framework of boarding schools are a primordial example to understand current realities and LEPs in general. Second, English *was* and *is still* spread to newcomers in a land that had many indigenous languages (the U.S.), an understanding than cat reveal useful precepts for LEP interpretation, especially considering the role of English now in the world. This includes the role of a dominant language in schooling and the marginalization of other languages, particularly for Indigenous people who have faced violent histories of cultural assimilation through schooling and through media representations of 'Indians' or 'immigrants' which do not correspond with their own self-knowledge. Given this context, the goal is to promote multilingualism through education (i.e. MLE to promote dynamic multilingualism) and to this end the MEMES project has been proposed to expand MLE and respond to the growing demand for educational (including linguistic) autonomy and community education projects rather than rigidly standardized (and monolingual) education and knowledge systems.

References

Adams, D. W. (1995). *Education for extinction: American Indians and the boarding school experience 1875–1928*. Lawrence: University Press of Kansas.

Adams, R. M. (1995). Foreward. In V. L. Hyatt (Ed.), *Race, discourse, and the origin of the Americas: A new world view* (pp. vii–ix). Washington: Smithsonian Institution Press.

Baker, D., & Wiseman, A. (2007). *International perspectives on education: Vol. 8. Education for all: Global promises, national challenges*. New York: JAI Press.

Beaulieu, D. (2008). Native American education research and policy development in an era of No Child Left Behind: Native language and culture during the administrations of Presidents Clinton and Bush. *Journal of American Indian Education, 47*, 10–45.

Cajete, G. (1994). *Look to the mountain: An ecology of indigenous education*. Durango: Kivaki Press.

Celic, C., & Seltzer, K. (2012/2013). *Translanguaging: A CUNY-NYSIEB guide for educators*. New York: CUNY-NYSIEB, The Graduate Center, The City University of New York. Retrieved January 6, 2014 from https://www.cuny-nysieb.org/translanguaging-resources/translanguaging-guides/.

Cherubini, L. (2010). An analysis of Ontario Aboriginal education policy: Critical and interpretive perspectives. *McGill Journal of Education/ Revue des Sciences de l'Éducation de McGill, 45*(1), 9–26.

Chilisa, B. (2012). *Indigenous research methodologies*. Thousand Oaks: SAGE.

Churchill, W. (September 6, 1943). *The gift of a common tongue*. Speech at Harvard University. Retrieved January 9, 2014 from https://winstonchurchill.org/resources/speeches/1941-1945-war-leader/the-price-of-greatness-is-responsibility/.

Cummins, J. (2009). Fundamental psycholinguistic and sociological principles underlying educational success for linguistic minority students. In T. Skutnabb-Kangas, R. Phillipson, A. K. Mohanty & M. Panda (Eds.), *Social justice through multilingual education* (pp. 19–35). Bristol: Multilingual Matters.

Dawson, G., & Farber, S. (2012). *Forcible displacement throughout the ages: Towards an international convention for the prevention and punishment of the crime of forcible displacement*. Leiden: Martinus Nijhoff Publishers.

Foucault, M. (1970). *The order of things: An archaeology of the human sciences*. New York: Vintage.

Haig-Brown, C. (2008). Taking Indigenous thought seriously: A rant on globalization with some cautionary notes. *Journal of the Canadian Association for Curriculum Studies, 6*(2), 8–24.

Harper, L. & Rawlins, N. (2016). *Comments from the national coalition of Native American language schools and programs*. Retrieved November 18, 2018 from http://www.ncnalsp.org/know-the-laws.

Harrison, K. M. (2009). *Isomorphisms in world education: Is this (UNESCO) education for all?* (Unpublished master's thesis). Madison: University of Wisconsin-Madison.

Harrison, K. M. (2016). *Educational imperialism: Schooling and indigenous identity in Puerto Rico*. Blue Mounds: Deep Education Press.

Harrison, K. M. (2018a). Conclusion-storytelling, plurilingual practices and pedagogy in schools of a thousand languages: Listening to displaced languages. In K. Harrison, M. Sadiku & F. Tochon (Eds.), *Displacement planet earth: Plurilingual education and identity for 21st century schools* (pp. 296–309). Blue Mounds: Deep Education Press.

Harrison, K. M. (2018b). Introduction: A 21st century continuum of displacement, school practices and experiences: Language education, identity, and a call for action. In K. Harrison, M. Sadiku & F. Tochon (Eds.), *Displacement planet earth: Plurilingual education and identity for 21st century schools* (pp. 16–26). Blue Mounds: Deep Education Press.

Harrison, K. M. (2018c). Language education policy and teachers in Puerto Rico: Implications for identity, sovereignty, and community in a context of displacements. *Journal for Educators, Teachers, and Trainers, 9*, 73–86.

Harrison, K. M., & Tochon, F. V. (2015). Interpreting language education policies: Conceptual, disciplinary, indigenous, and deep parameters for multilingual environments. In F. V. Tochon (Ed.), *Language education policy unlimited: Global perspectives and local practices* (pp. 351–390). Blue Mounds: Deep University Press.

Harrison, K. M. & Tochon, F. V. (in press). Diversity or displacement: Plurilingual pedagogy in transcultural classrooms. *Migration and Language Education*.

Hornberger, N. H. (2009). Multilingual education policy and practice: Ten certainties (grounded in Indigenous experience). *Language Teaching, 42*,197–211.

Illich, I. (1971). *Deschooling society*. New York: Harper & Row.

MacSwan, J. (2000). The threshold hypothesis, semilingualism, and other contributions to a deficit view of linguistic minorities. *Hispanic Journal of Behavioral Sciences, 20*(1), 3–45.

Maffi, L. (Ed.). (2001). *On biocultural diversity: Linking language, knowledge, and the environment*. Washington: Smithsonian.

McCarty, T. L. (2002). *A place to be Navajo: Rough rock and the struggle for self-determination in Indigenous schooling*. Mahwah: Lawrence Erlbaum Associates.

McCarty, T. L. (2012). Indigenous languages and cultures in Native American student achievement: Promising practices and cautionary findings. In B. Klug (Ed.), *Standing together: American Indian education as culturally responsive pedagogy* (pp. 97–119). Lanham: Rowman and Littlefield.

McCarty, T. L. (2013). *Language planning and policy in Native America: History, theory, praxis*. Buffalo: Multilingual Matters.

Menken, K. (2017). High stakes tests as de facto language education policies. In E. Shohamy, I. Or & S. May (Eds.), *Language testing and assessment, encyclopedia of language and education*. New York: Springer.

Miller, S. (2008). Native America writes back: The origin of the Indigenous paradigm in historiography. *Wicazo Sa Review*, *23*(2), 9–28.

Mundy, K. (2007). Education for all: Paradoxes and prospects of a global promise. In D. Baker & A. Wiseman (Eds.), *International perspectives on education: Vol. 8. Education for all: Global promises, national challenges* (pp. 1–30). New York: JAI Press.

National Alliance for Public Charter Schools (2019). *Public charter schools growing on Native American reservations*. Retrieved April 10, 2019 from http://www.publiccharters.org/press/public-charter-schools-growing-native-american-reservations/.

Nelson, F. C. (n/d). The school controversy among Norweign immigrants. *NAHA-Norge (Norwegian-American Historical Association)*, *26*, 206. Retrieved January 22, 2014 from https://www.naha.stolaf.edu/pubs/nas/volume26/vol26_10.htm.

Phillipson, R. (1992). *Linguistic imperialism*. Oxford: Oxford University Press.

Phillipson, R. (2008). The linguistic imperialism of neoliberal empire. *Critical Inquiry in Language Studies*, *5*(1), 1–43.

Phillipson, R. (2014). English, the *Lingua Nullius* of global hegemony. In P. A. Kraus & F. Grin (Eds.), *The politics of multilingualism: Europeanisation, globalization and linguistic governance* (pp. 275–303). Amsterdam: John Benjamins Publishing Company.

Phillipson, R. (2019). Professionalism and myths in TESOL. *TESOL (Teachers of English to Speakers of Other Languages) International Convention & English Language Expo*. Atlanta, GA (USA). 12–15 March 2019. Retrieved April 12, 2019 from http://www.linguistic-rights.org/robert-phillipson/.

Phillipson, R., & Skutnabb-Kangas, T. (2013). Linguistic imperialism and endangered languages. In T. Bhatia & W. Ritchie (Eds.), *The handbook of bilingualism and multilingualism* (pp. 495–515). Hoboken: Blackwell Publishing.

Popkewitz, T. (2008). *Cosmopolitanism and the age of school reform: Science, education and making society by making the child.* New York: Routledge.

Sallabank, J. (2010). Language endangerment: Problems and solutions. *eSharp*, Special Issue: Communicating change: Representing self and community in a technological world, 50–87.

Schabas, W. (2001). Symposium: Universal jurisdiction: Myths, realities, and prospects: Problems of international codification – Were the atrocities in Cambodia and Kosovo genocide? *New England Review, 35*(2), 287–302.

Schmidt, R. (2000). *Language policy & identity politics in the United States.* Philadelphia: Temple University Press.

Schwartz-Shea, P., & Yanow, D. (2012). *Interpretive research design: Concepts and processes.* New York: Routledge.

Skutnabb-Kangas, T. (2000). *Linguistic genocide in education – or worldwide diversity and human rights?* Mahwah: Lawrence Erlbaum Associates.

Skutnabb-Kangas, T. (2012a). Linguistic human rights. In L. Solan & P. Tiersma (Eds.), *Oxford handbook on language and law* (pp. 235–247). Oxford: Oxford University Press.

Skutnabb-Kangas, T. (2012b). The role of mother tongues: Educational goals and models, linguistic diversity, and language rights. In K. Gya, A. Snavely & E. Sperling (Eds.), *Minority language in today's global society* (pp. 127–161). New York: Trace Foundation.

Skutnabb-Kangas, T., Maffi, L., & Harmon, D. (2006). *Sharing a world of difference. The earth's linguistic, cultural and biological diversity.* Paris: Terra Lingua, WWF & UNESCO.

Skutnabb-Kangas, T. & McCarty, T. (2008). Clarification, ideological/epistemological underpinnings and implications of some concepts in bilingual education. In J. Cummins & N. Hornberger (Eds.), *Encyclopedia of language and education* (pp. 3–17). 2nd edition. New York: Springer.

Skutnabb-Kangas, T., Phillipson, R., Mohanty, A. K., & Panda, M. (2009). *Social justice through multilingual education.* Bristol: Multilingual Matters.

Smith, L. T. (1999). *Decolonizing methodologies: Research and indigenous peoples.* New York: Zed Books.

Tochon, F. V. (2018). Transcultural reasoning and social harmony: Moral paradoxes of intercultural education. In K. M. Harrison, M. Sadiku & F. V. Tochon (Eds.), *Displacement planet earth: Plurilingual education and identity for 21st century schools* (pp. 23–53). Blue Mounds: Deep Education Press.

Trudell, B. (2014). The multilingual education (MLE) network phenomenon: Advocacy and action for minoritized language communities. *Multilingual Education*, *4*(1), 17.

UNESCO. (2016). Education 2030: Incheon Declaration and framework for action for the implementation of Sustainable Development Goal 4: Ensure inclusive and equitable quality education and promote lifelong learning opportunities for all. Paris: UNESCO. Retrieved November 17, 2018 from https://unesdoc.unesco.org/ark:/48223/pf0000245656.

UNESCO. (2019). *UNESCO atlas of the world's languages in danger*. Retrieved April 16, 2019 from http://www.unesco.org/culture/languages-atlas/.

UNHCR. (2018). *Forced displacement above 68m in 2017, new global deal on refugees critical*. Retrieved April 12, 2019 from https://www.unhcr.org/news/press/2018/6/5b27c2434/forced-displacement-above-68m-2017-new-global-deal-refugees-critical.html.

Vertovec, S. (2007). Super-diversity and its implications. *Ethnic and Racial Studies*, *30*(6), 1024–1054.

Warhol, L. (2011). Native American language education as policy-in-practice: An interpretative policy analysis of the Native American Languages Act of 1990/1992. *International Journal of Bilingual Education and Bilingualism*, *14*(3), 279–299.

Warhol, L. (2012). Creating official language policy from local practice: The example of the Native American Languages Act 1990/1992. *Language Policy*, *11*(3), 235–252.

Warrior, R. A. (2005). *The people and the word*. Minneapolis: University of Minnesota Press.

Wynter, S. (1992). 1492: A new world view. In V. L. Hyatt (Ed.), *Race, discourse, and the origin of the Americas: A new world view* (pp. 5–57). Washington: Smithsonian Institute Press.

Yanow, D. (2000). *Conducting interpretive policy analysis*. Thousand Oaks: Sage.

Bertha Du-Babcock

Hong Kong language policy and its relationship to and effect on language use in Hong Kong

Abstract: The major aim of the present chapter is to describe and analyse the current language policy and language use in Hong Kong. Thus, the chapter begins by setting forth background factors related to the Hong Kong language environment and summarises, adopting a critical perspective, the different assessments measuring the language competence of Hong Kong citizens so as to communicate in Cantonese, English, and Mandarin. Next, it describes the various language policies set by the government, the educational sector, and business enterprises and their effect on communication in Hong Kong. By drawing on the language-based communication zones model, it further analyses several business communication situations, underlining the need for developing different language competence levels in order to communicate effectively in these situations. To conclude, the chapter ties together Hong Kong language policy and its relationship with present and future language use in the area.

Keywords: Communication zones, business communication, language competence assessment, language proficiency

1 Introduction

Hong Kong faces the challenge of developing and implementing a language policy that facilitates the acquisition of adequate levels of competency in three languages: Cantonese, English, and Mandarin. Language policy has historically been developed against a backdrop where English and Cantonese competencies were both needed, but, with the rise of Mainland China as a global economic and political power, competency in Mandarin is now also essential. In an increasing competitive global business communication environment, sound language policy is needed to enable Hong Kong to maintain and further its position in a multilingual global business communication environment. To ensure continued economic prosperity, a multilingual work force is needed comprising English speakers to compete in global business, Mandarin speakers to take part in business and governmental relationships with Mainland China, and Cantonese speakers for local Hong Kong business. English-speaking ability has long been believed to be a key competitive advantage in the financial services industry and in establishing itself as a regional center for multinational corporations. Mandarin-speaking ability is needed to serve as the gateway to Mainland China in regard to business and governmental relationships, in addition to serving Mainland China tourists. Cantonese-speaking ability allows local business to operate more effectively by facilitating better cooperation among employees and communication with customers. The need to develop English competencies was recognized earlier and the need to develop Mandarin later, as Mainland China has now emerged as a major economic power. At the same time, language policy needs to be sensitive to social concerns that revolve around protecting and preserving Cantonese, as it is the native language of Hong Kong. Furthermore, language policy needs to facilitate the development of adequate competency levels rather than setting and striving to achieve the unrealistic goal of achieving full competency in three languages. That is, differing areas and levels of language competency are needed in varied workplace settings, and language policy should be aimed at developing these useable language competencies.

Competing interests come into play in the development and implementation of language policy in Hong Kong. Emotional arguments are introduced into the discussion of language policy formulation, and critics point to an alleged decline in both English and Cantonese competency levels, especially in English as compared to other Asian countries. Results of a recent survey (2016) reflected that English proficiency among Hong Kong people has declined with the increased focus on Mandarin highlighted as the cause[1]. To frame and provide perspective for discussion, my focus is on introducing a theoretical framework for my analysis and on clarifying factors and analyzing the need for language competency in different work settings. I do not set forth language policy proposals, but hope to have provided useful perspectives and a framework for the further discussion of language policy and use in Hong Kong.

In the following sections of the paper, I outline Hong Kong language policy and its relationship to and effect on language use in Hong Kong. Section 2 sets forth background factors, including a historical perspective, relating to the Hong Kong language environment to set the stage for my analysis. Section 3 summarizes and critiques various assessments of language competency. Section 4 describes Hong Kong language policies set by the Hong Kong government, the educational sector, and business enterprises that collectively impact communication in Hong Kong. Section 5 lists and explains various communication situations that develop in the business sector and show how varying levels of language competency are needed to communicate effectively in these different

---

1 https://coconuts.co/hongkong/news/hku-survey-reflects-decline-english-proficiency-among-hongkongers-increased-focus.

situations and industries. Section 6 concludes the paper by tying together language policy and its relationship to present and future language use.

1.1 Conceptual framework

Two prominent models from business communication and business administration theory guide my analysis: the language-based communication zones model (Babcock & Du-Babcock, 2001; Du-Babcock, 2007; Du-Babcock & Babcock, 1996, 2001, 2007) and the generic corporate strategy model (Porter, 1985). The language-based model classifies and describes the required language competency levels in order to adequately communicate in different communication situations and tasks. According to the competency match of the interlocutors, this model classifies the speaker's competency into three levels: Zone One, Zone Two, and Zone Three. Hence, using the language-based communication zones model as a framework, the level of second language competency determines the ability to take part in business communication situations.

In the language-based communication zones model, two types of second-language competency co-exist: general-language competency and genre competency. General language competency refers to the language used for general purposes (LGP). Speakers may also use language in professional contexts where individuals exchange messages within their specialized areas, or discourse community (Bhatia, 2004). Genre competency thus refers to the language that is used for professional purposes and in professional contexts. While general language competency is seen as a broad category of any given language, the genre language competency of LSP is defined as the specialized language contained within the language and used in professional contexts (e.g. business and management, manufacturing), or in business transactions (e.g. buyer-seller, negotiating partners, company-auditor).

Professional genres are recognizable communicative events characterized by a set of 'communicative purposes' that are identified and mutually understood by members of identified language or discourse communities (ibid.). These professional genres can vary in scope from very wide (specialized professional genres such as legal or medical genres) to very narrow (customers ordering food in a fast-food restaurant).

Language competency determines the overall ability to communicate in a given communication environment and task, and is divided into three categories: Zone One where second-language competency is limited or extremely low, Zone Two where second-language competency is at an intermediate level, and Zone Three where second-language competency is full or fluent. Applying the language-based communication zones model in the Zone One communication situation, the monolingual Cantonese speakers may possess limited second-language communication ability and cannot carry out an extended, interactive conversation. These Zone One speakers, although lacking general language competency, may still be likely to communicate adequately if they encounter the communication situation where Zone One genre language competency is required. Such genres are characterized by having a knowable background context, nouns and phrases in the oral language, and sometimes an artificial language. Taking food orders in fast-food restaurants is an example of Zone One communication.

In Zone Two, Cantonese speakers possess intermediate language competency. These individuals may not be able to carry out conversations in all areas of the general language but, with an intermediate level of genre competence, could communicate in the language area constituted by the specific genre in their fields. In Zone Three, Cantonese speakers may be able to easily carry out general conversations in all situations, but may not be able to communicate effectively in a specific genre. The Zone Three communicator may also need to have the specialized vocabulary and knowledge of different topics related to specific genres.

The generic corporate strategy model distinguishes how business enterprises compete in order to gain a competitive advantage in the marketplace. In this model, firms attempt to compete by using one of four contrasting generic strategies: cost leadership, differentiation, cost focus, and differentiation focus. Regarding the generic corporate strategies of cost leadership and differentiation generic corporate strategies, firms concentrate on the whole market (wide scope); while in cost focus and differentiation focus strategies, firms target a specific niche or segment of the market (narrow scope). For cost strategies, the competitive advantage is gained through efficiency that results in lower cost, whereas, for differentiation strategies, competitive advantage is gained through offering unique products or services. In my analysis, I show how Hong Kong enterprises with differing generic corporate strategies require differing second-language competency needs for their workforce.

1.2 Data collection

The data for the paper were collected through the examination of public documents and through empirical research. I used interview methodology to gather data for Zone Two and Zone Three business transactions and an audio recording of a communication for Zone One. For Zone One, I observed expatriates over a six-month period and then conducted a field experiment. In the experiment, I had an English speaker make an order to a monolingual

Cantonese order taker. I then confirmed the second-language competency of the order taker by initiating and attempting to have an English conversation with her.

2 Description of the language environment

In this section I trace the historical description of the Hong Kong language environment, trace the evolution of business communication, provide a description of current language use in Hong Kong, and describe the social norms affecting language use in Hong Kong.

2.1 Historical perspective in general

The history of Hong Kong as a British colony (1843 to 1997) has influenced the Hong Kong language environment. Following the practice within both Britain and its empire, there was no statutory provision for what constituted the official language(s) in Hong Kong until 1974. However, "English was by practice the sole language used for all official matters within all three (executive, judicial and legislative) branches of the government during the period" (Dickson & Cumming, 1996: 41). In 1974, Cantonese became the second official language. With the handover to Mainland China in 1997, Mandarin or *Putonghua* entered the picture as Hong Kong administrators needed to interact with the central government.

Historically, English was the principal medium of communication in government, with English governors heading the government and English-speaking expatriates being located at high- and middle-level ranks of the civil service hierarchy; but, at the same time, competency in English did not spread through the general population. Although Hong Kong was governed by Britain until 1997, the spread of English was restricted to the local elites who acquired the English language mostly by way of a formal education. The 1991 census reported that 29.4 % of the people of Hong Kong were able to speak English (Dickson & Cumming, 1996). With the rapid expansion of university education in the 1990s the percentage of the population with competency in English has risen significantly. The results of the 2012 Census (Thematic Household Survey Report 51, 2013) relating to language use in Hong Kong show that 23.7 % of the respondents perceived that their spoken English-language competence was very good or good, with 36.9 % considering it to be average. As reflected by a comparison of the 2002 and 2012 census data, the reported ability to communicate in English broadened and increased substantially over this ten-year period.

Leading up to the handover to Mainland China in 1997 and continuing thereafter, a policy of localization was adopted and most expatriates who had occupied higher-level positions in the government bureaucracy returned to their home countries and were replaced by Hong Kong locals. Without the expatriate presence, Cantonese has now supplanted English as the principal medium of communication in Hong Kong government circles and this phenomenon has extended to the legislative council and the executive branch, including Carrie Lam, who is the present Chief Executive of the Hong Kong Special Administrative Region (HKSAR).

Although Cantonese and Mandarin have gradually replaced English in the Post-Colonial period, the importance of English in Hong Kong is still evident in its public social media, public discourse, and the courts. In Hong Kong, there are two free Cantonese and two free English TV channels. Similarly, for printed media, Hong Kong has two English newspapers (South China Morning Post and the Standard) together with several Chinese newspapers. For important public speeches, both Cantonese and English versions are provided through simultaneous translation. English is the language used in courts, but speakers can request that proceedings be entirely conducted in Cantonese.

2.2 Historical perspective on business communication

Language used in business and commerce has changed over the years. In the 1960s through to the 1980s Hong Kong became a manufacturing hub centered on an export market and also an international retail center known for competitive pricing (such as quality tailored men's and women's suits), and as a tourist destination (having the unique appeal of being a mix of Oriental and English culture). In manufacturing enterprises, this global positioning necessitated English-speaking competency requirements because personnel from the marketing departments of Hong Kong companies used English to establish overseas markets and top executives used English to communicate with government officials. Internal company language use was often based on Cantonese in day-to-day business operations, but English was prevalent for written communication. In retailing, the developments during the period of 1960 to 1980 required English-speaking competency as clerks and other personnel such as tailors needed to communicate with their customers in English.

In the 1990s, manufacturing facilities were moved north to Mainland China and Hong Kong transitioned up the value-added scale to become a major international banking and financial center and operated as a regional headquarters for multinational corporations. These dual developments brought forth an increasing need for staff with high or at least adequate English competency. Concurrently, as the need for English speakers increased, Mandarin Chinese became a new element in the Hong Kong language environment. In those enterprises where manufacturing facilities moved to Mainland China while retaining their headquarters in Hong Kong, Hong Kong executives and staff (whether stationed in Hong Kong, in Mainland China, or in both locations traveling back and forth) needed Mandarin competency for internal company communication with their Mainland staff and with China governmental officials. In addition, from the 2000s and accelerating in recent years, Mandarin-speaking Mainland China tourists have become a major component of the retail market, especially for luxury items.

2.3 Current language environment and use

In the Hong Kong communication environment, Cantonese, English, and Mandarin are the three major languages of everyday personal, business, government, and legal affairs. In everyday personal and family communication, the Hong Kong Cantonese, regardless of their competency levels in other languages and disregarding frequent code-switching, speak almost exclusively in their native language. There are three exceptions to this general pattern: when they speak with non-Cantonese speaking maids, when teaching English to young children, and for those returning to Hong Kong after spending an extensive period of time in western countries. In addition, some Chinese speak other Chinese dialects (e.g. Hakka, Shanghainese) and non-Chinese as their native languages (e.g. English, Hindi) in their home environments.

In the work environment, as Hong Kong Chinese compose about 95 % of the work force, they engage primarily in Cantonese language conversations with their fellow colleagues. However, these bilingual Chinese also have English conversations with local expatriates, business travelers and tourists visiting Hong Kong, and with overseas customers or suppliers via telephone, as well as sometimes Mandarin conversations with Chinese business travelers and tourists from Mainland China or Taiwan. As Mandarin is the national language of Mainland China, bilingual Cantonese business people and government civil servants accommodate and use Mandarin in their discussions with Mainland governmental personnel. This situation results in a commonly observed code-mixing phenomenon in which bilingual Cantonese individuals switch between two languages (Cantonese and English), and possibly a third language (Mandarin) on a daily basis, while using Cantonese whenever possible. In sum, apart from the use of Cantonese in the workplace Cantonese workers may use English (especially those working in financial services and in branches of multinational corporations) or Mandarin (especially those serving Mainland Chinese in the retail sector and in intra-organizational communication with Mainland China branches of Hong Kong companies).

2.3.1 Social norms affecting language use

Although the three languages co-exist, the dominance of Cantonese oral communication is reinforced by a cultural norm that restricts and sanctions the use of English in their conversations among Cantonese-speaking individuals (see, for example, Bond & Young, 1982; Du-Babcock, 1999; Gibbons, 1987; Pennington et al., 1992). Li (2000) stated that native Cantonese speakers are "subject to strong norms disapproving the use of English for intra-ethnic communication" (p. 305). Because of this societal pressure on Cantonese first-language speakers in the Cantonese-dominant language environment, they refrain from the use of English language communication with other Cantonese-speaking individuals (Bond &Young, 1982; Gibbons, 1987). Given these conditions, even conscientious Hong Kong Chinese individuals have difficulty in developing and maintaining high level interactive English-language communication skills, and especially in striking a proficiency balance between Cantonese and English-language communication competencies (Du-Babcock, 1999). This informal social norm restricting the use of English extends through all levels of society, although it is reduced at the higher levels in the society. As such, Cantonese bilinguals do not face a conducive environment in which to maintain and improve their English-language competency; and, consequently, even conscientious Cantonese bilinguals who are motivated to use English are discouraged from doing so.

3 Measurements of language competency

In this section I summarize available information on assessments relating to languages used and the abilities of Hong Kong residents to communicate in English, Cantonese, and Mandarin (the three major languages). This is intended to provide background information and the frame of reference for my discussion on language policy and its relationship to language use. Against a backdrop of contradictory and inconclusive evidence, critics point to an alleged decline in both Cantonese and English competency and especially in English, as compared to other Asian countries. The conclusions are derived from overall language proficiency, as measured by standardized tests of student populations and census data about the general public conducted by the Census and Statistics Department.

While language tests taken by students to measure aspects of language competency may generally indicate communicative competence for the workplace, these tests are administered prior to their working lives (with the exception of part-time working students). Thus, these standardized tests may at best reflect general language competency and do not directly measure workplace communication competency. Meanwhile, opinion surveys on perceived language competency and language use in Hong Kong can provide interesting data; these data, however, reflect self-assessment of language competency, which may or may not be indicative of workplace communicative competence.

It is my position, and the premise on which this paper is based, that measurements of language competency should indicate the ability to communicate in real-world workplace situations related to the business context or "economic activities status" (Thematic Household Survey Report 56, 2013). As such measurements are not currently conclusive, in this paper, I hope to redirect and frame the discussion and debate surrounding Hong Kong language policy toward ascertaining the requisite language competencies needed in business contexts.

3.1 English-language competency as measured by the standardized tests and survey data

In Hong Kong, English language proficiency has been systematically assessed among secondary school student populations. In this section, I provide an overview of the test scores of standardized tests adopted by the Hong Kong Education Bureau to assess students' language proficiencies. While the Hong Kong Advanced Level Examination (HKALE) operated until 2012, the Hong Kong Diploma of Secondary Education Examination (HKDSE) has been offered since 2012. In addition to these two Hong Kong-based public examinations, two internationally adopted tests that are also widely accepted by Hong Kong tertiary institutions are the International English Language Testing System (IELTS) and the Test of English as a Foreign Language (TOEFL).

3.1.1 Hong Kong public examinations: Advanced Level Examinations and Diploma of Secondary Education Examination

The Hong Kong Education Policy stipulates that for admission to the University's undergraduate degree programs, applicants are required to pass public examinations. The Hong Kong Advanced Level Examinations and the Hong Kong Diploma of Secondary Education Examination are standardized, norm-referenced, and centralized assessments of students' language proficiency conducted by the Hong Kong Education Bureau. The HKALE public

Table 1: A comparison of the use of English in A-level examination of the HKALE between 2008 and 2012

HKALE statistics of candidates' results						
		Year (Grade distribution in %)				
		2008	**2009**	**2010**	**2011**	**2012**
English	A	0.9	0.9	1	1	1
	C or above	15.4	16.4	15.7	15.4	15.6
	E or above	74.4	76.5	75	75	74.9

Table 2: A list of the English Language of the HKDSE between 2012 and 2015

HKDSE statistics of candidates' results					
		Year (Level distribution in %)			
Language	**Level**	**2012**	**2013**	**2014**	**2015**
English	5**	0.7	0.9	0.9	0.8
	5*	2.4	2.7	2.8	2.4
	5	5.2	5.3	5.4	4.9
	4	15.7	15.7	16.2	16.9
	3	26.0	23.9	27.2	26.7
	2	29.3	29.6	25.9	27.7
	1	10.5	13.1	12.0	12.6
	U	10.4	8.8	9.6	8.0

examination was phased out and replaced by the HKDSE in 2012 due to a structural change in the Hong Kong tertiary education system from a three-year tertiary education system to four years. Table 1 lists the grade distribution of the English Use of the HKALE between 2008 and 2012. Table 2 lists the results of the English Use of HKDSE scores and percentages between 2012 and 2015.

Table 1 shows that approximately 75 % of the A-Level examination test takers obtained a pass score of Grade E, and that about 16 % of the test takers obtained Grade C or above of the English Use, which corresponds to an IELTS score of 6.5 or above. The results also show that students performed fairly consistently in the use of English and the percentage of the grade distribution remained consistent between 2008 and 2012.

Table 2 lists the level distribution of the HKDSE English language since its inception in 2012. In examining the HKDSE English language, the results show

Appendix 1: Conversion table of standardized English language tests

Qualifications/ Framework of Reference	International English Language Testing System (IELTS)	Hong Kong Diploma of Secondary Education (HKDSE)	Hong Kong Advanced Level Examination (HKALE)	Test of English as a Foreign Language (TOEFL)
English Language: Foundation English for University Studies				
Common European Framework of Reference for Languages: Learning, Teaching, Assessment (CEFR) Level C2	Score 7.5 or above with no sub-scores below 7.0	Level 5* or above in English Language	Grade A in Use of English	590 or above (paper); or 243 or above (CBT); or 96 or above
CEFR Level C1 or above	Score 6.5 or above	Level 5 or above in English Language	Grade C or above in Use of English	550 or above (paper); or 213 or above (CBT); or 79 or above (IBT)

that approximately 8 % to 9 % of the test takers received Levels 5, 5*, and 5** of the English Use. The Level 5, 5* and 5** is corresponding to Grade C or above of the HKALE, or corresponding to IELTs 6.5 or above.

When comparing the results of the two Hong Kong Public Examinations over a five-year period (see Table 1 and Table 2), the result shows a slight decline in the test scores. While approximately 16 % of HKALE test takers received Grade C or above, less than 10 % of the HKDSE test takers obtained Level 5 or above. For information regarding the corresponding table, Appendix 1 provides a conversion table among various standardized tests, such as IELTS, TOEFL, HKALE, and HKDSE, and the individual test score equivalency to The Common European Framework of Reference for Languages (CEFR), an international standard for describing language ability for a reference.

3.1.2 IELTS and TOEFL

In looking at the IELTS and TOEFL test scores (see Fig. 1) between 2008 and 2014, Hong Kong's IELTS' score generally surpassed other Asian countries, although its TOEFL scores are very close to that of South Korea, China, and Taiwan. In contrast with the TOEFL test scores, the results show that

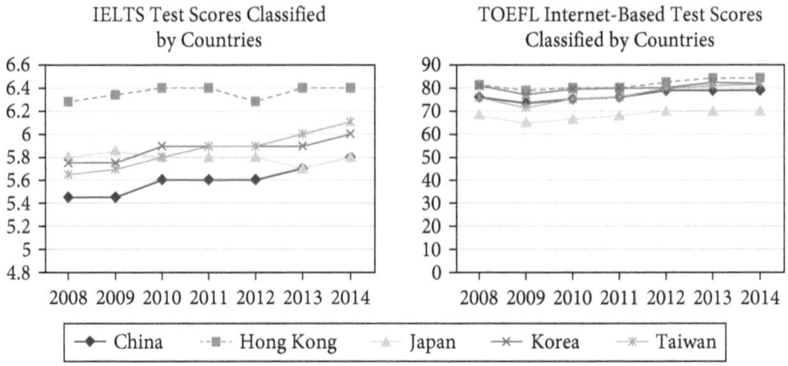

Fig. 1: IELTS and TOEFL test scores by countries between 2008 and 2014

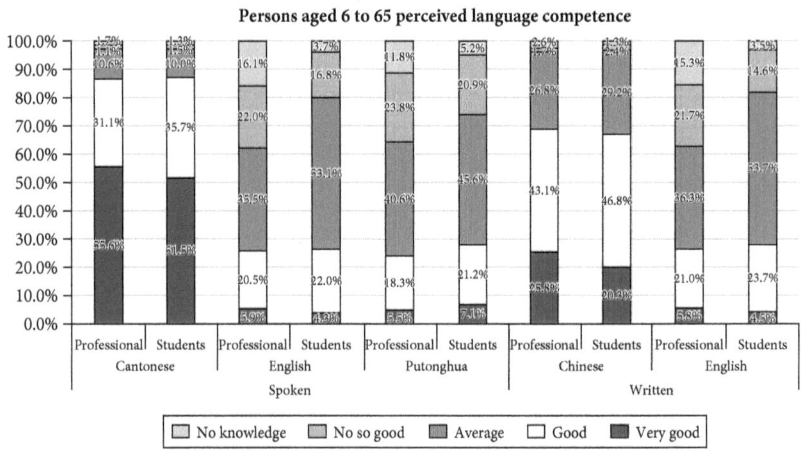

Fig. 2: A comparison of perceived language competence

the historic English-language competency advantage enjoyed by Hong Kong in comparison to other Asian countries has gradually decreased, with Hong Kong's English competency being exceeded by Singapore and Malaysia and the gap being closed with other Asian countries including Taiwan, Korea, and Japan (see Fig. 1).

Table 3: The world's top 60 countries in English according to the English Proficiency Index (EPI) scores (Source: http://www.ef.com.hk/__/~/media/efcom/epi/2014/full-reports/ef-epi-2013-report-master.pdf)

Country	Rank	EPI	Country	Rank	EPI
Malaysia	11	58.99	Indonesia	25	53.44
Singapore	12	58.92	Japan	26	53.21
India	21	54.38	Taiwan	33	50.95
Hong Kong	22	53.54	China	34	50.77
S. Korea	24	53.46	Thailand	55	44.44

3.1.3 Survey data

The Thematic Household Survey Report published in 2013 (see Fig. 2) presents the results of self-reported survey data from students and professionals. The results of the survey show that when using spoken English 26 % of the professionals perceived their spoken English competency to be good or very good, while 24 % of the students perceived that their spoken English competencies were good or very good. As for their perceived written English competence, about 27 % of the professionals and students perceived their written English competency as good or very good. It is interesting to note that more than half of the students felt their spoken and written English was average and only one-third of the professionals felt their spoken and written English was average.

The English Proficiency Index (EPI) published in May 2013 further confirms the results of Hong Kong English-language proficiency tests. Table 3 shows that Hong Kong ranked 22 out of the top 60 countries, a comparatively lower score than other Asian countries where English is the second language. Yet, the results of the EPI show that Hong Kong ranked higher than countries such as Korea, Indonesia, Japan, China, and Thailand where English is a foreign language (EPI 2013 Report).

3.2 Chinese-language (Cantonese and Mandarin) competency as measured by the standardized tests and survey data

To discuss language competency in Chinese, a distinction must be made between the oral (Cantonese and Mandarin or *Putonghua*) and the written language (traditional and simplified characters). Although Cantonese and Mandarin share some common vocabulary, and both are tonal languages (eight tones in

Table 4: A comparison of the A-level examination of written Chinese

HKALE statistics of candidates' results						
		Year (Level distribution in %)				
Language	**Level**	**2008**	**2009**	**2010**	**2011**	**2012**
Chinese	A	2.3	2.4	2.5	2.3	1.9
	C or above	24.8	25.0	26.8	27.1	26.6
	E or above	94.3	94.9	95.4	95.3	96.1

Table 5: A comparison of the Chinese language of the HKDSE scores between 2012 and 2015

HKDSE statistics of candidates' results					
		Year (Level distribution in %)			
Language	**Level**	**2012**	**2013**	**2014**	**2015**
English	5**	0.8	0.8	0.7	0.7
	5*	2.6	2.5	2.2	2.1
	5	4.9	4.9	4.5	4.2
	4	18.0	18.2	17.2	17.2
	3	22.7	25.0	26.1	27.0
	2	29.5	28.9	29.2	30.0
	1	17.2	15.8	16.3	15.6
	U	4.3	3.9	3.8	3.2

Cantonese and four tones in Mandarin), these Chinese dialects are so different that speakers of Cantonese and Mandarin may not be able to engage in an interactive conversation. The written language situation is similar in both Hong Kong and Mainland China to a large extent, except that Hong Kong uses traditional characters and adds some localized characters, whereas Mainland China uses simplified characters.

3.2.1 Hong Kong public examinations: Advanced Level Examinations and Diploma of Secondary Education Examination

As stipulated by Hong Kong Education Policy, for admission to a University undergraduate degree program, applicants are required to pass public examinations in both English and Chinese language subjects. In this section, the results of the HKALE and the HKDSE are reported. Due to a structural change in the Hong Kong tertiary education system from a three- year tertiary education system to four years, the HKALE public examination was phased out and replaced by the HKDSE in 2012. Table 4 lists the grade distribution of the Chinese language of the HKALE between 2008 and 2012, and Table 5 lists the results of the Chinese language of HKDSE scores and percentages between 2012 and 2015.

When comparing the results of the two Hong Kong Public Examinations in Chinese language subject (see Table 4 and Table 5), the result shows that approximately 25 % of the test takers received Grade C or above in Hong Kong A-Level Examination while about 25 % of the HKDSE test takers received Level 4 or above. As there is no information available in regard to the corresponding levels between HKALE and HKDSE, the same comparison cannot be made, as was the case with English.

3.2.2 *Survey data*

In comparison to English, the competency levels in Cantonese and Mandarin have not been systematically measured by standardized tests in addition to the public examinations. The Thematic Household Survey Report published in 2013 (see Fig. 2) is included to provide a different perspective by presenting the results of self-reported survey data from students and professionals. The results of the survey show that 86 % of the professionals and students perceived that their spoken Cantonese proficiency was good or very good, while 23 % of the professionals and students felt that their spoken Mandarin proficiency was good or very good. Hong Kong Cantonese are naturally fluent in their native language, thereby easily allowing them to always engage in everyday social conversations in Cantonese. In contrast, Mandarin is a second language.

In regard to written Chinese competency, the Thematic Household Survey Report data (see Fig. 2) indicates that Hong Kong citizens perceived that they possess proficiency in written Chinese, with a strong majority of respondents fitting into the average, good, and very good categories.

It should be noted that the survey and test data refer to measuring competency in using traditional characters and that Mainland China uses simplified characters. Nevertheless, the data regarding traditional characters may well represent valid surrogate data for the ability of Cantonese to communicate in written language with Mainland Chinese. In writing and understanding simplified characters, Cantonese speakers are aided by computer technology that converts traditional characters to simplified characters. Consequently, except for handwritten notes and messages, computer technology provides instantaneous translation enabling Chinese who only know either traditional or simplified characters to exchange messages.

4 Language policy

In this section I outline governmental, educational, and business language policy in Hong Kong.

4.1 Governmental policy

Governmental policy provides the basis for an impetus toward developing a multilingual society. The current language policy originating in 1974 designated English (because of historical reasons and influences) and Chinese as "the official languages of Hong Kong for the purposes of communication between the Government or any public officer and members of the public." (Legislative Counsel Paper No. CB(4)545/12-13(05), 2013: 1). It also declared that the "official languages possess equal status" and "enjoy equality of use". In 1990, the relationship between the Chinese and English languages was defined as follows: "in addition to the Chinese language, English may also be used as an official language by the executive authorities, legislature and judiciary of the Hong Kong Special Administrative Region" (Dickson & Cumming, 1996: 45). It could be argued, therefore, that Chinese was given an implicit position of superiority over English. In 1997, the current language policy was adopted: biliterate in written Chinese and English and trilingual in oral Cantonese, Putonghua and spoken English (兩文三語). Under this policy, both Chinese and English are acknowledged as official languages, with Cantonese being acknowledged as the de facto official spoken variety of Chinese, while also accepting Mandarin or *Putonghua* as one of the recognized spoken languages.

4.2 Language educational policy

Language educational policy is directed toward developing competency in Cantonese, English, and Mandarin. In this section, I summarize Hong Kong language educational policy in regard to (a) primary and secondary schools and (b) universities.

4.2.1 Primary and secondary schools

Primary and secondary schools are divided into Chinese Medium Instruction (CMI) and English Medium Instruction (EMI) schools. There are no designated schools using Mandarin as the medium of instruction. In CMI and EMI schools, Mandarin is taught as a subject. In CMI schools, English is taught as a subject. However, in many of these EMI schools, Cantonese can be used to a varying extent together with English in classroom instruction, although textbooks and assessments are mainly in English.

4.2.1.1 *Language policy for primary and secondary schools between 1998 and 2010*

In 1998, the Hong Kong Government issued a language policy which was based on the premise that having students learn a subject matter in their native language enhances overall learning. This language policy stated that "the mother tongue should primarily be predominantly adopted as the medium of instruction (MOI) for secondary schools" (Education Bureau, 2010: 6). Accordingly, 'firm guidance' from the government was given to all schools in regard to the appropriate medium of instruction for the schools. With the policy change, the number of EMI schools dropped from 450 to 104; and in doing so, the proportion of EMI schools was reduced to less than a quarter of its earlier size.

4.2.1.2 *Fine-tuning MOI policy in 2010*

In 2010, the revised MOI policy gave secondary schools greater flexibility in devising their MOI arrangements. With these new arrangements regarding the method of instruction, schools at secondary levels (FORM 4 to FORM 6) are not required to adopt a uniform teaching medium; that is, schools can have both CMI and EMI classes. Consequently, the choice and number of EMI subjects can vary between individual classes within the same school and between schools as a whole.

The revised policy has the dual purposes of "upholding mother-tongue teaching while enhancing students' proficiency in both Chinese and English". This policy aims to enhance students' exposure to learning and using English, and consequently to prepare the graduates to "embrace new challenges and enhance Hong Kong's status as an international city." (Education Bureau, 2010: 4).

4.2.2 *Language policy at the tertiary level*

At the university level, English is the prescribed medium of instruction and is used for teaching materials at the University Grants Committee (UGC) funded universities, although there is some variation in language policy and use. Mandarin may be used in China-related courses and in selected situations. In non-UGC universities and colleges, teaching may be conducted in Cantonese but most teaching materials are in English. However, based on personal observation and information accessed on the grapevine, Cantonese-speaking instructors may revert to code switching in class. Out of class, Cantonese conversations represent the norm in teacher-student or student-student communication (see, for example, Du-Babcock & Feng, 2015).

4.3 Corporate language policies and language use patterns

Companies establish language policies based on anticipated language use. The corporate language policies and language use patterns among Hong Kong companies vary widely but can be generally related to the organizational strategy followed by a particular company, either global where there are worldwide product divisions or multinational corporations where there are semi-autonomous geographical divisions. In branches of companies operating in global industries, English is often designated as an official company language. These companies set English competency standards in their hiring policies. In branch offices of multinational corporations and for local firms, Cantonese is the working language and there is not, generally speaking, a policy requiring high-level competency in English or Mandarin. If companies have business connections (plants or customers) from Mainland China, Mandarin competency requirements are set out in the hiring policy and training for those dealing directly with Mainland China may be conducted in Mandarin. Provision is made for English speaking customers in most companies. For example, business telephones call services are answered in Cantonese but provision is often made allowing callers to switch to English or Mandarin.

5 Language competency influenced patterns of business and commercial language use

In this section, I make the connection between language competency levels and the competencies needed to carry out designated tasks and activities in Hong Kong business and commerce. I draw on the language-based communication zones model to illustrate second-language (English or Mandarin) business and commercial related communication patterns in the Hong Kong business context. In these communication situations, bilingual Cantonese with varying second-language competency levels are able to communicate effectively and efficiently in English or Mandarin with non-Cantonese speakers. I present a series of examples to illustrate the need for differing levels of competency in English or Mandarin. These examples illustrate that full second-language competency may not be necessary for all communication tasks, but that competency needs to be related to and be sufficient to complete the communication tasks at hand.

5.1 Zone one communication episode

The first example illustrating Zone One communication has to do with ordering at a fast-food restaurant. The customer was a monolingual English speaker who could not speak Cantonese and the order taker was a Cantonese person with limited English competency. The food ordering occurs as the monolingual English-speaking customer goes to the counter to place a breakfast order. 'I would like scrambled eggs, orange juice, hash browns, and coffee, and I would like it to go,' said the customer. The order taker replied to the customer by saying, 'Number 3, stay here; take away.' The customer replied, 'Stay here'.

In this episode, the order taker picked out and separated keywords contained in the genre vocabulary to discover what the customer meant: eggs, orange juice, hash browns, coffee, and to go. The order taker then reinterpreted the customer's order (i.e. Number 3 for scrambled eggs, hash browns, and coffee) and then asked: stay here? or take away? The phrase of 'to go' which is commonly used in English-speaking countries was outside of her learned vocabulary and therefore could not be understood. 'Stay here' refers to dining in the restaurant and 'to go' or 'take away' refers to taking the food out of the restaurant. Number 3 represents an artificial language where breakfast sets are associated and listed by numbers and are posted on a wall behind the counter on a laminated sheet. 'Stay here' and 'take away' are the understandable words in the genre and substitute the phrase 'to go' which is not part of the genre vocabulary. The customer also learned some Zone One genre during the brief communication encounter. When the order taker said Number 3, the customer looked at the wall and saw the items that were included in the order. The order was generally acceptable, but the customer did not get orange juice. Genre competence is evidenced here as Zone One communicators develop the ability to sort out words and phrases constituting the Zone One linguistic component of the genre and, in the process, they disregard extra words and phrases that lie outside of the vocabulary of genre patterns.

This example illustrates a communication situation where second-language (e.g. English or Mandarin) competency can be brought up to the desired level through repeated experience and corporate training of order takers and through the development of artificial Zone One genre. As illustrated in this example, items can be combined into a category and given an associated number or letter. Posting item categories in a place where they are easily visible to customers is also an essential component of the genre communication transaction.

5.2 Zone two communication episode

My second example illustrating Zone Two communication is a Mandarin dialogue between a Cantonese salesperson and a Mainland China customer about purchasing expensive jewelry (with gold and precious stones) that was primarily being purchased as an investment. The Cantonese salesperson was partially proficient in Mandarin, and the Mainland Chinese customer could not speak or understand Cantonese. This general-language match placed the two interlocutors into Zone Two because the Cantonese salesperson possessed full genre competency in a language area revolving around jewelry-related conversation, but could not carry out interactive conversations in other areas of the general language.

In the Mandarin language discussion, the Cantonese salesperson explained the manufacturing process and the product specifications of the jewelry in an advanced genre language that the salesperson had learned through being exposed to these specialized product terms in Mandarin over a three-year period. During the communication process, the Cantonese salesperson also controlled the communication flow as she was able to adjust her genre language level to fit the comprehension capacity of her Mainland China customers. However, when the discussion involved a query related to whether it could be guaranteed that the gold was genuine and the warranty could be trusted, the conversation faltered as the Cantonese salesperson did not have an adequate general-language or professional-genre competency to communicate in the relevant legal genre. Consequently, the Cantonese salesperson sought the assistance of a nearby colleague who had competency in legal genre and who entered into the conversation successfully responding to the concerns of the Mainland China customer. After successfully completing the sale and in closing the conversation, the Cantonese salesperson had difficulty answering questions relating to tourist attractions that the Mainland China customer wanted to visit next.

This example illustrates that the Cantonese salesperson was able to have an interactive conversation about jewelry, price, and related matters as she possessed a genre competency in jewelry-related deliberations, but was unable to engage in legal or tourist discourse due to her lack of legal and tourist genre competency. Her advanced genre competency was confined to the subjects contained in a jewelry-related genre, where she could integrate genre and supporting general language in an interactive conversation comprising a full information exchange. However, she did not have the adequate vocabulary in legal- and tourist-related genres and also could not transfer her general-language competency to the discussion in these genres. In other words, her genre communication competence was limited to the industry/product-related genre and did not extend to legal discussions (a professional genre) or tourist-related conversations (a commercial genre).

5.3 Zone two and zone three episodes

In my third example, I contrast how varying levels of competency in English, Mandarin Chinese, and Cantonese Chinese can impact on language use and the effectiveness and efficiency of communication with customers in Hong Kong financial institutions. A trilingual language environment of Cantonese, English, and Mandarin exists in these financial institutions, but there are significant differences in language competency and language use among these banks. In this example, I contrast the language environments and communication patterns within these banks.

Bank A is an international bank with headquarters in London and concentrates on multinational clients, but also has a retail segment serving all income levels with a concentration on upscale customers (such as expatriates). The language communication patterns comprise a mix of English communication (among staff and with foreign and expatriate clients), Cantonese communication (among staff and with Hong Kong customers), and Mandarin communication (with Mainland and overseas Chinese customers). Although English has not been designated as the official company language, the presence of English-speaking expatriates influences the use of English in internal communication. Also, English-speaking customers in external communication provide continuing practice in English communication and are therefore a driving force in maintaining and increasing English language competency.

Bank A has a hiring policy requiring interactive English competency. Since the staff regularly use Cantonese and written Chinese with Cantonese customers, there is also a driving force that maintains and increases Cantonese and written Chinese competencies. The deficiency in language proficiency arises with limited Mandarin-speaking abilities as only specialists dealing with Mainland-China customers speak intermediate to fluent Mandarin.

The company follows a generic corporate strategy of broad differentiation (serving the whole market by offering superior service) and its language policy and staff language competency levels have matched this generic strategy. However, with the probable growth in Mainland China business, Bank A is facing a mismatch with its external environment and needs to develop Mandarin competencies to rectify this mismatch to better interact with Mainland clients.

Bank B is the leading domestic bank. Its customer base comprises Hong Kong Chinese enterprises and Hong Kong locals. The bank has fewer upscale retail customers compared with Bank A. The English language competencies of the staff are comparatively lower than those at Bank A, and Cantonese is the primary language internally and with customers. Bank B does not have a hiring policy requiring interactive English competency, and successful applicants only have to show passing scores on the *Hong Kong Certificate of Education Examination*. The bank's employees also do not have to demonstrate their Mandarin-speaking ability. Because Bank B does not set a high second-language (English or Mandarin) competency level in its hiring policy, a larger applicant pool becomes available which can be screened to select the best qualified candidates in terms of serving Cantonese customers. These policies are consistent with the bank's generic strategy of cost focus (competing by being the low cost leader in a particular market segment). The company's language policy has served it well and has resulted in the bank being highly profitable. This policy, however, has the disadvantage of largely limiting growth to the service of Cantonese-speaking customers, as the bank does not possess the language skills to efficiently serve other English and Mandarin-speaking customers.

Bank C is a Mainland China-based bank that has expanded into Hong Kong and whose major source of business is derived from Mainland Chinese firms that have export offices in Hong Kong. The bank has also started to expand its retail operations. Communication within the bank is in Cantonese and Mandarin, and there is relatively little English communication. Mandarin communication takes precedence because of the presence of Mandarin-speaking staff at higher levels, the need for internal organization between Hong Kong and the Mainland China headquarters, and with the client base of Mainland Chinese in Hong Kong. The high-level Mandarin competency of the staff facilitates this communication. The Mandarin communication skills are considerably higher than at Bank A or Bank B, while the English language competencies are comparatively low.

Bank C has followed a differentiation focus generic strategy (providing distinct services to a market segment) in its expansion into Hong Kong, but is now attempting to move beyond this designated focus on Mainland customers to a broader market segment (from focused to broad differentiation). To facilitate this change, the development of a staff possessing English and Cantonese competencies is essential, but finding employees with these competencies, alongside Mandarin competencies, might prove extremely challenging. I see a real possibility for the development of a mismatch between the generic strategy and the language proficiencies needed to execute this language strategy.

5.3.1 Language competency and communication effectiveness

Moving from the macro level (entire firm) to the micro level (individual communicators) of analysis, I next show how language competence enhances or hinders communication efficacy. In doing so, I concentrate on communication transactions requiring the competency to communicate in Zone Three. My example compares the communication between investment advisors and a client in three banks. The example illustrates how language proficiencies affect the efficacy of their interactions.

In Bank A, a financial advisor provided sophisticated investment advice to a discerning but non-expert investor. Both interlocutors were fully proficient in English general-language conversation, while the advisor had a professional understanding and the investor had an intermediate, but not professional knowledge of investment theory and terminology. In the conversation, the advisor was able to lower her professional genre to a language level that was comprehensible to the investor. Using layman's language, she provided a comprehensive picture of the investor's financial portfolio so that the options and financial position were completely understood by the end of the meeting. Mutual understanding was thus achieved in this communication episode. Notably, the advisor addressed conditional 'what if' questions systematically and adjusted to new issues as they arose. The interlocutors carried on an interactive discussion of various investment opportunities and options, in particular whether to sell particular investments. In this conversation, the advisor utilized her fluent Zone Three general and professional English-language competence to successfully execute the communication requirements of the task and situation.

In Bank B, another financial advisor had a conversation with the same investor about her investment opportunities. In this incident, the financial advisor had full professional genre competency or specialized financial language in financial analysis that was equivalent to the Bank A financial advisor, but only had intermediate general-English language competency. Although the financial advisor possessed a full professional genre competency in financial analysis, his intermediate general English language proficiency constrained him from engaging in a free flowing interactive dialogue, and specifically prevented him from fully responding adequately to the inquiries of the investor. The financial advisor kept responding to the investor's inquiries with 'Just do it'.

Unlike the Bank A financial advisor, he could not achieve mutual understanding in the communication transaction and left the investor with unanswered questions. In this situation, the Bank B financial advisor's limited general English proficiency constrained the communication effectiveness of the interaction. The financial advisor at Bank A had sufficient general language competency to communicate effectively in this situation, whereas the Bank B financial advisor with intermediate general language competency frustrated his investor client.

In Bank C, the investor met with a financial planner who was fully fluent in Mandarin and who had low to intermediate English competence. The investor was bilingual with both English and Mandarin competencies, and understood financial genre terminology in English, but not in Mandarin. The conversation was mainly conducted in English, as the site of conversation was in Hong Kong and the investor initiated the conversation in English. There was much difficulty in the communication process and the Bank C financial planner was not able to explain the nuances of different investment options effectively in English.

After attempting to communicate in English during a few exchanges, the investor switched to Mandarin, and the change of language made the financial planner much more comfortable. He then proceeded to explain the options in some detail, but the investor understood even less than when the financial planner had previously used English in his explanation. The investor did not understand the genre terminology even though she was fully bilingual in Mandarin. From that point, the conversation switched back and forth from Mandarin to English to attempt to communicate successfully. The overall result of the communication episode was unsatisfactory. The language competency mismatch of the financial planner and the investor did not allow for a successful exchange of information.

The three episodes above illustrate the need for interactive communication competency in English to successfully communicate in these situations. If the financial planners and the investors had had different language competencies, the communication results would have been different. Since the language environment puts communicators in touch with speakers of different languages who possess differing levels of competency in these languages, competencies in Cantonese, English and Mandarin are required to carry out business and professional communication in Hong Kong's trilingual communication environment.

6 Integration of language policy and language use

In this concluding section I connect Hong Kong language policy and its language use. My analysis is based on the premise that there should be a direct relationship between language policy (guiding the development of needed language competencies) and language use (applying language competencies in actual real-world communication situations).

6.1 Current language policy and competency development

The major thrust of the current governmental and educational language policy is to maintain a balance between the development of competencies in Cantonese and English, with a secondary concern directed toward developing Mandarin competencies. Other languages have not been considered in the development of Hong Kong language policy, with the minor exception of language courses (e.g. Spanish, French, German) being offered at university level. Language courses other than English, Cantonese, and Mandarin are not included in the curriculum at the primary and secondary level. Since 1998 the evolving educational policy has emphasized native language learning (teaching in Cantonese at CMI schools) at elementary and secondary education with the implicit assumption that Hong Kong people can acquire second language competence at the university level and on-the-job. At university level, the instructional language policy with exceptions has mandated English as the medium of instruction and this practice has continued except for Mainland China related courses, which are taught in Mandarin. This choice of English and Mandarin as the main instructional mediums has been based on economic motives; that is, to maintain and further develop Hong Kong's competitive position in global business (English) and with Mainland China business (Mandarin).

6.2 Future language competency needs and Hong Kong language policy

The second-language competency needs for business-related communication have changed dramatically since 1998, with a continuing and expanding need for English competency and the emerging need for competency in Mandarin. There now may be a mismatch between present language policy and its ability to facilitate the requisite language competency to communicate in needed areas and tasks. Forecasting the future language needs of Hong Kong is outside the scope of this paper, but suffice it to say that Hong Kong is facing a situation where there are competing demands to develop and maintain language competency in three languages, that is, to maintain English language competency so as to retain a competitive position in global business, to develop Mandarin Chinese competency to confirm its status as the gateway to Mainland China, and to maintain Cantonese Chinese for local business communication as well as for cultural preservation.

As an additional consideration, the development of competencies in other languages could prove beneficial both for economic and social reasons. For instance, competencies in European languages such as German, Spanish, and French could open up economic opportunities and encourage tourism from non-English speaking countries. Competencies in other Chinese dialects could provide economic benefits in regard to establishing commercial relationships with regions of Mainland China where these dialects are spoken, as well as providing social and cultural benefits to those in Hong Kong who might be interested in preserving their own dialects. Even though Mandarin is the national language in Mainland China, competency to speak other Chinese dialects could establish the personal relationships or *guanxi* to facilitate the development of future commercial ventures.

6.3 Evaluation of Hong Kong language policies

Through general observation, it can be stated that the combination of governmental, educational, and business policies has enabled Hong Kong to have developed (a) adequate English competencies in regard to securing a prominent position in the financial services industry, establishing itself as a regional headquarters center for multinational corporations, and becoming a major tourist destination and (b) adequate Mandarin competence in regard to establishing and maintaining governmental and commercial relationships with Mainland China. There certainly has been a positive relationship between Hong Kong language policy and the development of English and Mandarin competencies needed in Hong Kong business. Assessment of both general and genre language competencies and relating these competencies to tasks and situations is needed in order to make more accurate judgments of the effect of language competency on communication effectiveness and efficiency.

The development of English and Mandarin competencies provides an extremely interesting contrast. As pointed out in this paper, there has been a strong and longstanding commitment to the development of English competencies and a relatively recent commitment to the development of Mandarin competencies. Policy changes have only required Mandarin to be taught as a subject at the primary and secondary level and in China-related courses at the university level. With economic forces seemingly driving competency development in Mandarin, the Cantonese Chinese, in a relatively short period of time, have acquired adequate Mandarin competencies to serve a rapidly expanding retail trade with Mainland China and to engage in cross border business activities, especially in the management of Mainland Chinese factories.

Without the help and support of a language policy, Cantonese Chinese were able to gain Zone Two or intermediate levels of Mandarin competency in specific professional and commercial genres. Part of this rapid Mandarin acquisition process can possibly be attributed to the similarities between the two Chinese languages. But, surely another causal factor was that Cantonese had an immediate and ongoing economic motivation to master Mandarin. Research on this language enhancement could serve as an important input in determining the direction of future language policy.

6.4 Language policy based on competency needs in business and government

Current Hong Kong language policy is based on the implicit assumption that second-language development and measurement should be based on the general ability to speak and write a language. Reflecting this assumption, the current debate about the effectiveness of Hong Kong language policy is framed on the incorrect premise that general and uniformly high-level second-language competencies need to be developed, rather than relating the policy development to language use needs. In addition, reflecting this misconception, the measurement of language competency levels required to communicate effectively in different tasks, situations, and industries has not been undertaken. This paper hopefully will provide the framework and basis for developing and carrying out language competency measurement that can serve as a basis for developing and accessing language policy.

I have used the language-based communication zones model to discuss and analyze the second-language competency needs in various business and governmental related communication contexts. The zones model provides a framework to move toward defining the required genre and general language competency needed in different industries. As such, language policy can move away from attempting to expect all Hong Kong people to speak at high general language competency levels in their second language in order to meet economic needs.

I will next discuss language competency needs in fulfilling various communication tasks, namely Zone Three, Zone Two, and Zone One tasks, where high second-language competency is required in general and genre languages, as compared to Zone Two tasks where intermediate general language competency is adequate, but high genre competency is required, and Zone One language competency needs (where only Zone One professional genre is required).

6.4.1 Zone three English language competency required

Hong Kong wishes to remain an international business and financial center and commercial hub with international clients. Hence, as English is the world business language, emphasis needs to be placed on developing English competency in financial genres, while maintaining high-level competency in general English. That is, competency in both general language and financial genres is essential so that banking and financial professionals can communicate in Zone Three English with non-Cantonese speakers.

In the current period and probably more so in the future, as illustrated by the three commercial banking examples above, there is not a sufficient supply of fully fluent English speakers across banks and financial institutions in Hong Kong. However, discerning English-speaking clients may gravitate toward institutions having staff with the requisite English competencies. To completely analyze Zone Three communication competency needs, it is necessary to distinguish between the spoken and written language. Spoken competency is less of an issue than written language. Native-like second language oral communication is achieved through English instruction at university level and especially through an MBA education that develops genre competency in financial management and related business areas. However, preparing written technical English documents that meet advanced professional standards remains a problem even for professionals having advanced and native-like oral English competence.

6.4.2 Zone two Mandarin and English language competency

In areas of commerce such as retail and technical sales, bilingual Cantonese can communicate in Zone Two tasks if they have a high genre competency. These bilingual Cantonese do not need to have high general language competency as required in a situation where Zone Three genre language competency is essential. The need to possess only intermediate level general language competency is especially relevant where personnel need to be fluent in Mandarin as well as in English to interact with speakers of these languages, or even in other languages to attract and serve a wider range of global customers.

6.4.3 Zone one English and Mandarin language competency

Zone One communication does not require high second-language competency prior to employment. Consequently, governmental and educational policy does not apply to Zone One communication. To facilitate Zone One communication, companies can develop artificial Zone One genre language (as illustrated by the Zone One example in 5.1) and offer an on-the-job training to the use of Zone One genre language.

7 Concluding remarks

In this paper I have discussed the current Hong Kong language policy and its relationship to and effect on language use in an increasing competitive global communication environment. In doing so, I have offered an alternative way in which to view, analyze, and develop second language policy. First, language policy should focus on developing adequate general language and genre competencies in the target languages (English and Mandarin) in different business sectors rather than following a one-dimensional policy aimed exclusively at the development of high-level second general language competencies. Second, second language policy should concentrate on the genres in English and Mandarin that are related to real-world business and commercial needs in different business sectors.

To conclude, I want to note that Hong Kong may be facing a future policy making bind where more financial resources will have to be devoted to language competency development in order to remain competitive in world business. It is also confronted with a language environment where policy makers need to juggle the balance between the three major languages. In particular, the emergence of Mainland China as a larger and more significant player in the global business world, thereby signaling a growing need for more attention and funding to be allocated in developing Mandarin competency, becomes a significant challenge to the development of Hong Kong language policy. Therefore, the major obstacle to improving second-language competency, in my judgment, is to find ways to overcome the social norms that restrict the use of English.

References

Babcock, R., & Du-Babcock, B. (2001). Language-based communication zones in international business communication. *Journal of Business Communication*, *38*, 372–412.

Bhatia, V. (2004). *Worlds of written discourse: A genre-based view*. New York: Continuum.

Bond, M., & Young, K. (1982). Ethnic affirmation versus cross-cultural accommodation: The variable impact of questionnaire language on Chinese bilinguals in Hong Kong. *Journal of Cross-Cultural Psychology*, *13*, 169–185.

Department of Chinese and Bilingual Studies. (2014). English language education in Hong Kong. Retrieved March 10, 2014 from http://www.cbs.polyu.edu.hk/ctdso/paper/lang%20in%20ed%20hk%20.pdf.

Dickson, P., & Cumming, A. (Eds.). (1996). *Profiles of language education in 25 countries*. Berkshire: National Foundation for Educational Research.

Du-Babcock, B. (1999). Topic management and turn-taking in professional communication: First- versus second-language strategies. *Management Communication Quarterly*, *12*(4), 544–574.

Du-Babcock, B. (2007). Language-based communication zones and professional genre competence in business and organizational communication: A cross-cultural case approach. *Journal of Asia-pacific Communication, 17*(1), 149–171.

Du-Babcock, B., & Babcock, R. (1996). Patterns of expatriate-local personnel communication in multinational corporations. *Journal of Business Communication, 33*(2), 141–164.

Du-Babcock, B., & Babcock, R. (2007). Genre patterns in language-based communication zones. *Journal of Business Communication, 44*, 340–373.

Du-Babcock, B., & Feng, H. Y. (2015). Language in education policy and its impact on out-of-class language use and preferred communication media: A Hong Kong case of university education. In F. V. Tochon (Ed.), *Language education policy unlimited: Global perspectives and local practices* (pp. 181–218). Wisconsin: Deep University Press.

Education Bureau. (2010). Enriching our language environment, realizing our vision: Fine-tuning of medium of instruction for secondary schools. Retrieved March 10, 2014 from https://www.edb.gov.hk/attachment/sc/student-parents/ncs-students/about-ncs-students/moi%20booklet-eng-17apr2010.pdf.

EPI 2013 Report. (2013). English Proficiency Index 2013 Report. Retrieved March 12, 2014 from http://www.ef.com.hk/__/~/media/efcom/epi/2014/full-reports/ef-epi-2013-report-master.pdf.

Gibbons, J. (1987). *Code-mixing and code-choice: A Hong Kong case*. Clevedon: Multilingual Matters.

Legislative Counsel Paper No. CB(4)545/12-13(05). (2013). Legislative council panel on public service employment of ethnic minorities in the civil service. Retrieved March 15, 2014 from http://www.csb.gov.hk/english/info/files/Panel_Paper_on_Employment_of_EM_Eng.pdf.

Li, D. C. S. (2000). Cantonese-English code-switching research in Hong Kong: A Y2K review. *World Englishes, 19*, 305–322.

Pennington, M., Balla, J., Detaramani, C., Poon, A., & Tam, F. (1992). *Toward a model of language choice among Hong Kong tertiary students: A preliminary analysis* (Research Report No. 18). Hong Kong: City Polytechnic of Hong Kong, Department of English.

Porter, M. (1985). *Competitive advantage*. New York: The Free Press.

Thematic Household Survey Report 51. (2013). *Use of language in Hong Kong*. Hong Kong: Census and Statistics Department, Hong Kong Special Administrative Region. Retrieved March 2, 2014 from https://www.statistics.gov.hk/pub/B11302512013XXXXB0100.pdf.

University of Hong Kong Libraries. (2014). Historical laws of Hong Kong online: Official languages ordinance. Retrieved March 11, 2014 from http://oelawhk.lib.hku.hk/items/show/2203.

List of figures

List of tables

Foreign Language Teaching in Europe

Edited by:
Manuel Jiménez Raya, Terry Lamb and Flávia Vieira

Vol. 1 Pamela Faber / Wolf Gewehr / Manuel Jiménez Raya / Antony Peck (Eds.): English Teacher Education in Europe. New Trends and Developments. 1999.

Vol. 2 Stephan H. Gabel: Über- und Unterrepräsentation im Lernerenglisch. Untersuchungen zum Sprachgebrauch deutscher Schülerinnen und Schüler in interkulturellen Telekommunikationsprojekten. 2000.

Vol. 3 Winfried Bredenbröker: Förderung der fremdsprachlichen Kompetenz durch bilingualen Unterricht. Empirische Untersuchungen. 2000.

Vol. 4 Manuel Jiménez Raya / Pamela Faber / Wolf Gewehr / Antony J. Peck (eds.): Effective Foreign Language Teaching at the Primary Level. 2001.

Vol. 5 Yvette Coyle / Mercedes Verdú / Marisol Valcárcel: Teaching English to Children - Interactivity and Teaching Strategies in the Primary FL Classroom. 2002.

Vol. 6 Markus Kötter: Tandem learning on the Internet. Learner interactions in virtual online environments (MOOs). 2002.

Vol. 7 Manuel Jiménez Raya / Terry Lamb (eds.): Differentiation in the Modern Languages Classroom. 2003.

Vol. 8 Kees van Esch / Oliver St. John (eds.): A Framework for Freedom. Learner Autonomy in Foreign Language Teacher Education. 2003.

Vol. 9 Kees van Esch / Oliver St. John (eds.): New Insights into Foreign Language Learning and Teaching. 2004.

Vol. 10 Manuel Jiménez Raya / Lies Sercu (eds.): Challenges in Teacher Development: Learner Autonomy and Intercultural Competence. 2007.

Vol. 11 Flávia Vieira (ed.): Struggling for Autonomy in Language Education. Reflecting, Acting, and Being. 2009.

Vol. 12 María Luisa Pérez Cañado / Juan Ráez Padilla (eds.): Digital Competence Development in Higher Education. An International Perspective. 2014.

Vol. 13 Michał B. Paradowski (ed.): Productive Foreign Language Skills for an Intercultural World. A Guide (not only) for Teachers. 2015.

Vol. 14 Manuel Jiménez Raya / José Javier Martos Ramos / Maria Giovanna Tassinari (eds.): Learner and Teacher Autonomy in Higher Education: Perspectives from Modern Language Teaching. 2017.

Vol. 15 Hermann Funk / Manja Gerlach / Dorothea Spaniel-Weise (eds.): Handbook for Foreign Language Learning in Online Tandems and Educational Settings. 2017.

Vol. 16 Manuel Jiménez Raya / Terry Lamb / Flávia Vieira: Mapping Autonomy in Language Education. A Framework for Learner and Teacher Development. 2017.

Vol. 17 Tejedor-Cabrera, José Mª / Martos Ramos, José Javier / Trapassi, Leonarda (eds.): Aplicaciones de la metodología Tándem en la formación universitaria. 2018.

Vol. 18 Manuel Jiménez Raya / Terry Lamb / Borja Manzano Vázquez (eds.): Insights into Language Education Policies. 2020.

www.peterlang.com

www.ingramcontent.com/pod-product-compliance
Ingram Content Group UK Ltd.
Pitfield, Milton Keynes, MK11 3LW, UK
UKHW011005120926
8556IPUK00027B/84

9 783631 716069